P9-DGK-951

CONVICTION

The Determination of Guilt or Innocence Without Trial

CONVICTION

The Determination of Guilt or Innocence Without Trial

BY

DONALD J. NEWMAN

The Report of the American Bar Foundation's Survey of the Administration of Criminal Justice in the United States

* *

FRANK J. REMINGTON
Editor

LITTLE, BROWN AND COMPANY
BOSTON 1966 TORONTO

LIBRARY OF CONGRESS CATALOG CARD NO. 66-17210

Published simultaneously in Canada
by Little, Brown & Company (Canada) Limited

PRINTED IN THE UNITED STATES OF AMERICA

THE AMERICAN BAR FOUNDATION, CHICAGO

Survey of the Administration of Criminal Justice in the United States

PROJECT STAFF

Frank J. Remington, *Director*
Harry V. Ball
Robert O. Dawson
Wayne R. LaFave
Donald M. McIntyre, Jr.
Frank W. Miller
Donald J. Newman
Daniel L. Rotenberg
Lawrence P. Tiffany

PILOT PROJECT STAFF

Arthur H. Sherry, *Project Director*
John A. Pettis, Jr., *Assistant Project Director*
Frank J. Remington, *Director of Field Research*
Sanford Bates, *Consultant on Sentencing, Probation and Parole*
Edmund F. DeVine, *Special Consultant*
Fred E. Inbau, *Consultant on Prosecution and Defense*
Benjamin A. Matthews, *Consultant on Courts*
Lloyd E. Ohlin, *Consultant on Field Research*
O. W. Wilson, *Consultant on Police*

FIELD REPRESENTATIVES AND RESEARCH ASSOCIATES

Robert W. Cassidy
Herman Goldstein
Frank J. Hodges
William L. Hungate
Donald M. McIntyre, Jr.
Roy C. McLaren
Bruce T. Olson
Donnell M. Pappenfort
Arthur W. Schumacher
Louis P. Trent
James D. Turner
John Warner

DEDICATION

Dedicated to William J. Donovan, former chairman of the Project Advisory Committee, who, throughout his career as soldier, lawyer, and humanitarian, always emphasized the high ideals embodied in our system of jurisprudence.

> A proper and effective method of dealing with the criminal has always presented a question with which human society has had to struggle. Different methods have been prompted by the particular social philosophy of the time. But underlying all the philosophy has been the innate human disinclination to determine a man to be a criminal unless what is considered necessary procedure has been followed in order to determine whether or not our judgment is correct.
>
> William J. Donovan
> Speech before American
> Prison Association (1926)

PREFACE

Conviction is the second in order of appearance of the American Bar Foundation series on the Administration of Criminal Justice. The first volume to appear was *Arrest* by Professor Wayne R. LaFave, published early in 1965. The volumes that will complete the series are now in an advanced state of preparation and should follow not far behind the present work in publication. Taken as a whole, the series is an analysis in depth of the processes of criminal law administration from detection of crime to disposition of the convicted offender. In topical sequence, this volume dealing with the conviction in its administrative context is penultimate in the series.

The series is based upon the field data obtained in the Bar Foundation's Survey of the Administration of Criminal Justice. The survey originally contemplated a pilot field study to be followed by a nationwide survey. With funding from the Ford Foundation, pilot field work was undertaken in Michigan, Wisconsin, and Kansas in 1956 and 1957. A preliminary analysis of that work was prepared and disseminated among interested scholars and authorities in criminal law and its administration. It was then determined that, before any further field research should be pursued, it would be desirable to subject the data gathered in the pilot study to reflective analysis. This series on the Administration of Criminal Justice is the result.[1]

What was originally projected as a pilot study to be followed by a much broader survey has turned out to have provided far more material than anticipated, as the formidable character of this series attests. The pilot project has proved to be a study of major dimensions in its own right. Variant implications about the project as originally conceived arise from this turn of events. On the one hand, the survey as conceived appears in retrospect to have been astonishingly ambitious in its proposed scope. The fact that even its pilot phase proved difficult to digest should be a caution to any-

[1] A fuller account of the history of the Survey of the Administration of Criminal Justice is given in the Preface to the volume on Arrest. See LaFave, Arrest at ix-xiii (1965).

one venturing into the empirical study of legal institutions.[2] On the other hand, the provocative and enlightening riches of information produced in the pilot project fully justified the prediction that the survey would open new vistas in the administration of the criminal law. If anyone continues to doubt that not only the law's practical workings but also its formal content and its grounding in policy can be illuminated by empirical study of legal processes in action, surely the present studies should put such doubts to rest. At the very least, what is achieved in fact in the administration of criminal justice is a clue to what can be achieved by the instrumentality of the criminal law. This in turn establishes a factual predicate for consideration of the proper province of the criminal law as a device for social ordering.[3]

To see the criminal law in this light is, or at least surely ought to be, of professional concern to lawyers and legal academicians. But in this light it becomes equally clear that the criminal law cannot be regarded as a proprietary domain of the legal profession. The criminal law is and ought to be an object of concerned attention on the part of public officials and leaders, members of the general community, and scholars from other disciplines. In the ordinary political sense, of course, the criminal law is an object of general concern, but the attention it receives from the general public, as with most matters of persisting importance, is spasmodic, passionate, and wishful. If headway is to be made in the adaptation of the criminal law to the conditions in which it must be contemporaneously applied, then a more sustained, dispassionate, and hardheaded examination of its administration is required. And this examination should proceed from a broader intellectual base than the legal profession alone.

It is especially appropriate, therefore, that this volume in the Administration of Criminal Justice Series should have been the work of a criminologist rather than of a person whose training is in law. Professor Newman received his Ph.D. in sociology from the University of Wisconsin and is currently Professor of Social Work at that institution, with a joint appointment in its Law School. He has taught law school courses in criminal law and its administration for several years in collaboration with Frank Remington, Professor of Law at the University of Wisconsin and general editor of this series of volumes. Professor Newman has interested himself generally in the operational problems of criminal law administra-

[2] See Hazard, The Research Program of the American Bar Foundation, 51 A.B.A.J. 539 (1965).

[3] Compare Allen, The Borderland of Criminal Justice (1964).

tion and particularly in the problem of "plea bargaining." As this study shows, the process of negotiated disposition appears on field analysis to be as important in criminal cases as it has long been recognized to be in civil cases. Beyond this, Professor Newman brings forward the suggestive hypothesis that participation in plea bargaining may be crucially significant in the defendant's attitude toward his rehabilitation. This possibility is not only of obvious practical importance in considering reform of the criminal law but of general theoretical significance in considering the characteristics of a fair system of justice.

It is interesting, too, that Professor Newman has a message of importance to lawyers who represent criminal defendants in guilty plea cases, whether by bargaining or not. Representation of the guilty has traditionally seemed a simple, routine task of little other than symbolic significance. This work sees the role of the lawyer in the guilty plea process as extremely important for the defendant, for the court, and for postconviction agencies and a matter of professional responsibility no less vital in informal adjudication than in the adversary system of trial.

The format of the series on the Administration of Criminal Justice is such that the author has no opportunity to acknowledge his special indebtednesses to others. This arrangement proceeds not from a fixed antipathy to conventional scholarly amenities but from an attitude toward precedent and authority which is casual because it is familiar. In an undertaking of the scale of the project leading to these volumes, moreover, proper acknowledgment entails the risk of infinite regress. Nevertheless, it is appropriate to express certain acknowledgments on behalf both of the American Bar Foundation and of Professor Newman.

Professor Frank Remington is largely responsible for the fact that the writing of the series has been realized. He has provided each author with guidance, suggestions, editorial criticism, and intellectual stimulus. In the writing of this particular volume, Professor Newman has also sought the advice of Professor Frank Miller of Washington University Law School (St. Louis), who is now completing another volume in the series; of Professor Edward Kimball of the Law School of the University of Wisconsin; of Professor Lloyd Ohlin of the New York University School of Social Work; and of Dean Edward L. Barrett, Jr., of the Law School, University of California, Davis. The School of Social Work and the School of Law of the University of Wisconsin provided time and assistance to further Professor Newman's labors; the Russell Sage Foundation supported a program in law and social work at the University of Wisconsin that helped provide a productive milieu.

The Ford Foundation provided not only the funds for the original field work but also support for the subsequent analysis and exposition of the field data.

The Bar Foundation Committee on Administration of Criminal Justice under the chairmanship of Mr. Harold Smith of Chicago has approved this study for publication. The Foundation's standard practice is to submit each manuscript to review and approval, either by a special advisory committee or by the standing Research Committee of the Foundation. Members of these committees are given the opportunity to make recommendations to the author. This review of the research is an essential part of the Foundation research program. Nevertheless, neither the committees nor the Foundation assumes responsibility for the positions taken by the author, nor do they necessarily agree with all the statements in the text. These responsibilities are naturally assumed by the author himself.

Geoffrey C. Hazard, Jr.
Administrator

EDITOR'S FOREWORD

Conviction deals with the important stage in the criminal justice process at which an ultimate decision is made as to the guilt or innocence of a defendant. It is one of a series of volumes which, together, cover the major stages in criminal justice administration from the time a crime is committed until the offender is finally released from parole supervision. The other volumes concern Detection of Crime, Arrest, Prosecution, and Sentencing. *Arrest* was published in March of 1965; *Conviction* is the second volume of the series to appear.

The principal emphasis of the series is upon the total process of criminal justice administration and particularly upon those stages where decisions are made which are of vital significance to individual defendants and to the effectiveness of the administration of criminal justice as a whole. This emphasis reflects two assumptions which underlie this research: The first is that it is important, particularly for the legal profession, to be concerned about the process by which government applies the criminal sanction. If the American commitment to a government of law rather than men has meaning, it must relate to the procedural formality and regularity which characterize the process by which governmental power is applied to individual citizens. The second assumption is that understanding of the important issues which confront police, prosecutors, defense counsel, judges, and correctional workers requires that these issues be viewed not in isolation but rather as an integral part of the over-all process by which criminal justice is administered.

This commitment to the study of important decisions in the total criminal justice system is reflected in this volume, which stresses: (1) the guilty plea process, including bargaining for pleas of guilty, a process which accounts for the vast majority of criminal convictions but which is characterized by informality and wide variation in practice among trial judges; (2) the discretion which many trial judges exercise in acquitting or in reducing charges against defendants who are clearly guilty because it appears to the judge that conviction, or conviction of the more serious offense, would be inappropriate. This is a practice also characterized by informality and wide variation among trial judges and which gives rise to difficulty in the relationship between judges and law enforcement agencies and correctional administrators; (3) the use, by the trial judge, of his acquittal power to control the over-all system of criminal justice administration, a practice recognized as proper by the appellate court rule requiring the exclusion of illegally obtained evidence, but one which is also used informally by the trial judge to achieve other objectives which he thinks proper but which enforcement agencies often think improper; and (4) the role of defense counsel, particularly in serving the client whose interests may be more influenced by informal processes like plea bargaining than by the formal processes of trial.

Concentration on informal practices which are important to both individual defendants and the criminal justice system as a whole does not reflect the belief that study of the formal trial of contested cases is unimportant. It does, however, reflect the conclusion that too little attention has been given in research and by formal lawmaking agencies to these informal processes which form an important part of the criminal justice system. The consequence is that they are too little understood, too often characterized by wide disparity in practice among trial judges, and too often the basis for fundamental conflict and misunderstanding among the various criminal justice agencies and a cause of bewilderment and a sense of injustice on the part of too many defendants.

Understanding these largely informal processes and the role of counsel with respect to them is an important objective in itself. The description of practices found in Michigan, Kansas, and Wisconsin derives from over a year of careful observation in those states, and the decision to emphasize certain practices rather than others in this volume results from several years of effort to assess the significance of the descriptive data which were gathered.

Some of the research data are now several years old. For consistency and convenience, observed practices are described as if they were occurring today. Although some practices have been changed, most remain as they were and there is no doubt that the issues stressed in this volume are of continuing significance.

A word should be said about the references in this volume to the "acquittal of the guilty." This is the principal subject of Part IV, "The Decision Not to Convict the Guilty," and is referred to at various places elsewhere in the text. On its face, the term "acquittal of the guilty" is a legal contradiction, for in the strict sense one who is acquitted is not guilty, and a guilty defendant is one who has in fact been convicted rather than acquitted. Nevertheless, the field studies reveal a phenomenon frequently encountered in prac-

tice and extensively considered in the text for which the term seems descriptive: The discharge of a defendant, by the prosecutor's decision not to charge the suspect, by judicial acquittal, or by other disposition, despite the existence of evidence sufficient to convict him. Discharges of this sort are grounded upon a variety of considerations of fairness, public justice, and administrative expediency; they all have the effect of an acquittal; and they terminate prosecution against a defendant who, according to the formal criteria of the criminal law, might properly be convicted. In this sense, the disposition is an "acquittal of the guilty," and it seems useful and therefore appropriate to use this term, despite its formal anomaly, in place of one more cumbersome. The author should not be misunderstood as being ignorant of the distinction between acquittal and guilt, nor as suggesting that the courts systematically free offenders who ought to go to jail. On the contrary, the point is that "acquittal of the guilty" is a process by which defendants who are recognized as law violators are let free because, in the circumstances, punishment according to the formal terms of the law appears to the concerned officials to be useless, unduly harsh, or destructive of the very objectives the criminal law aims to achieve.

The objective in this volume is to describe the practices in a way that will demonstrate their significance and enhance understanding of them, thus, hopefully, providing a basis for making judgments about how needed improvements can be made. The focus is not upon rigorous, statistical measurement of practices but rather upon their relevance to an understanding of the over-all system of criminal justice administration and to the task of those professional practitioners, such as the policeman, the lawyer, and the social worker, who are responsible for maintaining the ongoing system.

This stress on accurate, objective description of significant practices does not indicate an assumption that quantitative measurement or the making of value judgments about existing practices is unimportant. It does indicate the belief that the identification, description, and understanding of important practices is a prerequisite to the measurement of their causes and consequences and to an assessment of their propriety and desirability.

Certainly what is said in this volume demonstrates that the conviction process, the role of the trial judge, and the function of defense counsel are much more complex than has generally been assumed, and that they deserve more attention than they have been given in the past.

SUMMARY OF CONTENTS

TABLE OF CONTENTS

CHAPTER 3

PART II

CHAPTER 4

CHAPTER 5

PART III

CHAPTER 6

CHAPTER 7

CHAPTER 8

PART IV

CHAPTER 9

CHAPTER 10

CHAPTER 11

CHAPTER 12

PART V

CHAPTER 13

CHAPTER 14

PART VI

CHAPTER 15

CHAPTER 16

CHAPTER 17

CHAPTER 18

CONCLUSION

CONVICTION

The Determination of Guilt or Innocence Without Trial

INTRODUCTION

Conviction and Acquittal Without Trial in Current Criminal Justice Administration

Conviction of a crime is a serious matter, especially for the person convicted, but also for the entire social order which defines and supports the conviction process. A great deal of attention has been given to the trial, particularly the jury trial, as a means of separating guilty defendants from those who are innocent. This is understandable, for the criminal trial is of great theoretical and practical significance. Important as it is, however, the trial is not the most common method of convicting or acquitting defendants. Roughly 90 per cent of all criminal convictions are by pleas of guilty,[1] and acquittals are commonly ordered by the trial judge as

[1] Precise data on the percentage of guilty pleas are difficult to establish, not only for the country as a whole but even for any given court. Court statistics are neither uniformly reported nor are standardized forms used. In addition, the fact that the percentage of pleas probably fluctuates from time to time necessarily makes it difficult to generalize. The percentage of guilty pleas in any single jurisdiction depends upon what crimes are tabulated and at what point in the conviction sequence statistics are taken. For example, if felony cases alone are used as the basis of calculation, the percentage of guilty pleas will probably fall in the range of 70 to 85 per cent. If misdemeanors are added, the percentage of guilty plea convictions may well climb as high as 95 per cent. If the tabulation is taken at the arraignment instead of at the final conviction the percentage of guilty pleas will be less, because some defendants plead not guilty initially but change their pleas before or during trial. The figure of 90 per cent includes all types of criminal cases and refers to the final plea. For some tabulations relevant to this statistic see Silverstein, Defense of the Poor 88-89 (1965). See also Administrative Office of the United States Courts, 1963 Annual Report of the Director 240; Judicial Council of California, 1963 Annual Report of the Administrative Office of the California Courts; Detroit Police Department, Annual Statistical Reports; Detroit Recorder's Court, Annual Statistics; Orfield, Criminal Procedure from Arrest to Appeal (1947); Laurent, The Business of a Trial Court: 100 Years of Cases (1959); and Newman, Pleading Guilty for Considerations: A Study of Bargain Justice, 46 J. Crim. L., C. & P.S. 780 (1956).

a matter of his discretion rather than because proof of guilt is lacking.[2]

These two processes of nontrial adjudication, the guilty plea and acquittal of the guilty, have tremendous administrative significance. Compared to the typically long, costly, and complex trial, the guilty plea is a model of efficiency, assuring conviction of defendants at small cost to all involved. In addition, acquittal of certain defendants who are actually guilty of criminal conduct keeps some sick, emotionally disturbed, untreatable, or "deserving" defendants from unnecessary or ineffective correctional treatment. Both processes are so important and so commonly employed that the entire criminal justice system comes to depend upon a high rate of guilty pleas and a systematic diversion of certain guilty defendants from correctional facilities. Prosecutors' offices are staffed, court calendars planned, and correctional facilities built in anticipation of these practices.

Efficiency alone is not the mark of proper administration of justice at the court level or at any other point in the criminal justice process. There are other very basic values involved. First, of course, there is a question of whether nontrial adjudication practices, particularly when they result in conviction, adequately fulfill such basic objectives as accurate and fair separation of the guilty from the innocent. No matter how administratively efficient, unless the guilty plea process is accurate in its task and fair in application, it is less than an adequate method of adjudication.

Second, there is a question of the propriety of nontrial adjudication practices even if they are efficient, accurate, and fair. The basic issue is the kind of conviction and acquittal process most fitting to a democratic society. We have a traditional commitment to the trial process with all of its protections of the defendant, its standard of proof of guilt beyond a reasonable doubt, and its procedures for assuring fairness to guilty and innocent alike. This is essentially a commitment to both process and proof. It is reliance on evidence fully and properly presented and tested by the adversary process.

Nontrial adjudication, in contrast, rests less on evidence of guilt

[2] Statistics in regard to acquittals and dismissals by the trial judge are even more difficult to obtain than statistics regarding guilty pleas. In many jurisdictions almost no records are kept when the court has no continuing interest in the defendant. One analysis of court practices in California showed that 7.3 per cent of all cases reaching the courts resulted in dismissal. See California Dept. of Justice, Bureau of Criminal Statistics, Crime in California 99 (1960). This does not, however, explain whether dismissals were for insufficient evidence or for other reasons, even if this percentage is correct. Observation of field practices leaves an impression that this percentage is approximately correct for the three states under analysis, although it would be somewhat higher if misdemeanors were included.

than on the consent of defendants and the exercise of trial court discretion not to convict at all or to convict of a lesser charge. It is a complex process in its own right, made up not simply of the guilty plea and acquittal of certain deserving defendants but also of the negotiated plea (charge reduction and promise of sentence leniency in exchange for a plea of guilty) and acquittal practices to achieve objectives such as the avoidance of legislative sentencing mandates and the control of police practices. Both process and proof are significantly different from those of the trial system.

The accuracy and fairness of nontrial adjudication and its appropriateness to our system of criminal justice are fully explored in the chapters which follow. Throughout, there is an attempt to do more than describe the nontrial adjudication process. Description of practice is organized around what are thought to be the questions of greatest significance, so that analysis of the guilty plea process, for example, is related to the central concern for the accuracy and fairness of this conviction procedure. In addition, analysis of the negotiated plea and acquittal practices of the trial judge is related to the broad question of the propriety of judicial discretion in convicting or acquitting defendants without trial.

There are also other aspects of nontrial adjudication which are important. One is whether the trial court assumes a central and controlling role in the total, over-all administrative system. At adjudication, the trial judge occupies a strategic administrative position. He not only controls the efficiency of his own court by encouraging guilty pleas through leniency in sentencing or by his support of the negotiated plea but also uses adjudication discretion to control other agencies, such as the police, or to avoid legislative controls on his own sentencing discretion. When his alternatives are limited by legislative sentences he can, and does, manipulate conviction to achieve sentencing flexibility where it seems desirable. When he dislikes enforcement methods of the police he can, and does, acquit defendants who have been subjected to those methods.

The central administrative position of the judge in the criminal justice system is not peculiar to nontrial adjudication. In contested cases, the judge is obviously a central figure in administering his own court, and he also uses his power to discipline and to control other agencies. Both the exclusionary rule of evidence and the defense of entrapment are formal recognitions of the responsibility of the trial judge to concern himself with the propriety of enforcement methods. In current practice, however, many judges do not limit the exercise of their acquittal power to cases involving these defenses. Particularly in minor cases, acquittals are likely to reflect a general dissatisfaction with police conduct without, however, any articulation by the judge of how such acquittals relate to either the exclusionary rule or entrapment. Even when acquittal practices become routine and systematic, they often rest on grounds that do not clearly fall within these two formal defenses. The informal use of judicial acquittal power, as well as the use of judicial discretion to avoid legislative sentencing mandates, is important in current practice, and both are dealt with in detail in this analysis.

Still another problem of importance in nontrial adjudication is the role of defense counsel, especially in guilty plea cases. There is currently a great deal of concern with the whole matter of right to counsel in criminal cases, particularly the right of indigent defendants to equal opportunity for representation. The importance of counsel, however, is traditionally evaluated in terms of the lawyer's function at trial or in preparation for trial. There has been little or no attention to the role of the defense lawyer in the much more common guilty plea process. Because the plea is the most frequent method of conviction, obviously crucial both to defendants themselves and to all who administer the criminal justice system, questions about what lawyers do or can do and what purposes they serve or can serve in nontrial conviction are of major importance.

All of these problems — the accuracy and fairness of guilty plea convictions, judicial discretion to reduce charges or to acquit the guilty, the central, controlling role of the trial court, and the function of the lawyer in guilty plea cases — form the skeleton of this book. Filling out this framework are the practices of nontrial adjudication, the daily court processing of hundreds of criminal cases through adjudication without trial.

PART I

Accuracy and Fairness of Guilty Plea Convictions

Court: You are charged in the information filed against you in this court with the crime of breaking and entering in the daytime, two counts. Do you understand what this means?

Defendant: Yes.

Court: And how do you plead to this charge?

Defendant: Guilty.

Court: Are you pleading guilty because you actually are guilty?

Defendant: Yes.

Court: Has the prosecuting attorney, any of the officers of this court, or any other person threatened you or made you any promises or inducements to influence you to plead guilty?

Defendant: No.

Court: You are pleading guilty freely and voluntarily?

Defendant: Yes.

Court: Prior to your plea did you understand that you had a consitutional right to a trial by jury and that if you were financially unable to employ counsel that the court would appoint a lawyer for you?

Defendant: Yes.

Court: You do not want a trial or a lawyer?

Defendant: No, sir.

Court: You understand that upon accepting your plea of guilty it is my duty to impose sentence on you?

Defendant: I understand.

Court: And that the penalty provided for daytime breaking and entering might involve a prison term up to five years?

Defendant: Yes.

Court: Very well, I will accept your plea of guilty and set the date for sentencing three weeks from today, that is, on December 10.

Arraignment in a Michigan Court

In practice, guilty pleas account for roughly 90 per cent of all criminal convictions. The process of pleading guilty is usually brief, with more or less routine questions asked by the court and monosyllabic responses given by defendants, who often plead guilty to even very serious crimes without the advice of defense counsel. There is no doubt that this process of conviction is efficient. In comparison to a contested case, the guilty plea puts little strain on the resources of the prosecutor and court. It is quicker, less costly, and often less subject to public attention than a trial; but the nature of the typical arraignment is such that the court really has little opportunity to learn much about the defendant or his crime. In deciding whether to accept a guilty plea the judge commonly faces the problem of having little information by which to assess the competency of the defendant to plead guilty or to evaluate the appropriateness of the plea to the particular charge. Unlike the trial, the plea-of-guilty process does not ordinarily require the presentation of evidence of guilt. The only formal requirement in most jurisdictions is that the plea be voluntarily entered by a competent defendant. This gives the process an apparent simplicity which does not accord with reality. It would be like saying that the only requirement for a trial is that it be "fair." Neither the term "voluntary" nor the term "fair" adequately reflects the complexity of conviction processes, whether by guilty plea or by trial.

While a good deal of attention has traditionally been given to the requirements for proper conviction at trial, relatively little attention has been given to conviction requirements for the plea-of-guilty process. This situation seems to be changing. A number of innovations now followed by some trial courts are designed to investigate the factual basis of the plea. An increasing number of trial judges rely upon the post-plea-of-guilty hearing, the presentence report, or other techniques to satisfy themselves that there is in fact adequate evidence to support the guilty plea. These techniques, however, are not consistently used in any court district but depend instead on the proclivities of individual judges. For the most part, trial judges take the voluntary requirement to mean that the defendant must freely consent to plead guilty and that if he so consents the resulting plea is likely to be trustworthy.

While the accurate separation of the guilty from the innocent is obviously a major objective of adjudication by trial or by plea, there is also increasing concern, particularly by appellate judges, over aspects of the guilty plea process not directly related to the guilt or innocence of the defendant. For example, it is generally required that the person pleading guilty do so only with full understanding of the consequences, which is usually interpreted to mean that it is necessary for the trial judge to warn the defendant of the maximum sentence that can be imposed if he is convicted on the charge. This reflects a fairness standard quite distinct from considerations of the truthfulness and accuracy of the plea. Likewise, fairness of the process also underlies much of the current appellate concern with "quick justice" convictions which involve arrest, plea of guilty, and sentencing within a period as short as a single day.

The accuracy as well as the fairness of guilty plea convictions is complicated by the negotiated plea process, common in many jurisdictions. Plea bargaining, which ordinarily involves charge reduction or a promise of a light sentence or both, not only presents problems of accurate, fair, and consistent convictions but raises a broader question of the propriety of such practices even if they result in truthful pleas. Some appellate judges take the position that "bartering" in the guilty plea process is intrinsically improper, whether or not the court honors its bargain and apart from the other considerations of accurate and fair separation of the guilty. This implies a propriety requirement in the guilty plea process that relates not so much to the fair treatment of individual defendants as to types of procedures that are proper and fitting in our system of criminal justice.

Increasing trial and appellate court concern about accuracy and fairness of guilty pleas and about the propriety of the bargaining process tends to make the guilty plea process more important, more complex, and certainly more difficult for the conscientious trial judge now than in the past. One experienced Wisconsin trial judge remarked that the risk of error is likely to be greater in a guilty plea case than in a case which is tried. Certainly, observation of current practice indicates that careful analysis of the guilty plea process is needed to afford an adequate basis for its appraisal.

The three chapters which follow deal in detail with current trial court practices designed to insure the accuracy of guilty pleas, with practices designed to insure that the process is fair even to guilty defendants, and with the issue of the propriety of plea bargaining practices. For purposes of analysis, the questions of accuracy, fairness, and the related but distinct matter of the consent of defendants to a plea of guilty are treated separately. In one sense this separation is artificial; in practice these issues are often, even usually, simultaneous concerns of the trial judge. The customary requirement that guilty pleas be voluntary, however, is so elusive of interpretation that its component parts need to be separated to permit full understanding of current practices.

CHAPTER 1

Concern for Accuracy in Guilty Plea Convictions

A. Formal Requirements Relating to the Accuracy of Guilty Pleas

A basic purpose of conviction procedures, whether by trial or by plea, is to separate accurately the guilty defendants from the innocent. Certainly the trial process is characterized by elaborate rules designed to insure that every safeguard is taken to avoid convicting an innocent person. Procedural requirements in the guilty plea process, however, are much less elaborate, and the customary emphasis on "voluntariness" as the test for proper conviction[1] tends to obscure the more specific objective of accuracy of the plea in both law and practice. The consequence of uncertainty about the dimensions of the voluntary requirement is that procedures for accepting guilty pleas vary from one court to another, with somewhat different emphases in the types of questions put to guilty plea defendants by trial courts.

There is, however, increasing concern with the accuracy of guilty plea convictions; that is, with examination into the factual basis for the plea as a major part of the so-called voluntary test. This is illustrated by the current proposal to revise Rule 11 of the Federal Rules of Criminal Procedure to read as follows (italics indicate proposed changes):

> A defendant may plead not guilty, guilty or, with the consent of the court, nolo contendere. The court may refuse to accept a plea of guilty, and shall not accept [the] *such* plea *or a plea of nolo contendere* without first *addressing the defendant personally and* determining that the plea is made voluntarily with un-

[1] See, for example, Machibroda v. United States, 368 U.S. 487, 82 Sup. Ct. 510, 7 L. Ed. 2d 473 (1962); Von Moltke v. Gillies, 332 U.S. 708, 68 Sup. Ct. 316, 92 L. Ed. 309 (1948); Johnson v. Zerbst, 304 U.S 458, 58 Sup. Ct. 1019, 82 L. Ed. 1461 (1938); Kercheval v. United States, 274 U.S. 220, 47 Sup. Ct. 582, 71 L. Ed. 1009 (1927).

> derstanding of the nature of the charge. *Notwithstanding the acceptance of a plea of guilty the court shall not enter a judgment upon such plea without making such inquiry as may satisfy it that there is a factual basis for the plea.* If a defendant refuses to plead or if the court refuses to accept a plea of guilty or if a defendant corporation fails to appear, the court shall enter a plea of not guilty.[2]

While the proposal does not spell out the nature of the inquiry which the judge must conduct nor give any indication of whether the court may properly consider evidence not admissible by trial standards, it does focus on whether a factual basis exists for the plea.[3]

Michigan has a similar provision, but the Michigan legislation, which has been in effect for some time, has been largely nullified by appellate interpretation. The Michigan statute provides:

> Whenever any person shall plead guilty to an information filed against him in any court, it shall be the duty of the judge of such court, before pronouncing judgment or sentence upon such plea, to become satisfied after such investigation as he may deem necessary for that purpose respecting the nature of the case, and the circumstances of such plea, that said plea was made freely, with full knowledge of the nature of the accusation, and without undue influence. And whenever said judge shall have reason to doubt the truth of such plea of guilty, it shall be his duty to vacate the same, direct a plea of not guilty to be entered and order a trial of the issue thus formed.[4]

An early interpretation of this provision held that the judge, in ascertaining the voluntary nature of the plea, must inquire what the respondent actually did which led to the charge.[5] At the present time, although the words of the statute make it mandatory for the judge to be "satisfied after such investigation as he may deem necessary . . . respecting the nature of the case, and the circumstances of such plea," it is sufficient to show that the examination was directed toward establishing that the defendant consented to plead guilty without improper inducement.[6] In practice in

[2] Second Preliminary Draft of Proposed Amendments to Rules of Criminal Procedure for the United States District Courts 5 (March, 1964).

[3] Walter E. Hoffman, Chief Judge of the United States District Court for the Eastern District of Virginia and a member of the Advisory Committee on Criminal Rules, commented, "The inquiry required is not to be restricted by rules of evidence and probably requires no more information than is already in the presentence report or the file of the attorney for the government." Hoffman, What Next in Federal Criminal Rules? 21 Wash. & Lee L. Rev. 1, 11 (1964).

[4] Mich. Comp. Laws §768.35 (1948).

[5] Edwards v. People, 39 Mich. 760 (1878).

[6] People v. Harris, 266 Mich. 317, 253 N.W. 312 (1934).

Michigan, thorough court inquiry into the facts supporting the guilty plea is made only in murder cases. The concern with murder cases resulted from a United States Supreme Court reversal of a "quick justice" guilty plea conviction of a seventeen-year-old defendant charged with murder.[7] In general, however, the judicial inquiry at arraignment in Michigan, as in most other state jurisdictions, currently relates primarily to the consensual basis for the plea rather than to its accuracy.

A recently adopted[8] instruction to trial judges in Wisconsin also indicates increasing concern with whether there is a factual basis for a plea of guilty:

> If [following questions relating to the consent of the defendant, his understanding of the charge, and his awareness of the possible penalty] the court is satisfied that the plea should be accepted, the court should state, "The plea is accepted and the clerk is ordered to enter it of record." While it is not required in Wisconsin, it is recommended that the court take evidence of defendant's guilt. This may be done by having the district attorney present evidence and introduce any statements or confessions which may have been obtained, or in such other manner as the court deems appropriate. The case may be adjourned by the court for this purpose if necessary.[9]

Although at present most trial courts are under no obligation to take evidence beyond the guilty plea itself (even under the Michigan statute requiring judicial investigation into the nature of the plea), in practice many judges do utilize informal devices designed to insure accuracy of guilty pleas.[10]

[7] De Meerleer v. Michigan, 329 U.S. 663, 67 Sup. Ct. 596, 91 L. Ed. 584 (1947), *rev'g* People v. De Meerleer, 313 Mich. 548, 21 N.W.2d 848 (1946).

[8] Wisconsin Jury Instructions — Criminal: Recommended Questions to Be Used When the Court Is Determining Whether to Appoint Counsel and Acceptance of Plea of Guilty or of Nolo Contendere (Proposed Final Draft, Aug. 10, 1964).

[9] Id. at 4.

[10] Attempts to change or interpret requirements for proper conviction by plea to include examination into the factual basis of the charge invariably create operational problems for the judge who desires to comply. The scope and procedure of the inquiry are left to judicial discretion. There is no hint of how the court should go about making such inquiry nor guidance on tests, if any, for proper, sufficient, and relevant evidence which may be considered by the court. There is an implicit question of the comparative weight to be given the willingness of the defendant to plead guilty in relation to the facts established by any inquiry. This problem occurs when the judge's inquiry raises some doubt about the accuracy of the conviction, enough for acquittal if the case were being tried, but the defendant insists that he wants to plead guilty, with, perhaps, the complicating factor of concurrence of his defense counsel. These and many other questions remain unanswered and, at present, only speculative.

B. Variations in Trial Court Techniques to Insure Accurate Guilty Pleas

1. *Assigning counsel to unrepresented defendants.* Judges in the three states studied, Kansas, Michigan, and Wisconsin, often assign counsel in cases where the defendant appears confused and uncertain in entering his plea, even though he has not requested a lawyer or has clearly denied wanting assistance. Often these cases involve defendants who appear to be ignorant or illiterate or who are of foreign extraction and have difficulty following the language of the court. In cases of minor offenses, the court may merely delay arraignment proceedings until some lawyer, present in the courtroom on other business, has an opportunity to confer privately with the defendant. Where more serious crimes are involved and where there is real doubt that the defendant understands the charge and can enter a trustworthy plea, the arraignment is postponed and counsel is assigned to the defendant.

Whether counsel actually does increase the probability of an accurate guilty plea depends, of course, upon how thoroughly and expertly he assesses the appropriateness of the plea decision, although in questionable cases the concurrence of counsel with the plea often resolves the doubts of the judge. In a Wisconsin case, for example, a woman charged with murder in the second degree admitted guilt at arraignment and, in response to inquiry by the judge, said she did not want an attorney even at state expense. She said, "I am guilty but I didn't plan or intend to kill anybody." After some discussion with her, the judge refused the plea, assigned counsel, and rescheduled arraignment. At the second arraignment the judge asked the defense attorney if he had conferred with his client and discussed the case with her. The attorney replied in the affirmative, stating that the defendant's recollection of what happened was vague, and in fact she could not remember any significant details. The judge then asked the defendant, "Do you wish to continue your plea of guilty?" The defendant answered, "Yes. I will plead guilty to get this over with. The suspense of not knowing what I have done is driving me crazy." The judge then asked the defense counsel: "Do you as counsel agree that defendant should continue in her plea of guilty?" The attorney answered: "Yes, I do," whereupon the court accepted the plea and sentenced the defendant to from fourteen to eighteen years in prison.[11]

[11] Conviction of defendant who pleaded guilty but "could not recall details" of the crime was upheld in Minnesota. State ex rel. Crossley v. Tahash, 263 Minn. 299,

The specific functions which counsel serves in guilty plea cases are discussed in detail in later chapters.[12] In general, however, there is little doubt that judges feel much more certain of the accuracy of guilty pleas when the defendant has been adequately represented, particularly if counsel has been in the case from the early stages. Some trial judges, nevertheless, require some evidentiary showing at arraignment or in a post-plea hearing that there is a factual basis for the plea.

It might be added that representation by counsel also affects other requirements of conviction by plea. Most judges feel more assured that the represented defendant has had his rights explained, has been informed as to the nature of the charge, and has been warned of the consequences of pleading guilty. While this advice of counsel relates in some degree to the accuracy of the plea, it also adds to the fairness of the whole proceeding. Furthermore, defense counsel is usually in a better position than any other participant in the guilty plea process to assess the competency of the defendant to plead guilty. In most cases the court sees the defendant only briefly; the prosecutor may be even less familiar with his personality. In the normal course of his duties, however, the defense attorney spends enough time with him to estimate, at least roughly, his intelligence and emotional stability. If counsel agrees with the defendant's decision to plead guilty, the judge has greater assurance that the defendant is in fact intellectually and emotionally competent to enter a truthful plea.

2. *Use of the pre-sentence report to assess the accuracy of the guilty plea.* The practice in a number of Michigan courts is to order the pre-sentence investigation to focus on evidence tending to prove or disprove the accuracy of the defendant's guilty plea. In routine practice, the court accepts a plea of guilty from the defendant but reconsiders its validity after receiving a pre-sentence investigation report. In some instances, however, trial judges do not accept a guilty plea, particularly where there is prima facie doubt of its accuracy, but take it "under advisement" until the pre-sentence report is received.[13] Another variation involves accepting an "open plea of guilty" to a particular category of offense, such as homicide, and using the pre-sentence investigation to determine

---

116 N.W.2d 666 (1962). But see State v. Jones, 267 Minn. 421, 127 N.W.2d 153 (1964), and State ex rel. Grattan v. Tahash, 262 Minn. 18, 113 N.W.2d 342 (1962).

[12] See Part VI.

[13] Judges often receive and read a probation investigation report prior to an adjudicative determination in juvenile delinquency proceedings, but this is less common in criminal actions where normally the pre-sentence investigation is not undertaken until after guilt has been determined. See Note, 58 Colum. L. Rev. 702 (1958).

the particular degree of the felony, whether manslaughter or murder in the second degree.

There is little doubt that a primary function of the pre-sentence investigation in these Michigan courts is to gather evidence that either supports or contradicts the plea of guilty. At least half, and often more, of the text of the pre-sentence report focuses on the facts of the offense. The approach is definitely investigative rather than diagnostic. The probation officers involved are referred to as investigators, and a high percentage of them are ex-policemen. To some professional social workers who viewed this practice, the function of the investigators appeared "prosecutory" with little effort to "diagnose or make a case analysis," the major attempt being to collect evidence to "refute [or support] defendant's own story" of his offense. The report usually contains a description of the offense and a statement as to whether the defendant "admits it," as well as a description of testimony of others relating to the circumstances of the crime. The report may make a recommendation as to guilt or innocence, as well as listing and describing any extenuating circumstances. One report ended with the quaint conclusion: "By now the court has perused the report . . . . [W]e believe any comment by us is superfluous other than to state that the defendant has, in our opinion, violated the most important of the ten commandments, that of the seventh commandment: 'Thou shalt not kill.' "

Occasionally such reports may cast doubt on the guilt of defendants. In one instance (in this case the defendant had been convicted at trial, but the same techniques are used with some guilty plea defendants) the officer conducting the pre-sentence report showed by use of handwriting comparisons, lie detector tests, and evidence of alibi that the defendant could not have been guilty of the crime. He was returned to court, where the charge against him was dismissed.[14] In most cases, the evidence gathered in the pre-sentence investigation supports the accuracy of the charge. The totally innocent guilty plea defendant is rare, although in a number of instances the pre-sentence report has cast doubt on the appropriateness of the specific charges to which defendants have

[14] An equally important function of the pre-sentence investigation is to document mitigating circumstances in the offense, which, while not casting doubt on the guilt of the accused, does give the court information relevant to discretion to reduce the charge or dismiss the case. For example, in one case in Detroit the pre-sentence investigation in a burglary case showed the defendant to be a college student from a respectable family who, however, was experiencing intense emotional disturbance. He was undergoing psychiatric treatment at the time of the burglary. The boy, his parents, and the psychiatrist all promised that psychiatric care would continue if the case were dismissed or probation granted. The judge dismissed the case in reliance upon this promise.

pleaded guilty, and in other instances the reports have indicated certain defenses or mitigating circumstances that could possibly have been raised at trial.

A judge usually will not refuse to accept a guilty plea on the grounds that the pre-sentence report shows that the actual conduct of the defendant was more serious than the crime to which he offers to plead guilty. In one felonious assault case, however, a judge refused to accept a plea to a charge of simple assault because the evidence in the pre-sentence report supported a higher charge. The defendant agreed to plead guilty to a slightly more serious charge of assault and battery (less serious than felonious assault), provided the judge gave him credit for jail time served. The court accepted the plea and the terms. More commonly, however, if there seems to be evidence to support a higher charge, judges who are concerned over the practice of reduction of charges take these pleas under advisement, although they ordinarily accept them in a day or two.

The use of the pre-sentence report to determine the degree of the crime after an "open plea" of guilty seems limited to homicide cases.[15] In general this procedure works as follows: A defendant, charged originally with murder in the first degree, offers to enter a plea of guilty to "some degree of homicide less than murder in the first degree." The judge may either accept the plea immediately and then order a pre-sentence investigation or may take the plea under advisement while awaiting the results of the pre-sentence investigation report. The following extracts from a case illustrate this procedure:

> Defendant was originally charged with first degree murder but at arraignment through his counsel and in the presence of the judge, the prosecutor, and the chief of police of the city in which the offense occurred, offered to plead guilty to homicide less than first degree murder.
>
> *Prosecutor:* "You want to enter a plea, Counsel?"
>
> *Counsel:* "Yes, enter a plea, withdraw original plea of not guilty to first degree murder and enter a plea for second degree or manslaughter depending upon the determination of the court."
>
> *Prosecutor:* "Of course you understand after the court hears the testimony, if he finds the testimony shows second degree he will so find and if he finds manslaughter, he will so find."
>
> *Counsel:* "Yes."
>
> *Prosecutor to police chief:* "And that situation is satisfactory to you, Officer?"
>
> *Officer:* "It is, yes, sir."

[15] Jayne, The Purpose of the Sentence, 2 N.P.P.A.J. 315 (1956). The "open plea" is also used in Iowa. See State v. Kelley, 253 Iowa 1314, 115 N.W.2d 184 (1962).

Prosecutor to defendant: "You understand this, do you?"

Defendant: "Yes."

Court: "You have counsel and have gone over it with your lawyer? You know you can have trial if you want it?"

Defendant: "I leave it up to him. Whatever he says will be all right with me."

Court: "You are pleading to either offense of murder or manslaughter as the court finds, understand that?"

Defendant: "I understand it."

Court: "And have you been offered any promises or had any threats to get you to make a plea?"

Defendant: "No."

Court: "All right I will accept your plea and set a hearing for such proof as you want to bring in."

A hearing was held,[16] but the court still did not make a decision as to the degree of the crime and referred the case to the probation department for a pre-sentence investigation. The report prepared by this agency was nine pages long; the first six pages were devoted to discussion of evidence concerning the offense, the remainder largely to the social circumstances of the offender and his family. When the report was received by the court, the defendant was summoned and the court said:

> I have given a great deal of thought to your case since I heard your testimony and taking into consideration your past very good record — of course you will always have to carry on your conscience the fact that you killed a man who was once your friend — those things happen — but I am satisfied that you had no malice in your heart which would make you guilty of murder. I find you guilty of manslaughter.

The defendant was placed on probation for five years and ordered to contribute to the support of the victim's family during this time. In this instance the pre-sentence report, in addition to elaborating the defendant's good reputation in the community, steady employment, and the like, suggested that he might have believed the victim was armed, and therefore, while it was not murder in self defense, there were mitigating circumstances. The victim had trailed the defendant in his car after a gambling game, had previously "pulled a knife" on the defendant, had stated in the past that he owned a pistol, and, when approached by the defendant, had his hand in his pocket. Although the defendant did not see a weapon, "taking no chances," he shot him. To substantiate this, the probation officer investigating the case interviewed the defendant, the police, witnesses to the crime, and other witnesses who

[16] To comply with Mich. Comp. Laws §750.318 (1948).

were in the bar where the gambling and the incident with the knife took place. While the pre-sentence report did not specifically recommend probation, it was certainly oriented toward mitigating circumstances leading in this direction.

One of the interesting aspects of the practice of pre-sentence investigation to determine the degree of homicide is that, although such investigations are carried out by the probation department of the court, the nature of the offenses almost always precludes the possibility of probation. The case above was exceptional. In most cases incarceration is imposed.

A variation on the use of the probation report or the open plea to determine the accuracy of the charge occurs in one Michigan metropolitan court for misdemeanants. This is a court where minor offenders (chiefly drunks and prostitutes) are heard, ordinarily without the presence of a prosecutor. Both the men's and women's divisions of the probation department assign a probation officer to interview the defendant in the bullpen before his court appearance and to stand beside and advise the judge during each case. The probation officers are thoroughly familiar with the habitués of the court and in their pretrial interviews tend to concentrate on newcomers. It is clear that their function is advisory in regard to adjudication as well as to sentence. They have, however sketchily, the facts and the evidence, and any gaps in information may be filled in by the arresting policeman, who is usually present at these hearings.

Pre-sentence reports are widely used by Wisconsin trial judges and are, in the main, diagnostically oriented. They are generally not used by the trial court to check upon the accuracy of the plea.[17] In some instances, however, they may raise doubts about the competency of the defendant to plead guilty and lead the court to seek psychiatric evaluation of the defendant. Pre-sentence reports are used rarely in Kansas, and they do not ordinarily focus on the question of guilt or innocence.[18]

[17] In certain cases in Wisconsin the probation agent conducting the pre-sentence investigation may come to doubt the actual guilt of the convicted offender and focus his investigation on the circumstances of the defendant's criminal conduct and on his decision to plead guilty. In one case in Milwaukee, a field agent came to doubt the actual guilt of a borderline feeble-minded defendant who had pleaded guilty and was allowed no post-plea hearing because he had been represented by an attorney. The defendant told the field agent that he was not guilty and had only pleaded guilty because his attorney had told him to do so. The probation agent arranged for the defendant to submit to a polygraph test, which showed him to be innocent of the offense. The probation agent took this evidence to the prosecutor, who in turn notified the court. The guilty plea was withdrawn and the case dismissed by the judge.

[18] In one case in a United States District Court in Kansas the hesitancy and apparent inconsistency of the defendant's statements at the time he entered a guilty plea to a forgery charge led the judge to question the accuracy of the charge and

3. *Post-plea-of-guilty hearings.* The post-plea-of-guilty hearing is a regular procedure in one metropolitan Wisconsin court.[19] It is used increasingly by other courts in Wisconsin and is now recommended procedure for all Wisconsin trial judges.[20] The post-plea hearing occurs occasionally in Michigan but was not observed in Kansas.[21]

The Wisconsin post-plea hearing is a fairly elaborate procedure, described by some observers as a "little trial." In general, it works in this way: After receiving and accepting a guilty plea from a defendant (defendants who, in the judge's opinion, have been adequately advised and represented by counsel are excluded) the court requires the defendant to take the stand, under oath, and

---

the actual willingness of the defendant to plead guilty. He ordered the plea withdrawn and referred the defendant to the probation department for "evaluation" of this matter. After receiving a report from the probation department, the court accepted the guilty plea.

19 The trial judge in this court reports that "several times" a year the post-plea hearing reveals that the defendant could not be convicted if he were to demand trial. In some cases the "conduct is not criminal," in others the "evidence would not support conviction." In both the guilty plea is withdrawn and the case dismissed. This judge also reports that he considers information learned during the hearing in determining the sentence if the defendant is in fact guilty, although in "most cases" he also requests a pre-sentence investigation.

20 Wisconsin Jury Instructions — Criminal: Recommended Questions to Be Used When the Court Is Determining Whether to Appoint Counsel and Acceptance of Plea of Guilty or of Nolo Contendere (Proposed Final Draft, Aug. 10, 1964).

21 Statutes in some states require the court to take evidence on a plea of guilty. The hearing is ordinarily like the post-plea-of-guilty hearing in Wisconsin; but in Alabama, for example, the code provides that the judge must find guilt "beyond a reasonable doubt." Ala. Code, tit. 15, §264 (1958) states: ". . . if, after hearing such testimony, the court believes beyond a reasonable doubt that the defendant is guilty, in manner and form, of the offense charged against him in the information . . . the court shall thereupon receive and enter the plea of guilty. . . ." Likewise, a statute in Virginia provides: "Upon a plea of guilty in a felony case, tendered in person by the accused after being advised by counsel, the court shall hear and determine the case without the intervention of a jury. . . ." Va. Code Ann. §19.1-192 (1950). See also McGrady v. Cunningham, 296 F.2d 600, 602 (4th Cir. 1961). The post-plea trial of misdemeanor cases is discretionary with the court. Va. Code Ann. §19.1-193 (1950).

In Tennessee, because of jury sentencing provisions (Tenn. Code Ann. §40-2707 [1955]), the criminal code provides: "Upon the plea of guilty, when the punishment is confinement in the penitentiary, a jury shall be impaneled to hear the evidence and fix the time of confinement, unless otherwise expressly provided by this Code." Tenn. Code Ann. §40-2310 (1955). The evidence heard by the jury relates to their determining an appropriate sentence rather than specifically to the guilt or innocence of the defendant. See Knowles v. State, 155 Tenn. 181, 290 S.W. 969 (1927).

Some post-plea inquiries are followed in federal district courts. However, in a recent case a circuit court of appeals held that "Post-plea inquiry into voluntariness is of uncertain value, and does not correct the error underlying receipt of the plea." Bishop v. United States, 349 F.2d 220, 222 (D.C. Cir. 1965). In this case the trial judge had not complied with Rule 11, Fed. R. Crim. P., by ascertaining whether the plea was voluntarily and freely entered with understanding of the charge before accepting it. When asked about this in a hearing on remand, the trial judge stated, "I don't ask those foolish questions. I don't go through that foolish ritual." Id. at 221.

state that he did commit the crime and exactly how he committed it. Questioning of the defendant is usually by the judge himself. Witnesses for the state are also sworn and required to testify in detail regarding the nature of the evidence of guilt which they hold. The defendant is asked if he wishes to cross-examine the state's witnesses or to call witnesses in his own behalf. In one court the judge explained that the state must put on a "full" case, but the most commonly expressed standard is that the state must present a prima facie case of guilt. In the great majority of cases the post-plea hearing leads to an affirmation of the guilty plea. Occasionally the judge will become convinced that the state's evidence is insufficient to sustain conviction or that the facts brought out in the hearing are inconsistent with the particular charge. In such cases he will entertain a motion for withdrawal of the plea and order the case either for trial or for rearraignment on a more accurate charge. Occasionally, also, he may become convinced by the hearing that the defendant is incompetent and request a psychiatric evaluation.

While the post-plea hearing is more time-consuming than the routine arraignment where evidence is not taken, most Wisconsin judges who use it feel that the time and extra work are worth the effort. The hearing not only gives the court an opportunity to examine evidence of the criminal conduct on which the plea is based but provides a more adequate record of the conviction process than does the customary arraignment. Commonly, the record of a guilty plea conviction is so sparse and contains so little information that it is virtually useless to appellate courts or to correctional agencies when they are later confronted with the defendant's allegations of unfair or otherwise improper conviction procedures. A judge who uses post-plea hearings remarked:

> The hearing not only protects the defendant, and certainly he is given opportunity to present any evidence or relevant information, but by providing a full record also protects public officials, like the police, the D.A. and the judge himself, and if there is one it protects the defense counsel too, from later accusations of improper conduct.

C. The Administrative Consequences of Trial Court Practices in Investigating the Accuracy of Guilty Pleas

The use of these trial court techniques and the current trend in court rules and recommended procedures in guilty plea cases indicate that the current, general "voluntary" test for proper conviction by plea is undergoing change. The major change in its form is directed toward the separation of consent and accuracy into two different considerations. The trend is toward a more detailed examination into the factual basis for guilty pleas, and the result of this is to increase the formalism of the plea process. What has been traditionally a quick and cursory procedure is becoming a more detailed exploration of the defendant's criminal conduct in relation to the formal charge to which he pleads guilty. The objective is to provide assurance that guilty pleas are accurate; that the defendant really did commit the crime, and that it is at least as serious as the one to which he is willing to plead guilty.

In addition, these techniques and new requirements have other administrative consequences. In the first place, investigation into the factual basis of guilty pleas acts to increase the visibility of charge reduction practices, a common form of plea bargaining in jurisdictions where sentences are legislatively fixed. Without a detailed inquiry at arraignment or without a post-plea hearing or a pre-sentence investigation focused on the facts of the crime, the frequency and extent of bargaining practices tend to remain largely unknown, invisible to court and correctional agency alike.

Furthermore, detailed investigation at arraignment or in the post-plea hearing provides a more adequate record of the conviction process than has been customary. A great many postconviction determinations about the defendant, from appeal to release on parole, rely heavily on the formal, official record of earlier court proceedings.

These devices also serve other purposes. Increased knowledge of the defendant and the circumstances of his offense provide the court with a better assessment of the competency of a defendant, of his willingness to plead guilty, and of his degree of understanding of the charges against him and the probable consequences of his plea. These other objectives of conviction, the consent and understanding of the defendant, are dealt with in the chapters that follow.

CHAPTER 2

Concern for Consent in Guilty Plea Convictions

A. Requirement of Consent in Guilty Plea Convictions

The requirement that a plea of guilty be voluntary reflects to some extent an assumption by some appellate and trial courts that conviction is proper if the plea is based upon consent, that is, upon the free and willing admission of guilt by the defendant.[1] It is not clear whether consent is thought to be adequate objective evidence that the person is in fact guilty of the crime, since a person presumably will not freely consent to plead guilty unless he is guilty, or whether it is thought proper to convict a person who consents regardless of whether he is really guilty.

In practice, the form and content of typical questions asked by most judges at the arraignment relate more directly to the conditions which preceded the defendant's decision to plead guilty than to the truthfulness and accuracy of the plea. It is common, for example, for the court to inquire whether the defendant has been threatened or induced in some way to plead guilty. A negative response is considered by many courts to be a sufficient basis for accepting the plea.

Consent plays an important part at various stages of the criminal justice process. Consent is a defense to false imprisonment actions growing out of unlawful police practices of stopping and questioning.[2] It is also a defense to allegations of illegal search,[3] and the

[1] See, for example, Machibroda v. United States, 368 U.S. 487, 82 Sup. Ct. 510, 7 L. Ed. 2d 473 (1962); Von Moltke v. Gillies, 332 U.S. 708, 68 Sup. Ct. 316, 92 L. Ed. 309 (1948); Johnson v. Zerbst, 304 U.S. 458, 58 Sup. Ct. 1019, 82 L. Ed. 1461 (1938); Kercheval v. United States, 274 U.S. 220, 47 Sup. Ct. 582, 71 L. Ed. 1009 (1927).

[2] For a discussion of the defense of consent, see Prosser, Torts, chap. 4, §18 (2d ed. 1955).

[3] Paquet v. United States, 236 F.2d 203 (9th Cir. 1956); Judd v. United States, 190 F.2d 649 (D.C. Cir. 1951); Holt v. State, 17 Wis. 2d 468, 117 N.W.2d 626 (1962). See also Note, 1964 Wis. L. Rev. 119.

validity of confessions rests largely on the extent to which they were freely given.[4] The competent defendant may consent to waive various rights including his right to counsel, his right to a preliminary hearing, or his right to a jury trial.[5] The consent of the defendant extends even to some postconviction processes, for example, where probation is viewed as a contract between the court and the offender or where the parolee signs an agreement to abide by the rules of parole supervision.[6] Some courts, including one in Wisconsin, even use consent probation in certain nonsupport cases as an alternative to prosecution and conviction.[7] The traditional stress on consent as the basis of the guilty plea is consistent with this pattern, but there are some conditions characteristic of guilty pleas that complicate the issue.

While a guilty plea is sometimes viewed as a form of confession,[8] there are important differences between a confession given to the police and a plea of guilty at arraignment. A confession relates a set of facts (i.e., "I shot him") , whereas a plea is an admission of all elements of a formal criminal charge (i.e., "guilty of murder in the second degree"). The confession requires knowledge of a factual situation; the plea, however, implies a sophisticated knowledge of law in relation to the facts.

There is also a major difference between consent to an official action, like a search, and consent to a plea of guilty. Consent of the suspect is the ultimate issue in the search situation, in that the search is considered proper if consent was freely given. In the guilty plea situation, however, there are two questions involved: whether the defendant freely consents, and whether he is in fact guilty of a crime at least as serious as the one to which he offers to plead guilty. These may be quite different things. It is possible to have a consensual plea to an offense of which the defendant is not guilty, particularly where the plea is made because the defendant is unaware of the technical requirements for conviction. All judges who use post-plea hearings, pre-sentence reports, and other methods of checking the accuracy of guilty pleas report cases in

[4] See McCormick, Evidence, chap. 12, §111 (1954). See also Lynumn v. Illinois, 372 U.S. 528, 83 Sup. Ct. 888, 9 L. Ed. 2d 966 (1963); Rogers v. Richmond, 365 U.S. 534, 81 Sup. Ct. 735, 5 L. Ed. 2d 760 (1961); Paulsen, The Fourteenth Amendment and the Third Degree, 6 Stan. L. Rev. 411 (1954).

[5] See Johnson v. Zerbst, 304 U.S. 458, 58 Sup. Ct. 1019, 82 L. Ed. 1461 (1938); also Note, 42 Colum. L. Rev. 271 (1942).

[6] See Lee v. Superior Court, 89 Cal. App. 2d 716, 201 P.2d 882 (Dist. Ct. App. 1949). For a discussion of the necessity of consent of the defendant to being placed on probation see Rubin, Weihofen, Edwards, and Rosenzweig, The Law of Criminal Correction, chap. 6, §6 (1963). For a discussion of the necessity of consent to parole, see id. §8.

[7] For discussion of consent probation, see id. §7.

[8] 2 Wharton, Criminal Evidence §622c (10th ed. 1912).

which the pleas are freely entered but where, upon examination, the defendant's conduct is found to be not as serious as the charge requires or where it appears that the defendant might have had a proper defense of his actions if the case had been tried. At present it is not possible to measure the incidence of such cases, since the accuracy of pleas is checked sporadically, but judges who do make the attempt uniformly report the incidence to be high enough to justify their continuing efforts to assess the accuracy of guilty pleas.

Freely entered but inaccurate pleas occur under other circumstances, in addition to lack of information on the part of the defendant about the legal requirements for conviction. These are (a) guilty pleas by innocent but emotionally disturbed individuals and (b) situations in which the defendant, clearly rational, hopes to achieve some goal by falsely pleading guilty. Some states, Massachusetts for example, require persons indicted for felonies that carry severe penalties to undergo mental examination where, presumably, delusional and other inaccurate confessions by emotionally disturbed defendants are detected.[9] Other states, such as New Jersey, refuse to accept guilty pleas in murder cases involving possible capital punishment.[10] These practices by no means fully answer the problem, and the number of false pleas made by emotionally disturbed defendants is not known. In theory, the severely disturbed defendant is not competent, and his plea therefore is not based upon consent. The difficulty is that the customary procedure at arraignment where the plea is entered is so brief and the contact of the court with the defendant is so minimal that it is virtually impossible for the trial judge to determine that the defendant is incompetent unless he is very obviously retarded or grossly psychotic. The defendant who, although apparently normal, is disturbed enough to plead guilty to a crime he did not commit is difficult to detect by a pro forma inquiry into whether or not the plea is willingly entered.

The rational defendant who enters a false plea is another matter. This has occurred in situations involving admission of one crime to avoid conviction for another which took place elsewhere at the same time, confessions to protect another person, and false pleas of guilty under the expectation of judicial leniency where the circumstantial case seems strong or where the defendant is otherwise afraid to submit his fate to a jury.[11]

[9] See Note, 28 Ind. L.J. 374 (1953), for a discussion of this.

[10] N.J. Rev. Stat. 2A: 113-3 (1951).

[11] See Borchard, Convicting the Innocent (1932); O'Donnell, Cavalcade of Justice (1952); Pollak, The Errors of Justice, 284 Annals 115 (1952); Note, 28 Ind. L.J. 374 (1953); Radin, The Innocents (1964).

B. Attitude of Appellate Courts Toward Consent and the Accuracy of the Guilty Plea

Some appellate courts have taken the position that subsequent doubt of the defendant's guilt is not sufficient to upset a consensual plea. For example, in a case in Wisconsin[12] the defendant pleaded guilty to assault with intent to rob while "armed with a dangerous weapon, to wit a loaded revolver." Upon a pre-sentence hearing it was alleged by the defendant that the revolver was not loaded, and the record is not clear as to whether this was established. After sentencing, the defendant sought to have his conviction set aside on numerous grounds, among them the allegation that the trial court had erred in receiving a guilty plea not warranted by the facts. The appellate court, however, affirmed the conviction, holding that proof that the gun was not loaded was not a sufficient basis to reverse the conviction. The majority conclusion was:

> In a criminal case if a plea of guilty is understandingly entered by a sane adult defendant no further trial than the proper pronouncement of a sentence is required. There is no issue to be tried, no need for a jury, nor for the waiver of a jury trial either orally or in writing, nor need the plea of guilty be in writing. The reception of such a plea and a lawful sentence thereon violates no guaranty of either our own or the federal constitution, but on the other hand constitutes due process of law. We deem it unnecessary to cite authorities to sustain the above elementary principles of criminal law.
>
> The only serious judicial inquiry presented by the record is whether or not the defendant was at the time of pleading to the information criminally responsible and mentally competent to enter the plea of guilty. The presumption is that a defendant is sane and mentally competent.[13]

While some courts will set aside a conviction when it appears that the commission of the crime in the way admitted by the defendant was impossible, there is nevertheless a strong dissenting position to reversing conviction even under such conditions. For example, in a Kansas case in which a defendant pleaded guilty to seven counts of murder (all other members of his family were slain), the appellate court, in reversing the conviction, said in part:

[12] Sorenson v. State, 178 Wis. 197, 188 N.W. 622 (1922).
[13] Id. at 201, 188 N.W. at 623.

> We have already remarked that the record does not reveal any of the facts of the seven crimes charged against the defendant. The corpus delicti was taken for granted. The most light we can glean is supplied by a dialogue between the trial court and the defendant. [Dialogue follows.] The foregoing dialogue prompts one observation, which is, however guilty this defendant may be, the court did not succeed in getting at the truth. No person can put *seven* bullets through the hearts of *seven* persons in *seven* shots *with his eyes shut*.[14]

In a dissent to the reversal, one justice argued:

> It is argued that the crimes could not have been committed in the way the defendant declared; that it was physically impossible. Perhaps so, but how can that exculpate the defendant? Suppose he did actually murder his little brothers and sisters in a more revolting manner than he disclosed. . . . Is that a good reason for holding that the trial court abused its discretion in not setting aside the defendant's plea of guilty? I do not think so.[15]

These two cases relate to the accuracy of the specific charge rather than to total innocence of any criminal conduct. Even when total innocence is alleged, however, the appellate court may still hold the conviction to be proper if the defendant freely admitted the crime at the arraignment. The Michigan Supreme Court has upheld a conviction of a defendant who, without counsel but fully informed of his rights, had pleaded guilty to rape and was sentenced to life imprisonment, although subsequently the victim filed an affidavit denying that the defendant had raped her.[16] The majority of the court said: "The record satisfactorily shows that defendant's plea was voluntarily made. There was no abuse of discretion in denying defendant's motion." [17]

If appellate decisions were all similar, it would seem clear that consent of the defendant is all that is needed, and the fact that some convictions are inaccurate is irrelevant if the defendant freely and willingly pleaded guilty. This is not always the case, however. In some instances appellate courts have reversed convictions where the defendants are apparently innocent although they willingly consented to plead guilty. In a case in Wisconsin, for example, the court, in contrast to the earlier "unloaded revolver" case referred to above, held that refusal to allow withdrawal of a guilty

[14] State v. Oberst, 127 Kan. 412, 423, 273 Pac. 490, 495 (1929).

[15] Id. at 422, 437, 273 Pac. at 495, 502. The reversal of this conviction was not solely because the criminal act described was impossible but was based in large part on the youth of the defendant and the severity of the sentence (seven consecutive life terms).

[16] People v. Vester, 309 Mich. 409, 15 N.W.2d 686 (1944).

[17] Id. at 413, 15 N.W.2d at 687.

plea after sentencing where defendant is in all likelihood innocent of the charge is an abuse of trial court discretion. In *LaFave v. State*[18] the defendant had pleaded guilty to a charge of arson based upon a fire he caused while drunk and stumbling in the dark around a friend's house that he had illegally entered. While the guilty plea was clearly consensual in the sense that it was freely entered, without inducement or coercion, the defendant had no counsel until the day after imposition of a prison sentence, at which time a motion to withdraw the guilty plea was made and denied. The Wisconsin Supreme Court, in reversing, said in part:

> Any competent attorney would have advised the defendant that the facts stated by him in these statements did not constitute arson. . . . No fact or facts were before the court when the instant motion was denied that showed anything more than that the defendant somehow accidentally but not intentionally set the fire. . . . Upon the whole situation we consider that the court should have granted the motion under review and that, even though the granting of motions to withdraw a plea of guilty is discretionary, it was an abuse of discretion not to vacate the judgment imposed in the instant case and permit the withdrawal of the plea and representation by counsel.[19]

The failure of appellate courts to clearly and consistently separate considerations of consent, truthfulness, and fairness has left determination of the proper procedures for accepting valid guilty pleas to the trial court judge, who is confronted with cases which on the one hand seem to say that the test is willingness to plead guilty without regard to truthfulness and, on the other hand, seem to stress truthfulness of the plea rather than the defendant's willingness to plead guilty at the time of arraignment.

C. Trial Court Practices to Insure That the Defendant Freely Consents to Plead Guilty

It is the common practice of trial court judges in all three of the states studied to ask each guilty plea defendant specifically whether his plea has been induced in any way by threats or promises. This inquiry is routinely made even by judges who conduct post-plea hearings, use the pre-sentence report to gather evidence in support of the plea, assign counsel to unrepresented defendants, or conduct more extensive interrogation into the facts supporting the charge. This indicates that consent is viewed by these judges as a requirement separate from that of the accuracy of the plea.

18 233 Wis. 432, 289 N.W. 670 (1940).
19 Id. at 439-440, 289 N.W. at 673.

In practice, trial court inquiry relating to consent relates both to whether there has been coercion and to whether there has been inducement, such as a promise of leniency, which led the defendant to plead guilty. These two questions may raise substantially different kinds of issues. While threats, force, or other forms of coercion are clearly improper at all stages of the criminal justice process, inducement by a promise of leniency is a common administrative practice throughout the criminal justice system, from police dealing with informants through the negotiated plea process. The promise of leniency raises a difficult conceptual issue for the trial judge. The consequence of promises may sometimes be to cast doubt upon the trustworthiness of the plea of guilty, since an innocent defendant may accept leniency rather than risk conviction and a severe sentence. Nevertheless, in the guilty plea process there is common use of charge and sentencing concessions in exchange for the plea of guilty.

The trial judge ordinarily has no doubt concerning the propriety of overt coercion. It is quite clear that pleas induced by force, threats of force, or other forms of coercion are improper, both because such pleas are likely to be inaccurate[20] and because coercion is inherently improper. It is, however, doubtful whether the brief arraignment and typical manner of questioning the defendant are sufficient to elicit much information about any coercion that might exist.

For the court, overt coercion has no administrative advantage.[21]

[20] See 3 Wigmore, Evidence §§822, 831-836 (3d ed. 1940). See also dissent in Shelton v. United States, 246 F.2d 571, 580 (5th Cir. 1957).

[21] Threats of more severe treatment should the defendant choose to go to trial rather than "cooperate" by pleading guilty do occur with some regularity. When this practice comes to the attention of the appellate court, convictions based on such coercive practices are typically reversed. See Euziere v. United States, 249 F.2d 293 (10th Cir. 1957) and United States v. Tateo, 214 F. Supp. 560 (S.D.N.Y. 1963). It was subsequently held that Tateo could be retried. See United States v. Tateo, 377 U.S. 463, 84 Sup. Ct. 1587, 12 L. Ed. 2d 448 (1964). For a case where the plea was voided because of threats by the prosecutor, see United States v. Taylor, 303 F.2d 165 (4th Cir. 1962), and see Waley v. Johnston, 316 U.S. 101, 62 Sup. Ct. 964, 86 L. Ed. 1302 (1942), for a case where the plea was voided because an FBI agent threatened to throw the defendant out a window unless he pleaded guilty.

The question of what constitutes coercion to the point of voiding a guilty plea is not easily definable. For example, in Kent v. United States, 272 F.2d 795 (1st Cir. 1959), the prosecutor told the defendant that unless he pleaded guilty the defendant's fiancée would be charged as an accessory. The defendant pleaded guilty and his fiancée was not prosecuted. The appellate court did not find this inducement improper, commenting, "We are not prepared to say that it can be coercion to inform a defendant that someone close to him who is guilty of a crime will be brought to book if he does not plead. If a defendant elects to sacrifice himself for such motives, that is his choice. . . ." Id. at 798. See also Comment, 31 U. Chi. L. Rev. 313 (1964).

While the practice of threatening defendants with long sentences may be established in some prosecutors' offices, the promise of leniency is safer from reversal by appellate court and more commonly employed. Thus pleas may be alleged involun-

The plea of guilty induced by a promise of leniency raises a more complex issue in practice. A promise by the prosecutor of sentence leniency or a charge reduction as a concession for a plea of guilty is a major characteristic of the negotiated plea process, which constitutes an administrative advantage for the court as well as for police and prosecuting agencies. A steady flow of guilty pleas and the corresponding avoidance of the time, expense, and uncertainty of trials is important to the smooth functioning of most criminal courts.[22]

From the point of view of the defendant, the most important thing about the guilty plea is not the conviction itself (although he may indeed be concerned with the criminal record and seek to have the charge reduced) but what will happen to him at sentencing. Prior knowledge of the likely sentence or a reasonable expectation of leniency in exchange for the plea of guilty is obviously important in the decision of whether or not to demand trial. In short, the guilty plea system rests on an expectation by the defendant of greater leniency than he would receive with a full trial. While there is some dissent, there is indication that many judges do feel that greater leniency should be shown the guilty plea defendant than one who has put the state to the time and expense of full proof at trial.[23]

The granting of leniency in sentencing after the plea of guilty is one thing; promising leniency to induce the plea of guilty is, or may be, another. The real issue is that prosecutors do promise leniency in many cases in order to induce defendants to plead guilty, and that some judges actively participate in the reduction of charges for the same purpose Yet, if inducement negates consent, the court is caught in the contradiction of supporting one system but testing the validity of the plea on other grounds. Furthermore, appellate court guidance in this matter is not at all clear, although in some recent decisions higher courts have attempted to distinguish proper from improper plea inducements. The test most often applied to inducement by promises of leniency is whether promises were proper and were kept. Inducement as such is not the measure of lack of consent; appellate courts distinguish between what has been called "honorable" plea arrange-

---

tary because of promise of leniency rather than threat, and, as noted, inducements are often viewed quite differently from threats and are much more acceptable if, in fact, the promises are honored. For these reasons, plea inducement is of great significance at the trial court level.

22 Orfield, Criminal Procedure from Arrest to Appeal 297 (1947).

23 Pilot Institute on Sentencing, 26 F.R.D. 231, 285-287 (1960). See also Comment, 66 Yale L.J. 204 (1956).

ments and those where the state does not fulfill its side of the bargain.[24]

In practice, the consequence of toleration of the honorable plea bargain, either promise of a lighter sentence or charge reduction, is that although the court routinely inquires whether any inducements have been made it does not intend to refuse a bargained plea on this basis if the inducement is proper and the defendant is guilty of a crime at least as serious as the one to which he is pleading guilty. In actual operation, a guilty plea is ordinarily considered sufficiently consensual and accurate if, for example, a defendant who is in fact guilty of armed robbery pleads guilty to unarmed robbery as a result of a bargain with the prosecutor or court or both. The real concern where such inducement is involved is whether the defendant really committed the more serious crime. The same is *not* true, however, of coercion. If a defendant is led to plead guilty to unarmed robbery because he has been threatened with severe punishment should he demand trial on an armed robbery charge, the conviction will ordinarily be overturned (or the original plea not accepted if it comes to the court's attention), even though the defendant may in fact be guilty of the offense. This distinction between threat of severity as improper but promise of leniency (if honored) as proper confuses the entire consent issue, but the two are rarely distinguished by the court in questioning the defendant at arraignment.

One of the problems which the trial judge confronts in assessing the consensual basis of the plea is an adequate procedure for discovering what inducements, if any, have been offered the defendant to obtain his plea and for assessing whether or not such inducements are proper. If the inducement involves a charge reduction of which the judge is aware, or, as in some Michigan courts, if it involves a charge reduction which the judge initiates, then there is no problem in discovering the inducement. The promise of sentence leniency, however, is another matter, and, as shall be more fully explored later, it is often solely a prosecutor's function without the knowledge of the court. In a general way trial court judges are aware that prosecutors commonly promise to "recommend" probation or some other sentence leniency if the defendant pleads guilty, but the court has no way of knowing, in any specific instance, what the defendant has been led to expect in the way of a sentence unless this question is put directly to him or to the prosecuting attorney. In no observed instances did the general question of whether anyone threatened or promised anything to the defendant elicit a response that revealed a sentence promise by

[24] See Note, 112 U. Pa. L. Rev. 865, 872 (1964).

a prosecutor. Judges ask the question as a matter of routine and almost invariably receive the monosyllabic negative reply. The only way an improper or unhonored plea inducement comes to the attention of the court is if the defendant complains at the time of sentencing or appeals his conviction because the bargain was not kept.

CHAPTER 3

Concern for the Fairness and Propriety of the Guilty Plea Process

A. Requirements of Fairness in Guilty Plea Convictions

The current requirement that a plea of guilty be voluntary relates only in part to concern for the accuracy of the conviction or to whether the defendant freely consented to plead guilty. Courts have insisted upon certain characteristics of fairness which do not relate directly to either accuracy or consent. Among these are the requirement that the trial judge advise the defendant of the possible sentence if he pleads guilty, the requirement that enough time elapse between arrest and plea to enable a defendant to consider adequately whether he wishes to plead guilty, and the requirement that bargaining agreements be honored by the court. In the aggregate, these have an important effect upon the procedure of the guilty plea process.

1. *The court's duty to advise the defendant of the consequences of a guilty plea.* Appellate courts have generally required trial judges to inform the defendant of the consequences of pleading guilty, even in the absence of legislation or a specific court rule making such a warning mandatory.[1] The requirement is only that the court indicate what penalty is possible under law, not what specific sentence the judge intends to impose.[2] This warning must be given even when a defendant is represented by counsel, who presumably has explained possible sentences.[3] Trial

[1] For a discussion of this duty and for a survey of cases to point, see Note, 97 A.L.R.2d 549 (1964).

[2] Id. at 571-581.

[3] Id. at 556-557.

court judges in Michigan,[4] Kansas,[5] and Wisconsin[6] are required to warn the defendant of the maximum sentence, and, in practice, they carefully comply before accepting a guilty plea.

While this requirement is usually included in the concept of the voluntary test, it does not relate primarily to whether the defendant has freely admitted his guilt or is actually guilty. It reflects instead a general concern by courts for fair play in the guilty plea process, a conclusion that fairness requires that a defendant be warned of the possible consequences of his waiver of right to trial.

2. *The duty to insure the defendant of sufficient time to consider his guilty plea decision.* "Quick justice" convictions are cases which are so rapidly processed from arrest through guilty plea to sentence that sober consideration of the defendant's guilt and of the consequences of the guilty plea seems unlikely. Although appellate courts have indicated the undesirability of excessively speedy justice, there has been no clear indication of whether speed is undesirable because it is likely to lead to inaccurate pleas, because it is inconsistent with the requirements of consent, or because it offends a sense of fair process. In some situations, as in the Michigan case of *People v. Mahler,*[7] the court seemed satisfied that the plea was accurate and that the defendant had capacity to freely consent to his conviction even though the entire proceedings from arrest to sentence took only three hours. The defendant was arrested at 5:30 P.M., pleaded guilty to murder in the first degree, was sentenced at 8:30 P.M. of the same evening, and began his imprisonment the following morning. When he appealed the trial court's denial of a new trial, the Supreme Court of Michigan found that the judge had properly informed the defendant of his rights and that the defendant was of sufficient age (twenty-seven) and experience (seven or eight years in the armed forces), of sound mind, and of normal intelligence. While not represented by counsel, he did know and understand the seriousness of the charge and the consequences of his plea, freely and voluntarily insisted upon pleading guilty, and related full details of the crime in open court. Under these conditions, the court found his rights duly safeguarded and the rapid processing of the case well within the requirements of due process.[8]

[4] People v. Barrows, 358 Mich. 267, 99 N.W.2d 347 (1959); People v. Bumpus, 355 Mich. 374, 94 N.W.2d 854 (1959); People v. Merhige, 212 Mich. 601, 180 N.W. 418 (1920).

[5] State v. Oberst, 127 Kan. 412, 273 Pac. 490 (1929).

[6] State ex rel. Burnett v. Burke, 22 Wis. 2d 486, 126 N.W.2d 91 (1964); Ailport v. State, 9 Wis. 2d 409, 100 N.W.2d 812 (1960).

[7] People v. Mahler, 329 Mich. 155, 45 N.W.2d 14 (1950).

[8] Id. at 158-159, 45 N.W.2d at 15-16.

Where the defendant is young, swiftness of adjudication is more likely to cast doubt upon the propriety of the plea-of-guilty process, although there are exceptions. In a Michigan case in the mid-thirties a boy fifteen years of age was arrested at school on a charge of murder in the first degree, taken to the police court where he waived examination (the juvenile court had waived its jurisdiction), arraigned in Superior Court where he pleaded guilty to murder, and sentenced to life imprisonment all on the same day. He was not represented by counsel nor was his father notified of his arrest and subsequent conviction. The Michigan Supreme Court refused to grant a new trial, saying:

> No claim is made by the defendant of coercion in obtaining the confession; neither does he now claim that the confession was not true.
>
> The procedure employed in the instance at bar was expeditious and might well, considering the age of the boy, have been less speedy and an opportunity [might have been] afforded the father to be present, but, if in accord with lawful action, we cannot set the same aside.[9]

One of the judges, in dissenting, argued:

> That one not yet sixteen should be taken from school in the morning, and before the setting of the sun, upon confession of guilt, be sentenced to life imprisonment, without the knowledge of his father, whose whereabouts were known to the officers, and without the benefit of counsel, does not, in my opinion, satisfy the requirement of what we term "due process of law." [10]

The position of the dissent was supported by the United States Supreme Court in a similar Michigan case decided some years later. In this case[11] a seventeen-year-old defendant was arrested and arraigned, pleaded guilty to murder, and was sentenced to life imprisonment on the same day without legal representation or adequate advice on the legal consequences of his plea. The United States Supreme Court, in reversing the decision, said in part:

> Here a seventeen-year-old defendant, confronted by a serious and complicated criminal charge, was hurried through unfamiliar legal proceedings without a word being said in his defense. At no time was the assistance of counsel offered or mentioned to him, nor was he apprised of the consequences of his plea. Under the

[9] People v. Crandell, 270 Mich. 124, 126-127, 258 N.W. 224, 225 (1935).

[10] Id. at 130-131, 258 N.W. at 226.

[11] DeMeerleer v. Michigan, 329 U.S. 663, 67 Sup. Ct. 596, 91 L. Ed. 584 (1947), *rev'g* People v. DeMeerleer, 313 Mich. 548, 21 N.W.2d 848 (1946).

holdings of this Court, petitioner was deprived of rights essential to a fair hearing under the Federal Constitution.[12]

This decision has made itself felt in terms of liberalizing the practice of court assignment of counsel [13] and influencing judges to make more thorough investigation and go more slowly in accepting pleas, at least in murder cases and where young defendants are involved.

Similarly, in a recent Wisconsin case[14] involving a defendant who pleaded guilty to murder in the first degree, sentence to life imprisonment was passed and the defendant began serving his sentence all in the course of one day. In releasing the defendant from prison after he had served almost eighteen years, the Wisconsin Supreme Court commented:

> There is a fleeting attractiveness to the rendition of "swift justice" wherein the alleged felon is brought into court shortly after his apprehension, enters his plea, and within minutes is whisked off to prison. The nub of judicial responsibility requires the trial court to stand between the accused and an impatient or inflamed community.[15]

The reversal in this case and in others, however, is not solely based on speed of conviction but is complicated by the lack of effective legal representation. Even so, the too speedy guilty plea process itself seems to be an independent matter of judicial concern, particularly in crimes that carry severe penalties.[16]

[12] DeMeerleer v. Michigan, 329 U.S. 663, 665, 67 Sup. Ct. 596, 597, 91 L. Ed. 584, 586 (1947).

[13] See Chapter 15 for a discussion of this. The decision also led to the adoption of Michigan Court Rule 35A, making it mandatory to inform the defendant of his right to counsel on arraignment.

[14] State ex rel. Burnett v. Burke, 22 Wis. 2d 486, 126 N.W.2d 91 (1964).

[15] Id. at 492, 126 N.W.2d at 94. The court also spoke to the duty of the trial court in accepting a plea of guilty: ". . . by appropriate questions and simply phrased comments, it is feasible for the trial court to do the following:

"1. To determine the extent of the defendant's education and general comprehension.

"2. To establish the accused's understanding of the nature of the crime with which he is charged and the range of punishments which it carries.

"3. To ascertain whether any promises or threats have been made to him in connection with his appearance, his refusal of counsel, and his proposed plea of guilty.

"4. To alert the accused to the possibility that a lawyer may discover defenses or mitigating circumstances which would not be apparent to a layman such as the accused.

"5. To make sure that the defendant understands that if a pauper, counsel will be provided at no expense to him.

"Finally, the trial judge should be certain that the record itself reflects the fact that careful consideration was given to the foregoing propositions." Id. at 494, 126 N.W.2d at 95-96.

[16] A rapid and perfunctory examination by the court of the basis of a guilty plea is not considered proper procedure in federal courts. See, for example, Domenica v.

3. *The duty to honor bargains made with the defendant to elicit his guilty plea.* In dealing with guilty pleas clearly induced by promises of leniency, appellate courts have generally required that the prosecution honor promises made.[17] When promises have not been kept convictions have been reversed, either on the somewhat misleading ground of improper inducement of the plea which "deprive[s] it of the character of a voluntary act" [18] or with only a general statement that the failure to fulfill the promise "violates due process." [19] In most such instances defendants do not seriously allege innocence of the crime; they appeal their convictions because they have received a sentence different from the one promised.[20] Nevertheless, the apparent basis of such reversal is an outraged sense of fairness, for where guilty pleas are induced by promises which are kept the conclusion of appellate courts is generally the opposite. Honored plea bargains rarely come to appellate court attention, because where the defendant is in fact guilty and could have been subject to a higher charge or a more severe sentence he has little reason to appeal his conviction. Notwithstanding, there have been some recent federal cases[21] in which this situation has arisen. In these cases appellate courts have upheld convictions where sentence promises and charge dismissal bargains have been made and honored and where the defendants have apparently benefited by the arrangements.

The propriety of plea bargains, honored or unhonored, is complicated somewhat by the characteristics of particular defendants and the question of whether or not they were represented by counsel. For example, a federal court saw no constitutional problem with a guilty plea conviction in which the defendant relied on a prosecutor's promise which was not honored by the court, commenting: "[Such promise] ought not to affect the prisoner's judg-

---

United States, 292 F.2d 483 (1st Cir. 1961), and the United States v. Lester, 247 F.2d 496 (2d Cir. 1957).

17 For a detailed discussion of sentence promises and the way appellate courts view the practice see Note, 112 U. Pa. L. Rev. 865 (1964).

18 Machibroda v. United States, 368 U.S. 487, 493, 82 Sup. Ct. 510, 513, 7 L. Ed. 2d 473, 478 (1962).

19 Dillon v. United States, 307 F.2d 445, 449 (9th Cir. 1962).

20 Some courts require an allegation of innocence for a guilty plea to be withdrawn. See Smith v. United States, 324 F.2d 436 (D.C. Cir. 1963); United States v. Cooper, 222 F. Supp. 661 (D.D.C. 1963); State v. Nichols, 167 Kan. 565, 207 P.2d 469 (1949).

21 Shelton v. United States, 234 F.2d 132 (5th Cir. 1956), 242 F.2d 101 (5th Cir. 1957), 246 F.2d 571 (5th Cir. 1957), and 356 U.S. 26, 78 Sup. Ct. 563, 2 L. Ed. 2d 579 (1958); Martin v. United States, 256 F.2d 345 (5th Cir. 1958). For an analysis of the Shelton case, see Note, 36 Tex. L. Rev. 97 (1957), and for a further discussion of the Martin case and the matter of voluntariness of a bargained plea, see Comment, 35 N.Y.U.L. Rev. 284 (1960).

ment in pleading . . . particularly where defendant is represented by counsel or is experienced in the ways of the criminal courts. . . ."[22] On the other hand, courts have reversed convictions of unrepresented defendants where there was no clear promise by the prosecutor or anyone else but where a "layman" might have misunderstood some statement of the prosecutor to be a promise of leniency.[23] In a recent Michigan case where the sentence promise was ambiguous, the court held:

> In this situation we do not require that the promise of leniency be established beyond any doubt whatever, or even beyond any reasonable doubt in the mind of one learned in the law and acquainted with judicial administration. The requirement is far less stringent: If the evidence establishes that the prosecutor or the judge has made a statement which fairly interpreted by the defendant (in our case of foreign extraction and with only an eighth-grade education, presumably in court for the first time) is a promise of leniency, and the assurance is unfulfilled, the plea may be withdrawn and the case proceed to trial.[24]

In general, a distinction is made between promises by the court, the prosecutor, the defense counsel, and the police, with promises by the police having little effect upon the propriety of the conviction. In a Michigan case[25] the defendant, sentenced to prison, alleged she relied upon the promise of the sheriff that she would receive probation if she pleaded guilty. Both the trial and the appellate courts held this insufficient to justify withdrawal of the plea. An unfulfilled promise by the trial judge is ordinarily grounds for reversal by the appellate court,[26] but an unfulfilled promise by a prosecuting attorney has not always been treated in the same way. In an old Wisconsin case in which a prosecutor had made an immunity agreement with a defendant without getting the trial court's sanction, the Wisconsin Supreme Court commented:

> A public prosecutor is a *quasi* judicial officer, retained by the public for the prosecution of persons accused of crime . . . ; never voluntarily to acquiesce in an acquittal upon certain presumption of guilt, or in conviction upon doubtful presumption of guilt . . . .
>
> Any agreement of the character here in question, unsanctioned

22 United States ex rel. Wissenfeld v. Wilkins, 281 F.2d 707, 712 (2d Cir. 1960).

23 United States v. Lester, 247 F.2d 496 (2d Cir. 1957).

24 In re Valle, 364 Mich. 471, 477-478, 110 N.W.2d 673, 677 (1961).

25 People v. Vasquez, 303 Mich. 340, 6 N.W.2d 538 (1942).

26 See Frank, Coram Nobis §3.01(d) (1953). However, see also State v. Ashby, 81 N.J. Super. 350, 195 A.2d 635 (App. Div. 1963), where bargain made with an acting judge was not honored by the regular judge upon his return from vacation.

> by the court, . . . between a public prosecutor and the attorney of the defendant . . . is an assumption of judicial function, a bargain for judicial action and judgment; hardly, if at all, distinguishable in principle from a direct sale of justice.[27]

In a recent Michigan case, however, the court held: "There is no doubt, of course, that where the prosecutor has in fact made a bargain as to the plea, on the faith of which the defendant pleads, the courts will permit the withdrawal of the plea if the bargain is not kept." [28]

The duty to warn of consequences, accept only a considered plea, and honor plea bargains sets an objective standard of fair treatment of guilty plea defendants quite apart from questions of the accuracy of conviction by plea. In addition to this concern for the fair treatment of individual guilty plea defendants, there is also concern about the propriety of the whole process of negotiating for pleas of guilty, even when bargains are kept.

B. Propriety of the Guilty Plea Process Even When Bargains Are Honored

In current practice there are a number of different viewpoints about the propriety of inducing or encouraging guilty pleas by charge reduction or sentence leniency for the defendant who waives his right to trial. These positions range from the practice in a Kansas court, where the judge conducts a "sentencing hearing" prior to accepting a plea and indicates what sentence he will give if the defendant pleads guilty, to the position that plea negotiation or greater leniency for the defendant who pleads guilty than for the one who demands trial is inherently improper. This raises the basic issue of whether a plea-of-guilty process characterized by negotiation, bargaining, or settlement of criminal actions is a proper form of criminal justice administration.

To a degree, opposition to a system of plea bargaining reflects concern with the possibility of inducing innocent persons to plead guilty. Some judges see no difference in principle between honored and unhonored bargains as plea inducements.[29] In their

[27] Wight v. Rindskopf, 43 Wis. 344, 354 (1877).

[28] In re Valle, 364 Mich. 471, 476, 110 N.W.2d 673, 676 (1961).

[29] In Shupe v. Sigler, 230 F. Supp. 601 (D. Neb. 1964), a defendant bargained for and received a sentence of nine years' imprisonment instead of the twenty years he would probably have received as an habitual criminal if convicted after trial. He appealed his conviction on the grounds that it was induced by a promise which, although honored by the sentencing judge, voided the "voluntary" basis of his plea. The court held: "The fact that the agreement was performed does not transform the plea, which the court holds involuntary, into one that meets the rigorous standards of the Fourteenth Amendment." Id. at 606.

opinion inducement is the wrongful element, for it might lead to an untrustworthy plea, and whether or not the promised sentence or leniency in charging actually follows is irrelevant. One judge commented: "[I]f, on judicial inquiry, the conclusion is that it was that promise [of the prosecutor], whether subsequently made good or not, that really brought about the guilty plea, then the plea was congenitally defective. . . ." [30] An article assessing appellate court distinctions between "fatherly, kind and scrupulously fair" court bargains and "biased judge" threats of severity commented: "The court's focus on the benefit to the defendant ignores the problem of inducing an innocent defendant to plead guilty, foregoing the protections of a trial. There is no such thing as a beneficial sentence for an innocent defendant." [31]

Some opposition to bargaining, however, relates less to the possibility of inducing untrustworthy pleas than to a general feeling that bargaining itself is an improper form of criminal justice administration.[32] The Wisconsin court has said, for example, that a prosecutor's promise of sentence leniency is "hardly, if at all, distinguishable in principle from a direct sale of justice";[33] and a federal judge stated flatly: "Justice and liberty are not the subjects of bargaining and barter." [34]

If tenaciously held, the position that any plea bargaining is improper presents an operational dilemma to the trial court. Plea negotiation, with bargains duly honored, is a device necessary to administration if a steady flow of guilty pleas is to be maintained. In a dissent to one of the opinions in the *Shelton* case,[35] Justice Tuttle distinguished between proper and improper bargains and presented the argument for the administrative necessity of plea bargaining:

> . . . although no man should be allowed to bargain away his life or liberty it is not apparent why any innocent person would plead guilty if not subjected to or threatened with illegal pressures (including exhaustive inquisitions or threats to "frame" evidence or a more serious charge), misled by promises not to be fulfilled, or induced by promises inherently improper, merely because he receives assurances that such a plea may lead to punishment less

30 Judge Rives in Shelton v. United States, 246 F.2d 571, 579 (5th Cir. 1957).

31 Comment, 32 U. Chi. L. Rev. 167, 181 (1964). See also Note, 112 U. Pa. L. Rev. 865, 878-882 (1964).

32 Among other reasons, the practice of plea bargaining has been criticized because it leaves with the defendant a feeling that "judges and prosecutors can be bought off" and furthermore that it undermines "the deterrent theory of punishment." See Dash, Cracks in the Foundation of Criminal Justice, 46 Ill. L. Rev. 385, 395 (1951).

33 Wight v. Rindskopf, 43 Wis. 344, 354 (1877).

34 Judge Rives in Shelton v. United States, 242 F.2d 101, 113 (5th Cir. 1957).

35 Shelton v. United States, 242 F.2d 101 (5th Cir. 1957).

severe than that which he would receive if unjustly (but fairly) convicted. . . .

. . . It is generally known that the great bulk of criminal cases are disposed of by pleas of guilty made after some discussion between the defendant and/or his counsel and the prosecuting attorney in which the latter frequently makes some commitment as to the sentence he will recommend or as to other charges or prosecutions he will drop; if this were not so, or if this Court holds that it may not be so, there would be few inducements for any person to plead guilty. Furthermore this decision would make it possible to impeach many now invulnerable sentences, and though in such a proceeding the burden of asserting innocence is at least preliminarily on the petitioner after many years he may be in a much better position to sustain it than the Government to oppose it.

In the present case it appears from the record and from his own appearance before us that the petitioner was an intelligent man, fully able to comprehend the alternatives open to him and the value of the prosecutor's promises. It also appears that the prosecutor in good faith tried to live up to his commitments and to a very large extent was successful in his efforts. . . . Nor can it be said that any of the promises were inherently improper for the offer to help obtain the dismissal of federal prosecutions in other districts does not differ fundamentally from the usual practice whereby a prosecutor agrees to nolle prosequi all except the charges on which a plea is to be entered.[36]

In an en banc rehearing of the *Shelton* case,[37] this dissent became the majority opinion and "proper" bargaining was recognized:

[A] plea of guilty entered by one fully aware of the direct consequences, including the actual value of any commitments made to him by the court, prosecutor or his own counsel, must stand unless induced by threats (or promises to discontinue improper harassment), misrepresentation (including unfulfilled or unfulfillable promises), or perhaps by promises that are by their nature improper as having no proper relationship to the prosecutor's business (e.g., bribes).[38]

In addition to maintaining the guilty plea process,[39] the plea bargain also has the advantage of allowing discretion in the charging and sentencing of worthy defendants, especially where severe mandatory sentences are fixed to certain crimes. The trial judge

[36] Id. at 115-116. [Footnotes omitted.]

[37] Shelton v. United States, 246 F.2d 571 (5th Cir. 1957).

[38] Id. at 572 n.2.

[39] In People v. Guiden, 5 App. Div. 2d 975, 976, 172 N.Y.S.2d 640, 642 (1958), the New York court said, "The acceptance of pleas of guilty to lesser offenses with consequent lighter sentences is perfectly appropriate where the proper and efficient administration of justice will best be served thereby."

may feel that although a particular defendant is guilty of criminal conduct and should be convicted he does not deserve the mandatory sentence.

While bargaining, implicit or explicit, is generally necessary to encourage guilty pleas, there is one major exception in cases with severe penalties. This occurs where the express purpose of the legislation is therapeutic, as, for example, in the Wisconsin sex crimes law.[40] Some defendants are willing to plead guilty to the maximum charge under this law because they desire treatment for their deviation and believe that conviction and sentencing will be beneficial in this regard.[41] This desire for treatment also occurs in certain minor cases, for example, where chronic alcoholics plead guilty because they need "drying out" time in jail. In routine cases of serious crimes, however, most defendants and most trial judges as well view conviction as punitive rather than therapeutic and consider charge and sentence concessions necessary to support the guilty plea system.

In both Michigan and Kansas, where mandatory sentences for particular crimes are common, plea negotiation not only is a widespread practice considered necessary to obtain guilty pleas but is generally accepted by both the prosecution and the trial courts as desirable in situations where charge reduction is necessary to avoid overly severe sentences. In general, the question of propriety of plea bargaining has not been squarely confronted by appellate courts, even though the practice is widespread and generally known.[42] In part, no doubt, this is because where a bargain has been reached and honored the defendant does not raise the issue of

[40] Wis. Stat. §959.15 (1963).

[41] The juvenile court process provides another example of a system where, apparently because its goals are benevolent and the judge has wide discretion, bargaining is almost unknown. Yet the percentage of juveniles who admit their delinquency, who in effect "plead guilty," is much higher than in the adult criminal system. See, for example, Schinitsky, The Role of the Lawyer in Children's Court, 17 Record of N.Y.C.B.A. 10 (1962).

[42] There is some evidence that appellate courts are at least recognizing the pervasiveness and administrative reality of plea bargaining. A federal district court said: "These are commonplace occurrences [of pleas to lesser offenses] in courts throughout the country. We do it in the Federal District Court. On multiple count indictments, we often accept pleas of guilty to one or two counts. . . . In many courts, particularly State courts, a defendant's lawyer and the prosecutor may bargain not only on the offense, but also on the length of the sentence which the prosecutor will recommend.

"It is an integral part of the administration of justice in the United States." Barber v. Gladden, 220 F. Supp. 308, 314 (D. Ore. 1963).

See also United States v. Cariola, 323 F.2d 180 (3d Cir. 1963); State v. Maberry, 93 Ariz. 306, 380 P.2d 604 (1963); In re Valle, 364 Mich. 471, 111 N.W.2d 673 (1961); People v. Guiden, 5 App. Div. 2d 975, 172 N.Y.S.2d 640 (1958); and Nagelberg v. United States, 377 U.S. 266, 84 Sup. Ct. 1252, 12 L. Ed. 2d 290 (1964).

propriety. Only rarely, as in the *Shelton* case,[43] does an appellate court consider a plea bargain which was kept and, thereby, consider the negotiation itself apart from the question of the honoring of the bargain.

C. Equal and Consistent Opportunity for Charge and Sentence Leniency

In both Michigan and Kansas, where plea negotiation is common, there is a question of the fair and consistent opportunity for all defendants to participate in the bargaining process. In the negotiated plea, state concessions in charging and sentencing must be sought by the defendant; that is, neither downgraded charges nor sentence promises are automatically awarded defendants without overt negotiation. Over a period of time, however, certain practices develop so that it becomes unusual for certain charges not to be reduced. In Michigan, for example, it is customary for a charge of armed robbery to be reduced to unarmed robbery if the defendant agrees to plead guilty to the lesser count. The same situation applies when other charges are brought: sale of narcotics is almost invariably reduced to possession, nighttime burglary to daytime burglary, and felonious assault to simple assault. Likewise it is common in Kansas to reduce armed robbery to a lesser offense and to promise bench parole to the defendant who is willing to plead guilty. Similar reductions occur in Wisconsin for offenses which carry mandatory sentences. In all three states, promises by prosecutors to recommend leniency in sentencing can often be obtained by negotiation.

The frequency of these practices raises the issue of whether the uninformed defendant should be told of the possibility of bargaining and of usual sentencing practices of the court. A defendant, naive or uninformed, sometimes pleads guilty to a charge and receives a mandatory sentence grossly inconsistent with the customary practices of the jurisdiction. A defendant in Michigan, for example, guilty of the sale of narcotics, who freely and willingly pleads guilty to this charge after having been warned of the mandatory sentence, stands properly convicted by all formal requirements. His plea is the result of neither coercion nor inducement. He is actually guilty as charged and he was fairly warned by the court. Yet in looking at the inconsistency between his conviction and sentence and usual practices in similar cases, it is clear that he

[43] Shelton v. United States, 234 F.2d 132 (5th Cir. 1956), 242 F.2d 101 (5th Cir. 1957), 246 F.2d 571 (5th Cir. 1957), and 356 U.S. 26, 78 Sup. Ct. 563, 2 L. Ed. 2d 579 (1958). See also Shupe v. Sigler, 230 F. Supp. 601 (D. Neb. 1964).

has received disparate treatment. The real question is whether the defendant should be told of customary practices of negotiation. No appellate court has required this, and the decision is thus left to the individual trial judge. In practice some judges not only inform certain defendants of bargaining possibilities but actively arrange a lesser charge to obtain greater flexibility in sentencing. This is a sporadic practice, however, occurring usually when the defendant is young (one judge explained that he regularly refused guilty pleas to the original charges from defendants "between the ages of 17 and 20") and the original offense carries a long mandatory sentence. Older defendants, perhaps equally uninformed, are allowed to plead guilty to the most serious charges with no effort at negotiation unless they initiate it, and in these cases the judge typically does not inform defendants of customary bargaining practices.

Differential opportunity for plea negotiation typically results in disparate sentences, a major problem for correctional authorities. In prison, particularly, offenders quickly learn of this "cop out" process and quite obviously compare their own sentences with those of other inmates guilty of similar crimes. It is a difficult correctional task to convince an inmate to accept a sentence perhaps three times as long as that of another who has successfully bargained. Not only is he likely to be embittered by his conviction, but the major lesson he learns is not remorse but that the system can be manipulated by the knowing offender. The consequence is that he is far from a good prospect for rehabilitation.[44]

[44] In a formal speech, a member of the Michigan parole board commented: "We are not unmindful of at least some of the problems which plague the prosecutor and his trial of cases. Crowded docket, pressure of work, uncertainty as to the reliability of key witnesses, and the time and expense involved in jury trials and the one thousand and one things that can go wrong in any trial. All these and more contribute to the necessity for, or at least the practice of, accepting pleas to reduced charges. If the offender counts himself fortunate and is motivated to mend his ways, no real problem to the Board is presented. If, on the other hand, such action results in his becoming smug in having at least partially outwitted the authorities and otherwise contributes to the state of mind which makes him a difficult person to approach or work with, this has resulted in further complications for the treatment personnel and the release authority. His subversive effect on those who pled guilty to the full extent of their crimes can also impede treatment efforts in those cases as they come to think of themselves as 'suckers' for their honesty in accepting full liability for their actions while the obstructionist, the 'wise guy,' has materially benefited from his nuisance value. Something of this same attitude can be discerned in those cases where the offender feels he was not able to hire as expert and highly touted counsel for his defense as were some 'better heeled' codefendants or criminal counterparts. While we recognize this as extraneous to the individual's basic problems, many of these people are crude realists, especially in the face of the possible difference in years of prison time, or indeed any conviction at all. It is very difficult to inculcate a sense of the basic values and truths in life when so often our society seems to reward the financially successful regardless of virtue."

Sentence disparity as a result of differential bargaining can, in some cases, be equalized by parole practices. This not only raises a question of the proper function of parole boards but, in practice, can have some curious consequences for the naive guilty plea offender. In Michigan, for example, downgrading the charge of armed robbery to unarmed robbery is such a common bargaining practice that parole authorities commonly assume that all inmates serving terms for the lesser offense are actually guilty of the greater. At parole hearings they often ask the supposedly unarmed robber what type of gun he used and, in general, respond knowingly to the bargaining practices of the courts. What of the robber who really was unarmed and who has pleaded guilty as correctly charged to unarmed robbery? Unless the board investigates his true conduct (which is not always easy to do from correctional records), the assumption is, as one board member expressed it, that he "has already received leniency from the court."

D. Subjective Aspects of Fairness

It is not only objective fairness that is important in the guilty plea process. The way defendants themselves perceive their treatment is important to both the conscientious trial judge and the postconviction authorities.[45] From a correctional perspective, it is obviously important that guilty pleas be consensual and accurate and that the various standards of objective fairness, such as warning of consequences and honoring plea bargains, are followed. Assuming an accurate plea, however, it is even more important that offenders sentenced to custody and treatment feel that they have been fairly convicted.[46] This does not mean that they necessarily feel contented. The realistic objective is less. Correctional personnel feel that it is desirable for an offender to enter the correc-

[45] Sanford Kadish remarked: "It has not escaped those who have been concerned with the institution of procedural regularity that one of its prime contributions is as a psychological stabilizer; acceptance of law is substantially furthered to the extent that those subject to its rule observe its workings with consistent, scrupulous fairness." Kadish, The Advocate and the Expert — Counsel in the Peno-Correctional Process, 45 Minn. L. Rev. 803, 836 (1961).

[46] It is obviously difficult to measure accurately subjective satisfaction or dissatisfaction of offenders with the criminal justice process. Part of the subjective assessment no doubt relates to the type and length of sentence a convicted defendant has received in comparison to what he might have received or what he expected when he was first apprehended and charged. See Newman, Pleading Guilty for Considerations: A Study of Bargain Justice, 46 J. Crim. L., C. & P.S. 780, 783 (1956). A study of inmates in the Iowa state penitentiary showed that 63 per cent of those offenders responding to questions about the fairness of their conviction procedures felt the process to have been unfair. See Lunden, Vox Convictus: What 107 Prisoners in the Iowa State Penitentiary Think About the Judicial Procedure in Criminal Cases (Governor's Committee on Penal Affairs, 1958).

tional process convinced that he has had his day in court, that all officials have acted fairly and decently to him, that his side of the story has been heard, and that he has not been railroaded or cheated of his rights in any way. Unless he has some sense of this, it becomes easy for him to rationalize his problem as unequal treatment in the court processes, and it may be difficult for him to accept responsibility for his own criminality and to take steps toward rehabilitation.[47]

The problem of embittered, confused, and disgruntled inmates is only too real. James V. Bennett, former director of the United States Bureau of Prisons, commented:

> It is a common experience of prison workers that defendants committed by the courts arrive with the attitude that they have been "bum-rapped." In most instances the prisoners do not really claim that they are innocent; their attitude stems from their feeling that they have had no meaningful representation in presenting their case to the court. They enter prison convinced that they have been denied a fair trial.
>
> In a fair trial it would seem that both sides should be about equally pitted against each other in the court's search for truth. But the resources of the Government are massive compared to those of the average defendant, particularly the impoverished. . . . As high a proportion as 90 per cent of the defendants in our Federal courts plead guilty. The very lopsidedness of this figure gives good cause to conjecture whether all of these defendants are even aware of the consequences of their plea.[48]

Even though the trial court is scrupulously fair in such matters as warning the defendant of the possible maximum sentence following his plea and notifying him of his right to trial and to court-assigned counsel if he is unrepresented and indigent, strong subjective feelings of unfairness may nevertheless result from three sources.

1. *The brevity and formalism of arraignment.* As has been pointed out, the typical arraignment at which a guilty plea is entered is brief and rather stereotyped. The offender is commonly

[47] Speaking in a somewhat different context from guilty plea convictions, namely, parole revocation, but relevant to this point, Justice Prettyman said: "Certainly no circumstance could further that purpose [rehabilitation] to a greater extent than a firm belief on the part of such offenders in the impartial, unhurried, objective, and thorough processes of the machinery of the law. And hardly any circumstance could with greater effect impede progress toward the desired end than a belief on their part that the machinery of the law is arbitrary, technical, too busy, or impervious to facts. The crisis in the rehabilitation of these men may very well be the treatment which they receive when accused of an act violative of the terms of what must be to them a precious privilege." Fleming v. Tate, 156 F.2d 848, 850 (D.C. Cir. 1946).

[48] Bennett, Of Prisons and Justice 364 (1964).

asked a series of routine questions about threats and inducements and asked to plead to the formal language of the statute describing his criminal conduct. Experienced defendants and those represented by lawyers may be able to follow the proceedings and understand the purpose of the procedures and the language of the court. To less experienced and unrepresented defendants, however, it may be confusing to confront an array of officialdom in unfamiliar surroundings and be asked to respond to a series of questions put in language not commonly used by the typical defendant.

Both judges and correctional personnel seem to be increasingly concerned over whether the defendant adequately knows what he is doing, what rights he is waiving, and what will be the consequences of his guilty plea. When the defendant is obviously confused or excessively hesitant, the court ordinarily will refuse to accept the plea, at least until the defendant has conferred with counsel. Unless there are overt signs of confusion or misunderstanding, however, the trial judge has no way of telling that the defendant does not understand what is happening.

2. *Unfamiliarity with alternatives.* Naive and inexperienced defendants plead guilty to offenses that are ordinarily downgraded to less serious crimes for more experienced defendants who have engaged in plea negotiation. A sense of unfairness is created in the defendant who did not know or was not told that his plea was negotiable. This relates not only to traditional plea bargaining but to the use of other alternatives to the criminal process, such as treatment by private or charitable organizations instead of by formal conviction and sentencing. Some experienced or sophisticated defendants, clearly guilty of criminal conduct, have charges dismissed or downgraded when they present the court with a workable plan for treatment or control in the community. Others, unaware of this possibility, plead guilty and accept the full, formal punishment.

3. *Lack of representation by counsel.* Most defendants who are guilty of criminal conduct and willing to plead guilty waive counsel. This is consistent with a common popular conception that the function of counsel is limited to litigation. The defendant who is guilty, knows that he can be convicted, and is willing to plead guilty and get on to sentencing ordinarily sees little advantage in retaining or requesting counsel; in fact, he may see disadvantages, such as unnecessary lawyers' fees if he can afford counsel, or possibly antagonizing the prosecutor or court if counsel is furnished at public expense. This refusal of counsel rests on the assumption that

a defense lawyer has no positive role in guilty plea cases and in fact may be unnecessarily costly. Yet the conditions of pleading that create a feeling of unfairness, the unbalanced and impersonal arraignment and unfamiliarity with procedures and with bargaining possibilities or other alternatives, are specific areas in which competent counsel can make a contribution to the defendant, the court, and the correctional authorities who ultimately receive custody of the defendant. The role of counsel in guilty plea convictions will receive more detailed treatment in later chapters. Here it is necessary only to make the point that much of the subjective feeling of unfairness held by guilty plea defendants relates to confusion, misunderstanding, and a sense of aloneness and disadvantage in their day in court, all of which could be alleviated by competent legal advice and counseling.

E. Court Practices to Achieve Fairness in Guilty Plea Convictions

While it can be fairly said that the major purpose of the trial judiciary in conducting post-plea hearings, directing pre-sentence investigations into the facts of the crime, or assigning counsel to unrepresented defendants is to increase assurance of the accuracy and trustworthiness of guilty pleas, these devices are also used to achieve a measure of fairness in the proceedings apart from the question of accuracy. Some of this is no doubt incidental and unplanned. But it is not unusual for information which is really irrelevant to the guilt or innocence of the defendant to be noted in the pre-sentence investigation or the post-plea hearing and, in turn, to be used by the court to modify the sentence or even the conviction itself in the interest of more equitable treatment. This information is often of a type that would be given by a competent defense counsel or a sophisticated defendant in moving to have a charge dismissed or in negotiating for a charge reduction. In this sense, the discovery of mitigating circumstances or other information which leads the court to modify the conviction acts to reduce disparity between defendants who are knowledgeable enough to raise these issues, or whose counsel raises them, and unrepresented and inexperienced defendants who plead guilty without mentioning them. The range of information discovered in this way is great. For example, a Michigan pre-sentence investigation of an alleged burglar showed his problem to be severe neurosis rather than completely volitional theft, and the court dismissed the charge even though the defendant had pleaded guilty. In another case, a defendant charged with larceny had the charge reduced because he was an alcoholic. This was not his "usual" offense, and he was otherwise a reputable person.

In general, while post-plea investigations are designed to increase assurance of the accuracy of the guilty plea, they also commonly present the defendant's own story and whatever mitigating circumstances might be present in the case. This gives the court opportunity to modify the charge or sentence if it seems equitable to do so, and it gives the offender an opportunity to make known the full context of and motivation for his offense.

In addition to this incidental discovery of mitigating factors, trial judges attempt to achieve fairness more directly in a number of ways.

1. *Explaining consequences of the plea.* Judges in all three states routinely tell defendants of the maximum penalties for their particular crimes and whether the sentences are mandatory. Most judges do not go much beyond this point. They neither tell nor hint at what a specific sentence might be in a particular case. There is a major exception in one Kansas court where the judge commonly holds an open pre-plea hearing, allowing the defendant and his family or friends to plead for bench parole (probation) if this is desired and indicating at the end of the hearing whether or not he will grant parole if the defendant pleads guilty. He commented: "This procedure gives a defendant and his counsel a more intelligent basis on which to decide whether to plead guilty or go to trial."

In most cases, however, judges do not indicate specific sentences, perhaps fearing that to do so would be interpreted as a wrongful inducement to plead guilty. At the same time, judges are fully aware that it is not at all unusual for the prosecutor to predict the sentence with a high degree of accuracy and to communicate this prediction to the defendant. As a matter of fact, a substantial part of the prosecutor's sentence promise as an inducement of the negotiated plea rests on familiarity with judicial sentencing practices. Because of this communication between prosecutor and defendant, most judges probably assume that the defendant who pleads guilty does have an idea of what sentence he will receive without the judge telling him. Warning of the maximum sentence serves to remind the defendant of the value he has received if the actual sentence is less severe.

The practice of warning of sentences, even in the context of the bargained sentence promise, does not always meet subjective aspects of fairness which are important to correctional personnel. Such warning or promises as occur ordinarily concern only the length of incarceration or whether probation is possible. The conditions of the sentence and the consequences of incarceration to the individual defendant, for example, are never explained, perhaps because these are not readily explainable. Yet some misunderstandings about the real consequences of the guilty plea occur that create problems for postconviction authorities. It is doubtful if an appellate court would hold it incumbent on the trial judge to explain the nature of conditions of imprisonment to a defendant, yet misunderstanding about what will take place in prison may play an important part in the defendant's decision to plead guilty. In Wisconsin, for example, the sex crimes law is predicated on the existence of a treatment program for sex offenders found in need of specialized treatment.[49] A serious attempt is made to fulfill this treatment mandate, but it is handicapped by the limits of a prison setting, shortage of personnel, and the inherent difficulty of developing effective therapy for such complex behavioral disorders as are manifested in sexual deviation.[50] A number of persons charged with sex crimes subsequently report that they pleaded guilty with virtually no knowledge of how the program actually operated but with expectation that they would be sent to a "hospital" or "psychiatric ward" and be treated for, even "cured" of, their sexual problems. Instead, they find themselves inmates in the general population of a maximum security prison, working like all other prisoners in the auto tag shop or other prison industry and serving a mandatory maximum term for their particular offense,[51] with, in addition, a possibility of an extended prison term if they are found to be "dangerous" upon completion of the statutory maximum.[52] Unlike ordinary inmates, sex deviates may receive treatment weekly or more frequently in the form of individual or group psychotherapy, but the prison is by no means a hospital, nor are routine in-prison activities in any way specifically related to the cure of their deviation.

The fact that a person actually guilty of a sex crime pleaded guilty under a misunderstanding of the nature of treatment is not an adequate basis for appellate reversal of the conviction. If the treatment were cruel or unusual or if no serious attempt were made to fulfill the legislative mandate the situation might be different, but such is certainly not the case in the Wisconsin sex

49 Wis. Stat. §959.15(6) (1963).

50 Halleck and Pacht, The Current Status of the Wisconsin State Sex Crimes Law, 33 Wis. B. Bull. 17 (Dec., 1960). See also Wis. Dept. of Public Welfare, Wisconsin's First Eleven Years of Experience With Its Sex Crimes Law (Statistical Bulletin C46, April, 1965).

51 Wis. Stat. §959.15(12) (1963).

52 Id. §959.15(13) (1963).

crimes program. Yet the problem of misunderstanding of the consequences of conviction remains and is bothersome. Most trial judges wish to give fair warning, and correctional personnel wish to receive inmates who feel that they have been fairly treated and whose expectations of correctional programs will be met.

2. *Refusal to accept guilty pleas from "deserving" defendants.* All trial court judges are occasionally confronted with defendants who are clearly guilty of criminal conduct and who are willing and competent to plead guilty but whose conviction of the particular charge seems somehow unfair and inappropriate. Criteria of inappropriate conviction depend greatly on how the individual judge looks at the total circumstances of such cases, but in general judges are unwilling to convict, at least of major crimes, when (a) the defendant is young, inexperienced, ignorant, or of low mentality and the offense charged is a serious one, (b) the offense charged carries a long mandatory sentence, or (c) the defendant, except for the present instance, is a "respectable" person who presents no threat of continued criminal activity and for whom the consequences of conviction would be devastating to reputation or career. Faced with such cases, it is not unusual for the court to refuse a guilty plea, not because of any doubt of the guilt of the accused, but because conviction and sentencing seem unnecessarily harsh, given all the circumstances in the particular case. The court chooses between the alternatives of outright dismissal and reduction of the charge to a lesser, perhaps even "illogical," offense. Judicial discretion to acquit the guilty and to downgrade the offense is detailed in subsequent chapters. The point here is that such discretion rests primarily on a desire to introduce a measure of fairness into what would otherwise be a relatively automatic process if the only issues were evidence sufficient to support a plea of guilty and the defendant's willingness to plead guilty.

3. *Assigning counsel to explain procedures and conduct plea negotiation.* Judges occasionally appoint lawyers to represent guilty plea defendants even when these defendants have indicated that they do not want counsel. This is done on some occasions when the judge has doubts about the actual guilt of the accused or about his competency to plead guilty. In other instances, however, lawyers are assigned to apparently hesitant, ignorant, or confused defendants in order to explain to them more precisely what is happening. Some Detroit judges, for example, are confronted with illiterate defendants, recent migrants from southern and border states, who have difficulty comprehending the court process. Ordinarily the court has no doubt of their guilt but assigns counsel to help them through the proceedings on the ground that the indi-

vidual lawyer can clarify what, to them, is a hopelessly confusing process.

In other cases, particularly those involving young or inexperienced defendants who are apparently willing to plead guilty to serious crimes that are commonly, almost routinely, downgraded in the negotiated plea process, counsel is assigned with frank instructions to work out an equitable charge reduction deal. A prosecuting attorney in Michigan commented:

> Frequently young and foolish defendants will enter pleas of guilty to robbery armed and the courts just will not accept the plea. Defense counsel will be assigned to work out a reduction. Most of the judges abhor the possibility of sending a young man to the penitentiary for a period of twenty years or more. Unless the defendant is flagrant in his violation, or has a long criminal record, the case will always be reduced.

One judge commented that he assigns counsel, even if none is requested, to all defendants under twenty years of age. Other judges have no such rule but assign lawyers to work out reduced charges on a case-by-case basis.

While accuracy and fairness of guilty plea convictions and consent of the defendant are analytically separable matters, it is clear that trial court practices designed to achieve more effectively one objective, greater assurance of accuracy for example, often contribute equally to the other objectives. Trial judges commonly accept guilty pleas from represented defendants with greater assurance that such pleas are accurate and that the defendant is in fact guilty of a crime at least as serious as the charge to which he is pleading. To the same extent, presence of defense counsel acts to assure the court that the defendant is freely and willingly pleading guilty. In addition, counsel serves to balance the system, to contribute to both objective and subjective aims of a fair proceeding. The same thing applies to the use of the pre-sentence report, where not only the evidence of the crime is presented but the defendant is given an opportunity to tell his own story and the crime is described in the total context of the defendant's background and personality and the circumstances surrounding his criminal behavior. Likewise, the post-plea hearing not only serves to assure the court of the factual basis of the plea and the consent of the defendant but also gives the defendant a chance to be fully heard and allows the court an opportunity to weigh any mitigating factors in the particular case.

These may not be the only or necessarily the best procedures to be followed in guilty plea cases. There are a number of current developments, such as the revision of Federal Rule 11, and the recommendation in Wisconsin that post-plea hearings become standard criminal court practice, which are primarily designed to increase assurance of accurate guilty plea convictions. The ultimate question, not yet resolved, is how much procedural formality and regularity the plea of guilty process will be given and, in this regard, to what extent formality will be consistent with other objectives of the guilty plea process.

PART II

Conviction of the Maximum Offense on a Plea of Guilty

A defendant was arrested by a policeman in the act of stealing electrical appliances from a warehouse at 3:00 A.M. He had gained entry to the building by forcing a rear door with a crowbar. Upon interrogation, he admitted four other recent burglaries.

This is a common type of burglary occurring in virtually all communities in Wisconsin, Michigan, and Kansas. The handling of this type of case at conviction, assuming a guilty plea, varies markedly among these states, however, and points up some differences in the relation of the guilty plea process to the sentencing structure of each particular state. In Wisconsin the defendant would probably be charged with burglary and plead guilty. If more than one count of burglary were charged, he would still plead guilty and in all likelihood would receive concurrent sentences. In Michigan, in contrast, the defendant would probably be charged in the information with breaking and entering in the nighttime but at arraignment would be allowed to plead guilty to the lesser offense of breaking and entering in the daytime, a charge inconsistent with the facts of the actual burglary. He would not ordinarily be charged with more than one burglary, even though he admitted four additional crimes. In Kansas the defendant would be arrested and charged in the warrant with one count of first degree burglary but, if the case were at all typical, prior to the filing of the information the charge would be reduced by the prosecutor to the lesser offense of third degree burglary in exchange for the defendant's agreement to plead guilty.

These differences in customary ways of dealing with defendants guilty of the same crimes point up both the complexity of the guilty plea process and the deceptive inferences that can be drawn from looking at only part of it. For example, if only the relationship between the charge contained in the information and the guilty plea is examined, both Wisconsin and Kansas would appear to be characterized by "on-the-nose" pleas, whereas charge reduction in Michigan would appear highly visible. Yet Kansas and Michigan are much more alike; both are characterized by common charge reduction practices, the only difference being the point in the conviction sequence at which the charge is reduced.

Differences between on-the-nose pleas, as in Wisconsin, and guilty pleas to lesser offenses, characteristic of the other two states, are largely a result of differences in sentencing structures of the states. Both Michigan and Kansas are characterized by legislatively fixed sentences, which seriously limit judicial discretion in sentencing; whereas Wisconsin law provides low minima for virtually all crimes, discretion of the court to fix the maximum term within legislative limits, and probation as an alternative to incarceration for all offenses. For example, Michigan statutes distinguish between nighttime and daytime breaking and entering, while Wisconsin statutes do not. In Michigan conviction of nighttime burglary carries a maximum penalty of fifteen years' imprisonment, the minimum to be set by the court, and probation is not allowed. On the other hand, in Wisconsin, burglary, whether committed day or night, carries a maximum penalty of ten years' imprisonment, with a low statutory minimum, the judge having discretion to lower the maximum and to grant probation. Kansas provides for three different degrees of burglary, each with substantially different sentences. These differences in sentences have an obvious effect on the willingness of defendants to plead guilty to burglary. Furthermore, judges in Wisconsin, unlike some Michigan and Kansas judges, show no hesitancy in accepting on-the-nose guilty pleas to the majority of offenses since there are few mandatory sentences and the court is allowed enough flexibility in sentencing to take account of the particular traits of a defendant or the peculiar circumstances of his case. Judges in Michigan and Kansas are often unwilling to accept a plea from a defendant who, while undoubtedly guilty of the crime, is not deserving in their opinion of as severe a sentence as is provided by legislation.

The close relationship of guilty plea practices to sentencing structure makes it difficult to assess adequately what is really involved in conviction of the maximum offense by a plea of guilty. Presumably a plea of guilty would be a plea to the maximum offense, as distinct from a negotiated plea, where the defendant pleads to a lesser crime than is called for by his actual conduct. Somehow, in the opinions of some appellate judges and probably of a fairly large segment of the public, the guilty plea and the negotiated plea are different. The former is right and proper, but the negotiated plea is a compromise with principle.

The essential difficulty with this distinction is that the negotiated plea and the on-the-nose plea cannot be so neatly separated. They are both variations of a single process, occurring because sentencing provisions for similar conduct differ from one state to another and because trial judges, desiring equity in sentencing, will achieve it by manipulating conviction labels if this is the only way it can be done. While the process of convicting burglars differs in the three states, the sentences received by burglars who have committed comparable crimes are about the same, even though this is achieved by downgrading the charge in Michigan and Kansas.

Conviction with an on-the-nose plea of guilty occurs with frequency only when the sentencing structure is such that the degree of a particular crime charged makes little difference to either the defendant or the sentencing judge, because the judge has discretion in sentencing that enables him to take into account the circumstances of the individual case, including the defendant's willingness to plead guilty. Of course there are exceptions; some defendants do not attempt to negotiate their guilty pleas even where this is customary, and some plea bargaining occurs in the most flexible sentencing system. In general, however, the distinction between a plea to the maximum charge and plea negotiation is structural, an artifact of differing legislation rather than a fundamental difference of process.

The determination of what constitutes a maximum charge is further complicated by the practical difficulty of obtaining jury verdicts of guilty if certain types of cases were to go to trial. Confronted with cases involving crimes like adultery or situations where a victim is more disreputable than the defendant, the prosecutor, doubtful of jury reaction, will often reduce the charge to a point where the defendant will plead guilty. In such instances conviction, like politics, can be defined as the art of the possible. This represents a form of maximum conviction, not in relation to the defendant's conduct, but in relation to the actual probability of conviction if the case went to trial. Reduction of charges because there is doubt that the defendant can be convicted of the more serious offense is different from the negotiated plea process. In the former the reduction is made because of an anticipated *inability* to convict; in the latter because it is thought more *desirable* to convict of the lesser rather than of the more serious charge.

In this way both an on-the-nose plea to the highest possible charge and a plea to a reduced charge because conviction of the more serious crime is improbable are forms of maximum conviction. Both are based on a desire to convict the defendant of the highest charge possible by a plea of guilty. Neither involves discretionary downgrading for the purpose of individualizing the consequences of conviction. The difference between them is primarily one of expediency rather than desirability. Both of these variations of maximum conviction by plea are dealt with in detail in the chapters which follow.

CHAPTER 4

Maximum Conviction on a Non-Negotiated Plea of Guilty

A. Variations in Maximum Conviction

The concept of maximum conviction on a plea of guilty, like that of the expectation of full enforcement of all laws by the police, raises some major problems in definition. The question of just what constitutes maximum conviction depends theoretically on the charging and sentencing provisions of the particular state and operationally on customary practices of the prosecutor and court. For example, while Michigan courts have forbidden consecutive sentences following conviction of multiple offenses,[1] they are permitted in Wisconsin.[2] In Michigan a plea of guilty to the single most serious offense supported by the evidence represents maximum conviction because, since the sentence is unaffected, there is little purpose in simultaneous convictions of other crimes. The same situation in Wisconsin might *not* be maximum conviction, for while a plea is to the most serious single offense supported by the evidence, it is theoretically less than maximum implementation, because in cases of multiple violations other offenses *could have been* charged, with the possible result of consecutive sentences. Likewise, in many states it is theoretically possible in cer-

[1] There is no general statutory authority for consecutive sentences in Michigan, and the Michigan Supreme Court has held that in the absence of such authority a sentence may not be imposed to commence at the completion or expiration of another sentence. In re Allison, 322 Mich. 491, 33 N.W.2d 917 (1948); In re Lamphere, 61 Mich. 105, 27 N.W. 882 (1886); 1943-1944 Mich. Ops. Atty. Gen. 174.

There are two exceptions to the no consecutive sentence rule in Michigan: (a) a sentence imposed for an escape from prison shall be served after the expiration of the sentence being served at the time of escape, Mich. Comp. Laws §§750.193 to 750.195 (1948), and (b) a prisoner who is convicted of committing a crime while on parole must be sentenced to serve the second sentence after completing the first sentence or after it is annulled. Mich. Comp. Laws §791.36 (1948). See also 1947-1948 Mich. Ops. Atty. Gen. 257.

[2] Wis. Stat. §959.07 (1963), which permits consecutive sentences.

tain cases to charge a defendant separately under repeater or habitual offender statutes, but this is rarely done in practice.

What is normally meant by a maximum, on-the-nose plea is that a defendant enters a guilty plea to the single highest charge supported by the evidence. Habitual offender actions and multiple offense prosecutions where the aim is accumulation of sentences all represent "extra-maximum" effort on the part of the prosecution and, in practice, are only occasionally used.[3] An on-the-nose plea, in a more operational sense, merely means that the defendant does not in any way attempt to arrange for a plea to an offense which reflects less than his actual conduct and less than is supported by the evidence held by the state. In effect this is the non-negotiated guilty plea.

The frequency of on-the-nose guilty pleas depends largely on the amount of sentencing discretion held by the judge. A defendant charged with a crime which carries a high mandatory sentence is usually reluctant to plead guilty because he has nothing to lose by putting the state to the trouble of a trial. His sentence will be the same whether he pleads guilty or is convicted by a jury and, of course, he always has the chance, remote perhaps, of acquittal at trial. The defendant who pleads guilty usually does so only if he has a reasonable expectation of greater sentence leniency than if he

[3] Defendants with a number of prior felony convictions are potentially susceptible to long sentences or separate convictions as habitual criminals. It is not an uncommon practice for prosecutors to mention this to recidivistic defendants, and there is little doubt that this exerts a strong pressure on them to "cooperate" with the state by pleading guilty. The question of the propriety of such pressures on the defendant is, like all plea negotiation, debatable. In a case in which the prosecutor threatened a severe sentence under an habitual offender statute unless the defendant pleaded guilty, and where the defendant did plead guilty but was sentenced as an habitual offender anyway, the appellate judge, in setting aside the conviction, commented: "It is the court's understanding that the practice of prosecuting attorneys of not filing prior convictions under prior offender statutes where the plea to the current charge is guilty, but filing such priors if the plea is not guilty and the case has to be tried, is quite common in Montana and elsewhere. It is debatable whether such practice involves a proper use of the prior offender statute. Undoubtedly the practice may result in many instances in coercing pleas of guilty which would not otherwise be entered. On the other hand, a defendant who would otherwise plead guilty in any event suffers no prejudice in not having his sentence extended by the pleading and proof of prior offenses. Where the practice is followed, fairness would seem to require that a defendant with prior convictions be advised of the practice in order that he could consider it, along with other relevant factors, in determining what his plea should be. However, without either approving or condemning the practice per se generally, the court in this case believes that the combination of the County Attorney informing petitioner, in effect, that his prior convictions would not be filed against him if he pled guilty, but that they would be filed if he pled not guilty, together with the failure of the State to provide the assistance of counsel at the preliminary hearing, resulted in pleas of guilty that cannot stand in the face of the due process requirements of the Fourteenth Amendment." Alden v. State, 234 F. Supp. 661, 670 (D. Mont. 1964).

were convicted of the same charge after trial. Unless the court can consider in its sentencing decision the willingness of the defendant to waive trial, he is often unwilling to admit his guilt, even though the evidence against him is overwhelming. Because judicial discretion in sentencing is much more limited in Michigan and Kansas than in Wisconsin, the on-the-nose plea occurs with frequency only in the latter state. Negotiation for charge reduction often takes place in Wisconsin in cases where defendants are charged with crimes carrying mandatory sentences, such as murder and driving while intoxicated.

In spite of the practice of downgrading charges, characteristic of Michigan and Kansas, and some plea bargaining in Wisconsin, some defendants plead guilty to whatever the crime charged, even if it is a serious felony carrying a long, mandatory prison sentence. This is one of the primary reasons for appellate court concern with "quick justice" convictions. These cases raise a real question of whether any defendant, particularly one who is not represented by counsel, should be allowed to plead guilty hastily to a crime which carries a mandatory sentence of life imprisonment.

Convictions of the maximum offense on a plea of guilty are perhaps commonest in all three states in cases of certain minor offenses, such as drunkenness and vagrancy, where persons plead guilty to charges consistent with their actual conduct. In fact, a number of chronic drunks and vagrants request conviction and incarceration, having no desire to manipulate the charge or to avoid sentencing consequences. However, on-the-nose guilty pleas do take place even in Michigan and Kansas in serious cases, where the more usual practice is to reduce the charge. This usually occurs when the state's case is strong, the offense or the offender is notorious, or the case is otherwise considered serious enough by the prosecutor and court for them to press for maximum conviction without any concessions in charges, and the defendant, because the evidence is conclusive or because of inexperience, does not desire trial. For example, in a Michigan case two defendants who were charged with breaking and entering in the nighttime pleaded guilty and each received the unusual and severe sentence of from fourteen and one half to fifteen years in prison. While the more usual practice is to reduce nighttime breaking and entering charges to a lesser offense, in this instance the burglaries occurred in a resort area and the court refused to concede a lesser charge, hoping to deter such crimes by making an example of these defendants. The state's case was strong so that there was little doubt of conviction even if the case went to trial and the defendants were both young and inexperienced men, neither one represented by counsel. In most cases which involve persistence in prosecuting a serious charge, such as sale of narcotics by notorious drug sellers, the defendants do not plead guilty but require the state to put on a full case at trial.

Like certain vagrants and drunks, there are some serious offenders who have no desire to modify their sentences but instead welcome them. Certain crimes of high emotional content, murder for example, are sometimes committed by persons eager to confess and to be punished. In these cases the desire for quick justice is not all on the part of the state but originates with the defendant, who wants to get it over with. Certain defendants charged with sex crimes plead guilty in an expectation of receiving treatment for their deviation. The frequency of attempts to withdraw guilty pleas in cases of murder and sex offenses no doubt reflects the effect of disillusionment of time and experience in prison on these motivations for on-the-nose pleas.

It can fairly be said that a plea of guilty to the highest charge with an expectation of the maximum sentence is not characteristic of any of the states. The frequency of on-the-nose guilty pleas in Wisconsin occurs in a context that allows wide judicial discretion in sentencing and early eligibility for parole. While occasionally defendants plead guilty to the few crimes in Wisconsin which carry mandatory sentences, the more common practice is either to plead guilty to a reduced charge or to demand trial.

For adequate understanding of either the negotiated plea or the on-the-nose plea, sentencing structure and reasonable sentencing expectations of defendants must be taken into account. Negotiation for charge reduction is an explicit, visible attempt to manipulate adjudication to achieve the sentence desired by the defendant and the court. This motivation is present in the on-the-nose plea as well, the only difference being that there is no reduction of the charge. It would be erroneous to suppose that only defendants who overtly bargain their pleas are interested in sentencing leniency. The routine defendant who pleads guilty on-the-nose usually expects, and receives, sentencing considerations for his waiver of trial.

B. The Implicit Bargain: Sentencing Considerations for Pleading Guilty Without Overt Negotiation

The negotiated plea implies a preconviction bargain between state and accused whereby the defendant trades a plea of guilty for a reduction in charge, a promise of sentence leniency, or some other concession from full, maximum implementation of the conviction and sentencing authority of the court. However, it should be noted that in any waiver of trial even without overt negotiation there may be an implicit bargain in the form of a reasonable expectation of sentencing leniency on the part of the offender and an established practice by the court of showing differential leniency to defendants who plead guilty in contrast to those who demand trial. For example, the Wisconsin sentencing structure is such that the trial judge has discretion to determine the maximum sentence within a statutory limit for each crime, there is a uniformly low statutory minimum sentence for virtually all offenses, and all convicted offenders are eligible for probation at the discretion of the trial judge.[4] In this setting the practice of charge reduction in order to obtain sentencing leniency is not necessary. Negotiation for a prosecutor's promise of leniency may indeed precede a guilty plea, but if the defendant knows that the plea itself may elicit the necessary leniency even a sentence promise may be superfluous.[5]

There is little doubt that, where possible, judges in all three states tend to show greater leniency in sentencing to the defendant who pleads guilty than to the defendant who demands a jury trial. Of course there are exceptional cases where, because of publicity about the crime, its nature or the circumstances under which it was committed, or some unusual traits of the defendant, the judge imposes a sentence as severe as would be likely if the defendant went to trial. Some judges have particularly strong aversions to certain types of crimes and tend to be severe when confronted with such cases. A judge in Milwaukee, for example, is customarily harsh with "gun cases," that is, with defendants who, whatever the offense, were armed at the time. A Michigan judge tends to be more severe with incest cases than some of his colleagues who view this offense more leniently as a cultural pattern among certain migrant "hillbilly" groups. One judge imposed sentences of from fourteen and one half to fifteen years on defendants who pleaded guilty to burglaries in a resort area where there was public clamor to stop such crimes. In spite of such exceptions, the more usual practice is to give the defendant who pleads guilty a "break."

[4] For authority of the trial judge to determine maximum sentences within statutory limits see Wis. Stat., chaps. 940 to 947 (1963). For low minimum terms see Wis. Stat. §57.06 (1963). For eligibilty of probation at court's discretion see Wis. Stat. §§57.01, 57.025, and 57.04 (1963).

[5] In Michigan where mandatory sentences are fixed by legislation and where probation cannot be granted for some offenses, a defendant who pleads guilty may nevertheless rely on judicial leniency in setting the minimum term. Even in Kansas where both minimum and maximum terms are fixed by law, the defendant who pleads guilty may hope to win "bench parole" (a form of probation) where his counterpart who goes to trial is imprisoned.

This leniency is not based only on the possibility that remorse is shown by the confession or the assumption that the plea of guilty is the beginning of rehabilitation, although it is sometimes explained this way.[6] In spite of such customary explanations to defendants, it is apparent that the overriding motivation in showing leniency to defendants who plead guilty is to encourage and maintain a steady flow of guilty pleas. This is perhaps most apparent in crowded metropolitan courts where cases are never lacking, but in general the guilty plea is just as welcome in rural courts.

C. The Propriety of Differential Sentences for Guilty Plea Defendants

The question of the propriety of showing differential leniency to defendants who plead guilty and those who demand trial has long been the subject of debate, particularly in the federal judiciary. The *Yale Law Review* sent a questionnaire to all 240 federal judges inquiring about this practice and received responses from 140. Sixty-six per cent of the respondents considered the defendant's plea "a relevant factor in local sentencing procedure," and the majority of them rewarded the defendant pleading guilty with a less severe sentence than his counterpart who had trial.[7]

Discussion among a group of federal judges of the influence of a guilty plea on sentencing led to three different points of view: (a)

[6] Conversely, severity (or, more accurately, lack of leniency) to a defendant convicted after trial is sometimes explained on the grounds that the offender has compounded his crime by committing perjury in denying it at trial. As a judge in Wisconsin said, "perjury and probation are not properly handmaidens."

A defendant may indeed be prosecuted for perjury committed in his own behalf without violating double jeopardy protections (see United States v. Williams, 341 U.S. 58, 71 Sup. Ct. 595, 95 L. Ed. 747 [1951]), but it is rare that a defendant who is convicted is subsequently prosecuted for perjury. The question ordinarily is not new prosecution for perjury, but increased punishment for the crime itself when compounded by the defendant's lying under oath. There are two different views about this. One is that the judge is imposing additional sentence because the defendant has committed the crime of perjury as well as the original offense. The other is that the perjury is a negative reflection on the character of the accused and is properly taken into account by the judge in concluding that the defendant who lies is more difficult to reform. For discussion of these viewpoints, and of the propriety of both, see Note, 66 Yale L.J. 204, 212-217 (1956).

There were a few examples in the field data of perjury charged as a separate offense after defendants were convicted following trial. In a Wisconsin case a defendant charged with burglary demanded a trial, which resulted in a hung jury. However, he was convicted following a second trial and sentenced to seven years' imprisonment. After his conviction the district attorney interviewed him in jail and requested him to "be honest now" and tell what he had actually done. The defendant admitted he was guilty, whereupon the prosecutor charged him with perjury. He was convicted and received a consecutive sentence of from two to five years.

[7] Note, 66 Yale L. J. 204 (1956).

the guilty plea should not have independent significance in sentencing; (b) the willingness to plead guilty *may* have sentencing significance, depending upon the total circumstances of the case, and (c) giving a shorter sentence to those who plead guilty rather than to those who demand jury trial is both "appropriate and practically necessary" in order to achieve the proper administration of justice.[8] The viewpoint that the guilty plea should not have independent significance in sentencing rested on the argument that a defendant seeking trial is merely exercising a constitutional right and should not be penalized in any way regardless of "practical necessity." The view that the defendant who pleads guilty should receive a *less* severe sentence was based on (1) the state costs saved by the guilty plea, (2) the chance of jury acquittal waived by the defendant pleading guilty (which some judges thought to be particularly great in income tax cases), (3) the necessity to encourage the practice of pleading guilty if larger numbers of criminal cases are to be effectively processed, and (4) the "realization of wrongdoing," a "step toward rehabilitation," evidenced by the plea. One of the judges illustrated his position:

> Take the example of two defendants charged with the same offense and one pleads guilty and the other stands trial. One, in effect, says: "I admit my crime, I stand repentant and place myself upon the mercy of the Court." The other, in effect, says: "I invoked every right the law afforded, took my chance, was found guilty and I now stand before you, unrepentant, yet asking the leniency of the Court." If the sentencing judge believes both to be guilty, hasn't he discriminated against the confessing defendant if both receive the same sentence? Therefore, I believe it is a logical and fair conclusion for a Court to reach when the judge shows more leniency to one who confesses his crime and disposes of his case without cost or consumption of the time of the Court. However, I do not think the Court should ever bargain with defendants or counsel, nor should the United States Attorney be informed that any concession will be made to those who plead guilty. The Court's practice will soon be found out without the Court making a statement of policy. The policy of stiffer sentences to those who stand trial, in the more congested districts at least, will help to solve some of the problems of that congestion.[9]

The middle-of-the-road position is that the total circumstances of the case should be considered in determining sentencing consequences of trial versus plea. This relates to whether the defendant who demands a trial has a reasonable or frivolous defense:

[8] Pilot Institute on Sentencing, 26 F.R.D. 231, 285 (1960).

[9] Id. at 289.

> I do not think any judge here would hold it against the defendant if he demanded a trial and presented a reasonable defense, either on the government's failure of proof or otherwise. On the other hand, if the defendant presents a fraudulent defense, or adds perjury to his other crimes, I think it ought to be considered in determining his sentence.[10]

In trying to summarize areas of consensus, a committee of judges composed a "Decalogue of Sentencing," one of which is:

> That the court is justified in giving a lesser sentence upon a plea of guilty than it would give on a plea of not guilty, upon conviction for the same offense, after a trial in which the testimony of the accused is proved to be false or in which there is some other circumstance chargeable to the accused evincing a lack of good faith.[11]

At the same time, the committee selected this as an "important, current issue which ought to receive attention in future institute programs." [12]

Regardless of the administrative practicality of lesser punishment on a plea of guilty, it is quite clearly improper for a court to induce a plea by threatening a defendant with a more severe sentence should he go to trial.[13] In a recent federal case[14] one of four defendants demanded trial while his three partners pleaded guilty. He was convicted by the judge and received a more severe prison sentence than any of the other three, although on the record both his actual participation in the crime and his criminal background were less serious than his cohorts'. Furthermore, the judge made it clear that the sentence was higher because the defendant had asked for a trial.[15] The judge said his "standard policy" was to refuse probation for defendants who demanded trial. The Circuit Court of Appeals reversed the conviction, one judge commenting:

> The trial judge announced from the bench that it was the standard policy of his court that once a defendant stands trial, probation for such a defendant would not be considered. This policy or rule is self-imposed. It is contrary to the statute and the rule

10 Id. at 287.

11 Id. at 379-380.

12 Id. at 383.

13 Euziere v. United States, 249 F.2d 293 (10th Cir. 1957).

14 United States v. Wiley, 278 F.2d 500 (7th Cir. 1960).

15 The judge remarked that if the defendant had demanded a jury trial rather than the bench trial, the sentence would have been even more severe. It was subsequently revealed, however, that the judge had some knowledge that the defendant's background was more criminal than the record showed, so that the actual sentence was not unrelated to this factor even though the express reason for denying probation was that the defendant had demanded trial rather than entering a guilty plea. United States v. Wiley, 184 F. Supp. 679, 686 (N.D. Ill. 1960).

of criminal procedure authorizing probation. Such a rule should not be followed. A defendant in a criminal case should not be punished by a heavy sentence merely because he exercises his constitutional right to be tried before an impartial judge or jury.

In the case at bar, McGhee, the four-time convicted felon, and the ringleader, received a two-year term. The three defendants other than Wiley, all of whom had criminal records, received sentences of one year and a day. Yet, Wiley, who had a good previous record except for one juvenile matter when he was thirteen years old, received a three-year term. A realistic appraisal of the situation compels the conclusion that Wiley's comparatively severe sentence was due to the fact that he stood trial. No other possible basis is suggested for the disparity. Consciously or not, the learned trial judge again applied the standard of his rule when he reimposed the three-year sentence. I agree this sentence should not be permitted to stand.[16]

In several cases in Michigan and Kansas it was generally held to be well within judicial sentencing discretion to grant leniency in guilty plea cases but improper for the judge either (a) to threaten a severe punishment should the defendant demand trial or (b) to give a more severe sentence to a defendant convicted after trial, solely because he requested trial, than would reasonably follow from the circumstances of the offense and the characteristics of the defendant, providing the defendant entered a good faith (not frivolous) defense.[17] In short, a policy of leniency following a plea of guilty is proper, but its converse, extra severity following trial, is not. This is not by any means a unanimous opinion, nor one that stands without reservation even if generally supported.

[16] United States v. Wiley, 278 F.2d 500, 504 (7th Cir. 1960).

[17] It is apparent in Michigan that it is improper for trial court to use threats of more severe punishment to induce a plea of guilty. In an early case the Michigan Supreme Court said that "no sort of pressure can be permitted to bring the party to forego any right or advantage however slight." O'Hara v. People, 41 Mich. 623, 624, 3 N.W. 161, 162 (1879). In People v. Brown, 54 Mich. 15, 19 N.W. 571 (1884), the court in dictum went on to say: "And even though not given by way of threat, had a sentence of great severity followed [trial], it might have been apparent that the defendant had been wronged." 54 Mich. at 29, 19 N.W. at 579. However, again in People v. Brown, a guilty plea should not be set aside merely because a judge has shown "disposition to inflict a milder punishment on confession of guilt, and has done so." 54 Mich. at 29, 19 N.W. at 579.

In a Kansas case complicated by the youth of the defendant and the lack of counsel, the defendant, seventeen years of age, was sentenced to seven *consecutive* life sentences after pleading guilty to seven counts of murder following the slaying of all other members of his family. The appellate court, in allowing the defendant to withdraw his guilty pleas, commented in part: ". . . where the charge is murder in the first degree and the punishment necessarily imprisonment for life, and no possible advantage of leniency to the defendant could be gained by pleading guilty thereto without the advice of counsel, such a plea should only be received with great circumspection. From a seventeen-year-old boy it should not be so received at all." State v. Oberst, 127 Kan. 412, 424, 273 Pac. 490, 496 (1929).

In addition to the objection that denying leniency to defendants who put the state to proof in effect discriminates against them for demanding their constitutional right to trial,[18] some observers argue that a practice of showing differential leniency to encourage guilty pleas may create a risk that defendants who are in fact not guilty may be induced to plead guilty because circumstantial evidence against them appears strong or because of their poor reputations or past records. If they deny guilt and are convicted they may lose their chance for probation or other leniency.[19] It is also said that the practice contributes to the problem of sentence disparity, a concern of courts and correctional authorities as well as of offenders adversely affected.[20]

Many judges, however, take the position that in practice problems of inaccurate guilty pleas and sentence disparity are not markedly affected by leniency shown to certain guilty plea defendants. Judges increasingly investigate the factual basis of guilty pleas before accepting them, so that a plea of guilty by an innocent defendant is rare. While it can happen that an innocent person is convicted by his own plea, the same thing can also occur after trial. Although different sentences result from this practice, they are not necessarily disparate. Few judges base leniency solely on the guilty plea; most judges consider it only one relevant factor among many in determining sentence. In general, the administrative advantages of the guilty plea process are felt to outweigh the small risk of increasing inaccurate pleas or disparate treatment. Realistically, the guilty plea process operates effectively only if defendants come to expect, and do receive, greater leniency in sentencing on a plea of guilty than if they demand trial.

[18] Note, 66 Yale L.J. 204, 222 (1956).

[19] See Newman, Pleading Guilty for Considerations: A Study of Bargain Justice, 46 J. Crim. L., C & P.S. 780, 783-784 (1956).

[20] Note, 66 Yale L.J. 204, 222 (1956).

CHAPTER 5

Plea of Guilty to a Reduced Charge Because Conviction on the Maximum Charge Is Unlikely

A. Determination of the Maximum Charge Likely to Be Sustained by Conviction

The prosecutor, in deciding upon what he feels to be the maximum charge supported by the available evidence, necessarily operates with less than total knowledge of the facts and possible trial situation. No matter how strong his case, he makes a probability decision, for no case is won until the final verdict. On the one hand he has the police department's skill in gathering evidence, police technological services, his own knowledge and experience of court customs and foibles, some limited discovery where defenses of alibi or insanity are to be used, and in many cases an early opportunity to interrogate the defendant or witnesses with the possibility of obtaining incriminating statements. On the other hand, he does not have total knowledge of defense tactics or strategy, which must merely raise doubts, not dispel them. In the first phases of a case he has no sure knowledge whether the defendant will plead guilty or seek trial. He can only estimate the relative skills of the defense counsel, if there is one, and at best make an educated guess about the sufficiency of his evidence to prove all elements of the crime he charges, including, for some offenses, the especially difficult requirements applying to the mental state of the defendant.

Under such circumstances a prosecutor can frame what he believes to be the most accurate maximum charge possible, with fair ease establish probable cause during the customarily brief, one-sided preliminary hearing that usually results in bindover of the defendant,[1] and yet have room for agonizing re-appraisal as the trial draws near. With this second sight he may well decide that the maximum offense will not be sustained and move that it be replaced by a lesser charge.

B. The Decision to Reduce the Charge Because of Insufficient Evidence

Except where deliberate (or sometimes inadvertent) overcharging is used to force a plea, the charge for a particular offense represents a decision by the prosecutor that, at the time, his evidence will probably be sufficient for conviction at trial. A later decision to reduce the charge is a re-assessment of this probability. One of the most important factors affecting such re-assessment is a change in his evidence, particularly the reluctance of a witness or complainant to testify at trial. Another is new perspective on the evidence given by the trial judge in a pretrial conference.

1. *Reduction because of reluctant witnesses.*

Illustration No. 1: A defendant in Detroit had stabbed and seriously wounded his girl friend, with whom he was living. He was charged with assault with intent to do great bodily harm less than murder, and at arraignment pleaded not guilty. On the date set for trial, the victim-complainant approached the prosecutor and said she did not want to testify against the defendant. The defendant, however, had a poor criminal record and the prosecutor's office, in consultation, decided to proceed with the trial. Just as the trial was about to begin, the prosecutor, realizing he "would probably get nowhere without the cooperation of the complainant," offered to let the defendant plead guilty to felonious assault, a lesser included offense. The defendant's attorney agreed that "under the circumstances this would probably be the best move" because there was a possibility of the state introducing another eyewitness to the fracas (who, only the prosecutor knew, was also reluctant to testify) and the defendant pleaded guilty to felonious assault.

The reluctance of the complainant-victim to testify is a common occurrence in family or lover assault cases. The victim, usually the real or "common-law" wife, swears out a complaint, expresses a willingness to testify, but after arraignment and before trial changes her mind, thus ruining the prosecutor's case. Under such conditions the prosecutor may dismiss the charge, requiring the victim to sign a statement attesting her desire not to proceed to

[1] While there is, of course, some variation from time to time and from one jurisdiction to another, estimates of prosecutors and judges typically put the rate of bindover to trial following preliminary hearing at between 90 and 95 per cent.

conviction. As an alternative, the prosecutor may decide to go ahead with the trial, swear in the witness, and bring prosecution for perjury if she does not tell the truth on the stand. Another alternative is to reduce the original charge sufficiently so that the defendant will plead guilty to it. In selecting among these alternatives, the factors most likely to result in proceeding with rather than dismissing the charge, which is more usual, are (a) the poor past record or future dangerousness of the defendant and (b) the seriousness of the criminal conduct involved. Where a serious crime, such as homicide, is the original charge or where an organized criminal is the defendant, the prosecutor may decide to proceed even with reluctant and hostile witnesses, hoping to force their testimony by threats of prosecution for perjury.

The last-moment reluctance of complainants to testify in assault cases growing out of lovers' quarrels and family disputes is such a common occurrence that most prosecutors prefer not to receive such cases initially. Use of the Misdemeanor Complaint Bureau of the Detroit Police Department, which handles the bulk of these cases at the police level, is a functional alternative to charging.[2]

Reluctance of the victim to testify is by no means limited to cases of assault and organized crime. In certain sex offenses, such as rape or indecent liberties, the victim (or if a child, its parents) may be unwilling to go through the trauma of a trial, yet will not consent to total dismissal. In such cases a lesser offense will typically be offered the defendant. In cases of accosting and soliciting and in larceny involving "respectable" citizens who are fleeced by prostitutes, homosexuals, or procurers, the victims may be unwilling to proceed to trial because of their own involvement in the offense but be satisfied with the relatively anonymous guilty plea to a reduced charge.

Restitution or payment of hospital bills or other expenses often is the primary concern of victims of crimes such as assault, bad checks, confidence games, and various forms of petty theft. Many of these victims are much more concerned with recovering their money than with having the defendant convicted of the highest charge and will gladly settle for a lesser charge, probation, and restitution rather than risk losing their money should the defendant be convicted and incarcerated after trial.

2. *Reduction on advice of the judge.*

Illustration No. 2: A Michigan prosecutor had what he felt was a strong case against three narcotics pushers. He tentatively decided to charge them with sale of narcotics and consulted with

[2] A more detailed discussion of this agency is found in the volume on Arrest, Chap. 7, n.1.

a trial judge as to the likelihood of conviction on this charge. After reviewing the case in chambers with the prosecutor, the judge expressed the opinion that the evidence would not fully support either sale or possession of narcotics and suggested a charge of conspiracy which, although carrying a shorter sentence than sale (a five-year maximum as compared with a twenty-year minimum for sale), would probably result in conviction and thus accomplish the general desire to "put them out of circulation." The prosecutor agreed.

Illustration No. 3: A prosecutor and the defendant's counsel met in conference with a trial judge to review the appropriateness of a charge of indecent liberties in a particular case. The prosecutor, while certain that indecent liberties best described the offense, revealed his own doubts about securing a conviction because both the victim and her mother were of low intelligence and would make poor witnesses. The judge agreed that the case was doubtful, that the testimony would likely be confusing, and that perhaps "some evidence [was] lacking." However, he insisted that the court wanted "control" of the defendant because he was "dangerous" and suggested a reduced charge of assault. Both prosecutor and defense counsel agreed to the lesser charge.

There is little doubt that the opinion of the trial judge in pretrial consultation with the prosecutor is critical in influencing charge reduction. The prosecutor often has access to the judge in chambers, and in some situations it is not unusual for him to request, informally, an opinion about the appropriateness of the charge in terms of the likelihood of conviction in a particular case. This ordinarily occurs where the case is serious or unusual in some way and the prosecutor wants an informed, "outside" opinion about his charging decision. In most cases he is clearly not asking for confirmation of whether the evidence is sufficient to charge the offense but is raising the broader question of whether the defendant would be likely to be convicted at trial. He may therefore raise questions about the credibility of witnesses and the probable effect they will have on a jury. He also, of course, is using the consultation to discover, if possible, the judge's opinion about the desirability of pressing the greater offense or of reducing it with the strong possibility of eliciting a guilty plea.

C. The Decision to Reduce the Charge Because Conviction Is Unlikely Even with Sufficient Evidence

Once a criminal case goes to trial, in theory the only issue involved in conviction or acquittal is the sufficiency or lack of evidence to convince a reasonable judge or jury of the guilt of the defendant beyond a reasonable doubt. The trouble with this theory, of course, is that judges and juries may not always be reasonable and may base their findings on technically irrelevant matters.[3] Where there is a conviction unsupported by sufficient evidence the defendant has recourse to various remedies to get his conviction reversed,[4] but where the finding is not guilty, even though there is evidence to the contrary, the state is barred from further seeking conviction.[5] Operationally, in deciding whether to prosecute a defendant on a particular charge, the prosecuting attorney must consider the probable sentiments of the judge or jury as well as the sufficiency of his evidence. Furthermore, given the vagaries of juries and the predilections of some judges, the manner in which the evidence would be presented and the skill with which it would be rebutted may be important considerations in the choice between trial on the higher charge or assured conviction by guilty plea on a lesser charge. The evidence amassed in the prosecutor's office must be realistically tested against the possibility of challenge by an aggressive and skilled defense counsel.

1. *Charge reduction where judge or jury is unlikely to convict in spite of sufficient evidence.*

Illustration No. 4: A seventeen-year-old defendant in Michigan was charged with sale of narcotics based upon the sale of some marijuana cigarettes to a friend. While the state's evidence was clearly sufficient to establish the crime of "sale," the prosecutor's office reduced the charge to "possession," a lesser offense. A prosecutor explained: "We can't take these kinds of cases to trial. In the first place the law isn't intended to cover this type of situation. In the second place, when juries find out that the mandatory penalty is twenty years to life they just won't convict. Who is going to send a seventeen year old to prison for twenty years? And the judges do not like the law either, because they are caught in the same bind."

Illustration No. 5: In Wisconsin an otherwise respectable couple was arrested in a parked automobile and charged with adultery. The prosecutor reduced the charge to disorderly conduct, explain-

[3] An intensive study of the bases of jury decisions is currently in progress at the University of Chicago. For a description of this project see Broeder, The University of Chicago Jury Project, 38 Neb. L. Rev. 744 (1959); for some preliminary results see Kalven, The Jury, the Law, and the Personal Injury Damage Award, 19 Ohio St. L.J. 158 (1958).

[4] For a general discussion of defendant's right to appeal in criminal cases, see 4 Am. Jur. 2d, Appeal and Error §267 (1962).

[5] Even in states which are lenient in allowing state appeal, such as Wisconsin, the reversal of an acquittal is limited to matters of law rather than to a finding of innocence. See for example State v. Evjue, 254 Wis. 581, 37 N.W.2d 50 (1949). For a further discussion of state's right to appeal see Chapter 9.

ing: "Adultery cases are probably the toughest to get convictions on. Where adults are involved and it's clearly a consensual situation juries just won't convict."

Illustration No. 6: A defendant was arrested for "accosting and soliciting" because of homosexual overtures made to an officer of the Detroit vice squad. The charge was reduced to "disorderly person investigation." A prosecutor commented: "In these kinds of cases, it is the officer who is on trial rather than the defendant. Judges claim that the vice squad entices these people into their criminal actions and they not only acquit them but bawl out the officer."

The experienced prosecutor, in anticipation that acquittal at trial is likely, will frequently reduce a charge in spite of evidence objectively sufficient to sustain it. In general, prosecutors hesitate to try cases where (a) a long mandatory sentence will follow conviction; the defendant is young, respectable, or inexperienced; and the offense is of a minor nature; (b) the conduct involved in the offense, while technically criminal, is not generally considered morally reprehensible; (c) the activities of the police in obtaining the evidence are likely to be viewed by the court or the jury as improper and perhaps more blameworthy than the conduct of the defendant; or (d) the characteristics of the defendant, such as youth or respectability, or the particular circumstances surrounding the offense are such that the criminal conduct will probably appear justified or mitigated to a jury. These factors, among others, are important in both the negotiated plea process and the acquittal of guilty defendants by the trial judge. Familiarity with these practices necessarily leads the prosecutor to an assessment of the convictability of the defendant beyond the question of sufficiency of evidence. Confronted with cases having these characteristics he typically concludes that there is little point in vigorous prosecution when acquittal by the jury or acquittal or charge reduction by the court is likely. The common practice, if conviction is desired at all, is to reduce the charge until a guilty plea is elicited.

Occasionally prosecutors will press a charge when the evidence permits, although they are perfectly aware that the case will probably be decided on extra-evidential factors. This usually occurs in cases involving a serious offense which has received a good deal of publicity. In these situations a prosecutor may prefer to try the case and have the charge reduction or acquittal decision made by the judge or jury. For example, in a small Michigan city, in a murder case where the facts clearly showed that a husband had killed his wife with a shotgun, the prosecuting attorney had strong doubts that the defendant would be convicted because he was an industrious, well-liked, solid citizen of the community, whereas his wife, the victim, had a reputation as a drunken and promiscuous person. Nevertheless, because the crime was so serious and had received widespread newspaper publicity, the prosecutor felt it his "public duty" to proceed to trial even though he referred to the case as a "defense attorney's dream." Sure enough, the defendant was found not guilty. Both the victim's mother and son testified for the defense, and, in spite of careful instructions by the judge on the lesser charges of murder in the second degree and manslaughter as well as on the original charge of murder in the first degree, the jury brought in an acquittal. The prosecutor noted that the jury's decision was so popular with the spectators that the defendant "received congratulations as though he had won a sweepstakes."

Unfavorable reputation may characterize a witness also. The credibility of state witnesses is always an important factor in trial, and where their characteristics or reputation make them of dubious value the decision may be to reduce the charge rather than risk acquittal. For example, in an armed robbery case the prosecution decided to reduce the charge because the complainant-witness was in jail by the time of trial, himself a defendant on a murder charge. The prosecutor asked the judge about the desirability of reducing the charge and the judge concurred, flatly stating: "No jury will convict of armed robbery on the testimony of an alleged murderer." In another case witnesses to an indecent liberties offense were three young men, all with felony records. The prosecutor decided that he could not risk using their testimony at trial so he reduced the charge. Prosecutors also reported difficulty in getting convictions in the areas of gambling, narcotics, prostitution, and similar vices because many times witnesses were themselves addicts or fringe underworld characters whose reputations weakened the state's case.

2. *Charge reduction when defense counsel is employed.*

Illustration No. 7: A defendant was charged with felonious assault based upon a fight in which he had stabbed the victim a number of times. In fact it was first thought that the victim would die, and the charge was not finally decided upon until it was clear he would recover. The defendant sought to have the charge reduced to simple assault, a misdemeanor, but the prosecutor was of the opinion that he had already given the defendant a "break" in that he "could have charged attempted murder" and refused to further reduce the charge. The defendant requested and received counsel, and his lawyer reopened negotiation over the charge, "threatening" trial unless it was reduced. The prosecutor eventually complied and reduced the charge to assault and battery.

The presence on the scene of a competent and aggressive defense counsel can decrease the likelihood of conviction. Some defense attorneys are of the opinion that prosecutors are more likely to reduce charges if a lawyer with a "good trial reputation" is employed by a defendant. They imply that the prosecutor is afraid to meet such an attorney as an adversary at trial. Some attorneys commented that this works both ways: A defense attorney remarked, "I have no desire to go to trial against a prosecutor who is both popular and eloquent. However, if I'm forced to trial, I'll always waive the jury because judges tend to be more objective."

Prosecutors in general denied any fear of "trial lawyers," while at the same time frankly admitting a willingness to negotiate with defense counsel for charge reduction. There is such a general desire to avoid trial that, as one prosecutor said, "All *any* lawyer has to do to get a reduced charge is to request a jury trial." This is not quite accurate for, of course, many cases do go to trial, just as numerous guilty pleas are entered without any charge reduction. Whether the prosecutor's decision to reduce the charge is based solely on the trial reputation of the defense counsel is doubtful because, as one prosecutor put it, "if a lawyer thinks of himself as a hot-shot at trial work he won't take a reduced charge." Furthermore, some prosecuting attorneys indicated markedly less willingness to negotiate for charge reduction with some "so-called criminal lawyers" because they are felt to be disreputable. A prosecutor commented:

> There are twelve to fifteen lawyers who hang around the courthouse day after day hoping to pick up cases. We refer to them as the ———— Street Bar. What they want to do is pick up a fee by pleading their clients guilty. I wouldn't give them the time of day.

While the retention of a defense lawyer is certainly not necessary either to the negotiated plea[6] or to charge reduction without negotiation, the presence of counsel does mean that the evidence will be more expertly scrutinized and does increase the probability of trial. Metropolitan prosecutors particularly are of the opinion that the early retention of a defense lawyer puts them at a disadvantage should the case go to trial. An assistant prosecutor in a large office explained:

[6] For plea bargaining practices with and without defense counsel see Newman, Pleading Guilty for Considerations: A Study of Bargain Justice, 46 J. Crim. L., C. & P.S. 780 (1956).

> Prosecuting attorneys are assigned to a given court. They have little or no opportunity to prepare a case for trial and must depend upon the investigating police officer in charge of the case to present them with the entire package which will be the essential core of the prosecution. The typical prosecuting attorney will have no more than two hours prior to trial to interview witnesses and prepare his case for trial. Furthermore, they are overburdened with cases. [In contrast] a defense counsel who might have been with a case from the initial stages would have had weeks in order to prepare a defense.

Charge reduction in such cases is an obvious alternative to this imbalance. Furthermore, the skilled defense counsel not only can threaten trial and develop sound defense strategy but also can use his knowledge of variations in judicial temperament to maneuver his client before a "favorable" judge. In Detroit, for example, defense attorneys whose clients are charged with accosting and soliciting often try, by postponements or affidavits of prejudice, to get before judges who are hostile to vice squad methods.

While some assigned counsel are young and inexperienced in comparison to many prosecutors, some prosecuting attorneys are of the opinion that this is a defense advantage. They feel that at trial such attorneys are given more "breaks" by judges and that because trial court judges determine who is assigned, an intrinsically friendly relationship exists between the bench and these lawyers.

Whether all of these suppositions are objectively accurate is difficult to assess. Accurate or not, they are so inextricably woven into the prosecutor's assessment of the convictability of the defendant that whether his decision to reduce a charge is based on insufficient evidence alone can never be clearly determined. Charge reductions because of reluctant or disreputable witnesses, uncertainty about jury behavior, or the presence of defense counsel are not part of the negotiated plea process where charges are reduced as a form of plea bargaining. Instead, these reductions occur because they appear to be the only way to get a conviction in cases where conviction of some crime is desired. Charge reduction as part of plea negotiation, in contrast, is essentially an exercise of discretion, a deliberate decision that conviction of the lesser offense is more desirable or more equitable than conviction of the maximum charge, even though this would be possible. The negotiated plea is discussed in detail in the chapters which follow.

PART III

The Negotiated Plea

Justice and liberty are not the subjects of bargaining and barter.

JUDGE RIVES
in *Shelton v. United States*
242 F.2d 101, 113 (5th Cir. 1957)

All law is compromise.

Michigan trial court judge

When defendants plead guilty, they expect more leniency than when convicted by a jury, and must receive it, or there will be no such pleas. The truth is, that a criminal court can operate only by inducing the great mass of actually guilty defendants to plead guilty, paying in leniency the price for the pleas.

JUSTICE HENRY T. LUMMUS,
The Trial Judge 46 (1937)

A major characteristic of criminal justice administration, particularly in jurisdictions characterized by legislatively fixed sentences, is charge reduction to elicit pleas of guilty. Not only does the efficient functioning of criminal justice rest upon a high proportion of guilty pleas, but plea bargaining is closely linked with attempts to individualize justice, to attain certain desirable conviction consequences, and to avoid undesirable ones such as "undeserved" mandatory sentences.

If, as one Michigan judge put it, "all law is compromise," then compromise in the conviction process is neither surprising nor less desirable than compromise exercised at other stages in the criminal justice process. Certainly the negotiated plea is only one of a series of discretionary decisions that characterize the administration of criminal justice. From the initial decision of whether to investigate a crime to the final decision of whether to revoke a parole, the entire administrative process rests upon discretionary choices, formally recognized or not, of men who must fit law to cases. A police officer may decide not to arrest a suspect for reasons unrecognized, perhaps, in the general legislative mandate to the police. A prosecutor may choose not to charge a suspect at all or to charge him with a crime less serious than his conduct objectively warrants in order to accomplish some end that a more accurate charge might prevent. The same process, somewhat more visible, occurs at the conviction stage when a defendant is allowed to plead guilty to a lesser offense than the one of which he is actually guilty, or where, in exchange for his plea, he is promised a less serious sentence than would otherwise be imposed.

In large part, the negotiated plea is motivated by a desire to individualize the consequences of conviction for deserving defendants. But this is not the sole reason for the practice. As the term implies, plea negotiation involves an exchange of concessions and advantages between the state and the accused. The defendant who pleads guilty is treated less severely than he would be if he were convicted of the maximum charge and assessed the most severe penalty. At the same time, he waives his right to trial, thereby losing his chance, no matter how slight, for outright acquittal. The state, at the relatively small cost of charge reduction or sentence leniency, gains the numerous administrative advantages of the guilty plea over a long, costly, and always uncertain trial. In this way the negotiated plea in a real sense answers two important objectives of criminal justice administration: the individualization of justice and the maintenance of the guilty plea system.

The exercise of discretion at the conviction stage raises most if not all of the same issues as the exercise of discretion elsewhere in the criminal justice process. At conviction these issues relate particularly to the propriety of plea bargaining in general; the propriety of charge reduction to avoid legislative mandates for sentencing; the question of the equality of opportunity for all defendants to negotiate for charge reduction or sentencing leniency; the function of defense counsel in the negotiated plea process; and the existence of effective controls on plea negotiation.

The chapters in Part III deal with plea negotiation as it occurs in practice in the three states studied. The essential focus is plea bargaining as a process whereby the court can individualize the labeling and sentencing consequences of conviction while maintaining a steady flow of guilty pleas. Charge reduction as a means of avoiding legislative controls on the court and the role of defense counsel in plea bargaining are analyzed in later chapters.

CHAPTER 6

The Negotiated Plea Process

A. Variations in Plea Bargaining Between Jurisdictions

The point in the pretrial process at which negotiation over the charge or sentence takes place varies somewhat between jurisdictions and may, in any given case, involve the prosecutor, the police, and directly or indirectly the trial judge.[1] In many instances negotiation in behalf of the defendant may be conducted by his counsel; in others the defendant himself may bargain directly with the prosecutor or court.[2] In any case, plea bargaining involves an informal confrontation of defense and prosecution where the compromise is struck. No matter how common, it is never an automatic process, with the exception of the situation where a guilty plea is entered with an expectation of leniency in sentencing but without an expressly agreed upon concession.

In some instances negotiation is vigorous and truly adversary, less formal than trial, but requiring on both sides competent knowledge of the law and skill in predicting the behavior of judge and jury. Most negotiated pleas are arranged under conditions

[1] For studies and analyses of plea bargaining see Schwartz, Cases and Materials on Professional Responsibility and the Administration of Criminal Justice, 24-29, 85-87 (1961); Dash, Cracks in the Foundation of Criminal Justice, 46 Ill. L. Rev. 385 (1951); Miller, The Compromise of Criminal Cases, 1 So. Calif. L. Rev. 1 (1927); Newman, Pleading Guilty for Considerations: A Study of Bargain Justice, 46 J. Crim. L., C. & P.S. 780 (1956); Polstein, How to "Settle" a Criminal Case, 8 Prac. Law. 35 (1962); Weintraub and Tough, Lesser Pleas Considered, 32 J. Crim. L., C. & P.S. 506 (1942); Note, 112 U. Pa. L. Rev. 865 (1964); and Comment, 32 U. Chi. L. Rev. 167 (1964).

[2] An earlier study indicated that defense counsel was by no means necessary for successful plea bargaining. In this study defendants who retained or requested assignment of counsel were typically first offenders or outsiders, unfamiliar with the personnel and operations of the particular court district. Recidivists and others wise in the ways of the courts commonly conducted their own negotiations and, in fact, unless denied an appropriate "break," felt that the retention of counsel might be deleterious, serving only to antagonize the prosecutor or the judge. See Newman, Pleading Guilty for Considerations: A Study of Bargain Justice, 46 J. Crim. L., C. & P.S. 780 (1956).

somewhat less intense and a great deal more routine. Common patterns of charge reduction or sentence promise emerge wherever the practice is frequent. Certain charges are almost invariably reduced, and certain classes of offenders are routinely promised that probation will be recommended. In Michigan, for example, when sale of narcotics or armed robbery is charged in the information, in routine cases, there is no real expectation or desire on the part of the prosecutor that the charge will be pushed to conviction. The expectation, rather, is that it will be reduced after minimal negotiation. The charges are filed to provide "leverage" to insure a guilty plea, and the only real issue is the range of the reduction.

The bargain, however, must be sought. The defendant or his counsel must explicitly trade a plea of guilty for a reduced charge or a sentence promise since, generally, the charge will not be automatically reduced even though the routine practice is to reduce if a request is made. There are some exceptions to this. In Michigan some pleas of guilty to armed robbery by young defendants have been refused by the court and counsel has been assigned to work out a reduced charge. Most plea bargains are overtly arranged at or prior to arraignment on the information. In routine cases this is not difficult, but in some instances a bargain is not agreed upon until after a trial on the highest charge has begun. Some bargains are so common, however, that one defense counsel commented that his strongest argument in bargaining is precedent.

Because of differences in both sentencing structure and customary practice, the actual mechanics of negotiation vary from one state to another and, to some extent, even from one court to another in the same state.[3] Common negotiation procedures are described below.

1. *Negotiation for charge reduction in Michigan.* Charge reduction is the most characteristic form of plea bargaining in Michigan courts. Negotiation occurs after an information has been filed charging the highest offense supported by the evidence. The negotiation takes place at or just prior to arraignment on the information, or between arraignment and trial when a not guilty plea is entered at the arraignment. Whether the charge is reduced at or following the arraignment depends primarily upon whether defense counsel pleads not guilty at the arraignment to "steer" the case to a judge believed more lenient in sentencing. This can sometimes be accomplished in a multiple judge court by a request for a trial with the hope that the defendant will be bound over to

[3] For an excellent analysis of the relationship of plea bargaining to sentencing structure see Ohlin and Remington, Sentencing Structure: Its Effect upon Systems for the Administration of Criminal Justice, 23 Law & Contemp. Prob. 495 (1958).

a more favorable judge than the one currently conducting arraignments. Once the bindover takes place, the plea of not guilty is withdrawn and a plea of guilty entered.

Plea bargaining in rural areas is relatively unstructured, since the judge knows all the lawyers by their first names and most of the defendants as well. The relative impersonality and great volume of cases in metropolitan districts require more structure and, to this extent, the process is more visible. There is one assistant in the Detroit prosecutor's office whose sole job it is to screen cases just prior to arraignment with the express purpose of obtaining guilty pleas to reduced charges. This assistant has been at the task for about fifteen years, is well known to defense attorneys, and is heavily relied on by the judges. His office is the hallway connecting various courtrooms:

> The hallway which runs between the court of Judge A and Judge B is used as conference quarters by the assistant prosecutor and the various defense attorneys who line up to talk with him and to discuss pleas and sentences. This is all done during the Judge's first docket call or immediately thereafter. The hallway is about 20 feet long and 4 or 5 feet wide. A door off one side is screened and barred and looks into the bullpen or detention quarters of the defendants awaiting hearings in the court. Through these bars and mesh the various defense counsel talk with their clients, telling them what they can obtain for them, what reductions of charges and what sentences they may anticipate, and learn whether or not their clients will consent to plead under those circumstances.

A typical negotiation conference between the assistant prosecutor and a defendant's counsel involved the following:

> A defendant was charged with possession of heroin, namely 19 caps, an offense carrying a 10 year maximum. Present in the hallway were defendant (in bullpen), his counsel, the police officer in charge of the case, and the assistant prosecutor, who offered defendant a reduced charge of addiction which would carry a one year maximum. Defense counsel thought this was a good deal and talked with his client, but the client, faced with the year sentence, backed off and said he wanted a jury trial on the possession charge. Defense counsel thought the evidence sufficient to convict him (he had had the heroin in a violin case and, when approached by the police, had thrown the case away, but they recovered it) and asked if the prosecutor would recommend probation on the one year user maximum if defendant pleaded guilty. The prosecutor snorted at this, stating that anyone having 19 caps of heroin had some to sell, and that no user would have this much for his own use alone. He said defendant, in spite of no prior convictions, was too old (28) to consider for probation and had had too much heroin. After some

haranguing back and forth, the prosecutor said he wouldn't favor or oppose probation and that he would go along if the court saw fit to grant it. He refused to change from this position and eventually defendant pleaded guilty to being an addict and was sentenced to one year in prison.

After the morning's negotiations have been completed, the assistant prosecutor enters the courtroom, explains the bargain to the court, and moves that the lesser offense (to which defendant has agreed to plead guilty) be added to the information. The judge in such proceedings regularly accepts the plea to the lesser count, provided he is satisfied that the prosecutor has approved the reduction. Occasionally, the prosecutor will not have completed his hallway duties before arraignments begin, and in these cases the defendant or his attorney will ordinarily inform the judge that the prosecutor has agreed to a lesser charge, and the judge in turn will send for the prosecutor to be sure the lesser offense has been okayed.

The bargaining prosecutor insists that the original charge in the information be as high as the evidence permits. Overcharging is not customarily used to induce pleas, but on the other hand no charging leniency is shown by the prosecutor who first determines what the charge will be. An assistant prosecutor whose job is to file the original charge explained:

The other day the bargaining prosecutor came in and told us: "For God's sakes, give me something to work with over there. Don't reduce these cases over here; let me do it over there or many of these guys will be tried on a misdemeanor." What he was referring to is, if we had graded a case at the lowest charge in the class of offenses in which it logically belonged, a defense attorney could conceivably get his man to plead to even a lower crime, a misdemeanor, for example. We will limit to the highest possible charge because we expect a reduction in court for a plea.

This results in a four-step adjudication process in Michigan: the issuance of a warrant, the filing of an information, negotiation for reduction after the information has been filed, and acceptance of the plea to a lesser offense to be added to the information. The fact that a defendant is originally charged with the maximum offense justified by the evidence prevents "double bargaining," which might occur if reduction took place both at the time of the issuance of the warrant or filing of the information and also at the time of the arraignment.

The technical procedures followed in charge reduction are simple and direct. If the information already contains two charges, the guilty plea is entered to the lesser count. The higher count is not then dismissed but remains potentially active (although with a promise of dismissal) until after sentence is passed so that the defendant cannot withdraw his plea and demand trial on the lesser charge. The bargaining prosecutor explained that the defense attorneys regularly practicing in his court understand this and rely on his promise to dismiss once sentence is passed. Sometimes lawyers less familiar with the practice will insist on immediate dismissal after the bargain is struck. One attorney was told:

> No, you may not be the attorney when the man comes in for sentencing two weeks from today. Under Michigan law he may withdraw his plea any time prior to sentencing and because of the presentence investigation it will be two weeks from the time he enters his plea until he is sentenced. If he should change his mind and obtain another attorney in the meanwhile, I do not want to be in the position of having dismissed the other counts.

If the lesser count is not already contained in the information, it is ordinarily typed in during the arraignment itself, or, if there is time between the agreement in the hallway and defendant's appearance before the judge, the information may be sent back to the prosecutor's office where the new count is added. Adding a count to the information is common even in situations where the lesser offense may be an included crime, which does not, therefore, have to be specifically charged. If the lesser offense is an included offense all that is required is a notation on the case file that the defendant "pleaded guilty to the lesser included offense of . . . ." The difficulty with this is that it is often difficult to be sure that a given offense is included in the original charge. The director of legal research of the court pointed to confusion in both statutory and case law regarding the included offense concept and concluded: "When there is any doubt it is always best to add the less severe count to the original one."

The prosecutor not only bargains over the charge but occasionally offers the additional inducement of a promise to recommend probation. While this is not an assurance of probation, the recommendation is communicated to the judge along with the pre-sentence report for his consideration. The experienced prosecutor can determine which defendants are likely to receive probation, and it is rare that he makes a probation promise in a case in which it would not ordinarily be considered.

The formal acceptance of a guilty plea to a reduced charge follows precisely the same routine pattern as acceptance of any guilty plea. Particularly striking, in view of the hallway negotiations, are the judge's questions as to whether the plea was induced by any promises or inducements. The following questions were asked of a defendant after he had pleaded guilty to unarmed robbery when the original charge was armed robbery. This reduction is common, and the judge was fully aware that the plea was negotiated:

Judge: You want to plead guilty to robbery unarmed?
Defendant: Yes, Sir.
Judge: Your plea of guilty is free and voluntary?
Defendant: Yes, Sir.
Judge: No one has promised you anything?
Defendant: No.
Judge: No one has induced you to plead guilty?
Defendant: No.
Judge: You're pleading guilty because you are guilty?
Defendant: Yes.
Judge: I'll accept your plea of guilty to robbery unarmed and refer it to the probation department for a report and for sentencing December 28.

This is a routine procedure designed to satisfy the statutory requirement and is not intended to disguise the process of charge reduction. If the defendant's plea is trustworthy and freely given, the fact that he pleads guilty to a less serious crime than his conduct might indicate does not ordinarily put the matter of his guilt in doubt. The question and answer sequence, however, is not likely to effectively satisfy the court that there is a factual basis for the plea. In practice such charge reductions commonly occur where there is little doubt that the defendant did commit the more serious crime, the reduction being merely a break for him in exchange for his plea.

2. *Plea bargaining in Kansas.* The charge reduction process in Kansas commonly occurs within the prosecutor's office and, except when no agreement can be reached, does not directly involve the trial judge. The compromise is commonly reached before the information is filed and is visible as a downgraded charge only when compared with the offense alleged in the warrant. When a bargain is reached, the lesser offense is the only charge contained in the original draft of the information to which the defendant pleads guilty at the arraignment. However, the original charge selected by the prosecutor and reflected in the warrant is typically the maximum possible on the facts of the case, regardless of anticipated difficulty in proving those facts. This is done to put the prosecutor's office in a position from which to negotiate a guilty plea, rather than with any real intention of prosecuting for the highest charge except in those cases where, for reasons of excessive publicity or some other factor, plea negotiation is not desired or practical.

Once the highest original charge is decided upon and incorporated in the warrant, negotiation for charge reduction begins. Usually this involves an informal conference between a member of the prosecutor's staff and the defense counsel and may occur in the county attorney's office, in a hallway, over the telephone, occasionally in the courtroom prior to entering of the plea, and in some cases at a pre-arraignment conference with the trial judge. This informal process in the prosecutor's office is a common daily occurrence. Various defense attorneys wander around the office looking for a particular deputy prosecutor in order to discuss a pending case. The discussions are often in the manner of good-natured kidding; the prosecutor asks whether the attorney is going to plead his client guilty to the charge, and the attorney in reply argues that the prosecutor should dismiss the case because he has no evidence. Eventually some kind of an arrangement is worked out, usually a charge reduction and a promise to recommend bench parole in return for a guilty plea. In cases where the defendant has a record of prior convictions, the prosecutor may assure the lawyer that the habitual criminal statute will not be invoked if his client pleads guilty. In all but very serious cases such as murder, rape, and armed robbery, the various deputy prosecutors are authorized to make whatever arrangements they wish without asking the permission of the prosecuting attorney. Arrangements in cases involving serious charges can be made only with his authorization. Thus the bargaining process in Kansas focuses primarily on reduction of the offense charged and promise of bench parole following a plea, both of which are often involved in a single negotiation.

It is a general practice of judges in Kansas to deny bench parole to offenders convicted of first degree murder, robbery, or rape; consequently, charge reductions in these serious cases are necessary if bench parole is to be considered. In other felonies and in misdemeanors charge reduction is not necessary in order that the defendant be eligible for bench parole, although there is no assurance that it will be granted without pre-arraignment bargaining. Except where there is a desire on the part of the defendant to avoid a felony record or some other consequence of conviction, such as loss of driver's license, negotiation in most felonies and misdemeanors is directed primarily to the promise of bench parole. Where the issue is not bench parole but rather the length of imprisonment, because of the seriousness of the crime or because the defendant has an extensive prior record, charge reduction is imperative from defendant's point of view, since both minimum and maximum terms in Kansas are fixed by legislation and must be imposed by the judge. In other cases negotiation may avoid long sentences or prosecution in other states. One deputy prosecuting attorney explained:

> Defendants who are wanted in some other state like Arkansas or Louisiana where prison conditions are known by them to be punitive are very amenable to pleading guilty here. When a defendant is picked up on a charge here and there is a hold order for Arkansas, I tell him, "Well, you can have a trial here or you can plead here. Then again maybe I'll just turn you over to Arkansas and forget the charge here." Invariably, he will decide to plead to the charge here in the hope that he will not later be returned to Arkansas.

If for lack of time or for some other reason an appropriate deal cannot be worked out in the prosecutor's office, negotiation may occur in the judge's chambers prior to preliminary hearing, arraignment, or in some cases just before trial. In these situations the judge plays a more central role in bargaining. Some Kansas pretrial conferences tend to be a group affair with all the defense attorneys whose clients are scheduled for some proceeding — preliminary hearing, arraignment, or trial — and all the opposing prosecutors assembled in the judge's chambers. The proceedings are extremely informal, with perhaps three to five or more cases under discussion simultaneously:

> Three defense attorneys and two deputy county attorneys were in the judge's chambers participating in their negotiations. The three cases discussed involved two felonies and one misdemeanor.
>
> While the judge was discussing a first degree murder case with the defense attorney, another attorney shouted across the room to the deputy prosecuting attorney, insisting that his client — an 18-year-old boy charged with petty larceny — be given a bench parole in exchange for a plea of guilty. The deputy prosecuting attorney had difficulty in following this argument since he was also discussing an assault case with another attorney. The prosecutor eventually gave in to the plea of guilty and parole arrangements to the larceny case, but he stood his ground on the assault case by insisting that the defendant be incarcerated for at least a short period of time due to the aggravating circumstances of the case. (The defendant in the assault case lured a 15-year-old girl into his automobile and proceeded to drive out to a lonely country road. After he had parked his car in what appeared to be a deserted area, he proceeded to remove her clothing by force. The girl escaped and the defendant was picked up several hours later.)
>
> The judge then informed the prosecutor that he would be inclined to parole the defendant charged with the assault due to the fact that he had a wife and two small children plus being a first

offender. The prosecutor then stated that he would not recommend that parole be granted but he "would keep his mouth shut in the courtroom when such a recommendation was made by the defense attorney."

Arrangements were made, under the court's supervision, in the larceny case — the defendant was caught siphoning gasoline from parked cars — to have the defendant plead guilty, receive a sentence of ten days in the county jail and be paroled for a period of one year. Later in the morning this sentence was imposed by the court and parole was granted with the condition that the defendant perform the usual conditions of parole plus "keeping out of trouble."

At least one Kansas judge holds an open court hearing to determine whether or not a defendant will be granted bench parole *prior* to his entering a plea. In most Kansas courts, in many borderline cases where a defendant is a questionable candidate for bench parole, a pre-sentence hearing is conducted *after* the defendant has pleaded guilty or has been convicted at trial, so that the defendant himself, his attorney, or his family and friends can introduce extenuating or mitigating evidence which might lead the judge to consider bench parole. The pre-plea hearings are much the same except, of course, the defendant has not yet decided upon his plea. A judge who follows the practice of conducting a pre-plea hearing explained:

> I think it is proper for me as a judge, upon sufficient facts, to indicate in advance of a plea whether a particular defendant is to be granted a parole from the sentence that is to be imposed on him. Upon inquiry as to the attitude of the court toward parole in a given case, I set the matter down for an informal hearing in open court to which the prosecutor, police or sheriff's department, relatives and friends, and others interested are invited to appear and have their say and to explore with the court the wisdom of a parole. After a full conference, I then indicate whether I think the defendant would or would not be a good parole risk. This procedure gives a defendant and his counsel a more intelligent basis on which to decide whether to plead guilty or go to trial. The open court nature of the hearing follows a very good principle of judicial administration which is that a judge should not hear argument, hold conferences, or make decisions in chambers when they can be done in open court. In this way the authorities and the court are protected from unjust criticisms.

Regardless of where or how the bargain has been struck, the actual entry of the plea of guilty follows much the same routine procedure as in Michigan. The defendant is informed of the charge in the information (which is commonly the agreed upon lesser offense) and is asked to plead. A plea of guilty is ordinarily accepted without further investigation, except perhaps a routine inquiry of the defendant as to whether his plea is "freely entered." If the bargain is bench parole, the prosecutor may at this point recommend it, and, because pre-sentence reports as such are rarely used in Kansas, the court usually follows the prosecutor's recommendation. One of the advantages for the defendant who bargains for bench parole is that his case is ordinarily processed rapidly so that he does not have to spend an excessive amount of time in jail. At the same time, this is one of the pressures to induce him to plead guilty. Because of calendar congestion, a defendant who cannot make bail may be forced to remain in jail for a number of weeks or even months before his case is heard. Once he indicates a willingness to plead guilty his case is moved up, and since there is ordinarily no delay for investigation between the guilty plea and the granting of bench parole, he will be released from custody immediately following arraignment.

3. *The negotiated plea in Wisconsin.* Wisconsin shows the greatest variation in bargaining procedures from one court to another. The Wisconsin sentencing structure is such that trial judges have discretion to set maximum terms of incarceration within statutory limits; there is a low statutory minimum for all but a few offenses; and all offenses are probationable at the discretion of the judge. Wisconsin has a highly developed correctional program including a policy of early release on parole for all but the most dangerous offenders.[4] Thus an offender sentenced to ten years' imprisonment and another sentenced to three years are both eligible for release at the same time, and, in the absence of factors affecting parole risk, the two prisoners would probably be released at about the same time, certainly with less disparity than the seven years between their maxima.

These characteristics of the Wisconsin system make charge reduction less necessary to obtain sentencing leniency than in Michigan or Kansas. However, even in Wisconsin when the judge has no discretion in sentencing, as in first degree murder or traffic cases where conviction results in the loss of a prescribed number of "points," charge reduction is the only way to avoid mandatory consequences which follow conviction. As a result, in such cases, especially in traffic cases, there is much heavier pressure on the prosecutor to negotiate for a plea of guilty.

[4] See, for example, how Wisconsin compares with other states and with the national average in the average time served by prisoners in correctional institutions in National Prisoner Statistics — Prisoners Released from State and Federal Institutions 3 (Federal Bureau of Prisons 1960).

The prosecutor's promise to recommend a light sentence is of less value to a defendant in Wisconsin than in Kansas, because Wisconsin trial judges typically have a detailed pre-sentence report. Consequently, granting probation or a low maximum sentence depends less on the prosecutor's recommendation than on the information contained in the pre-sentence report. The prosecutor's recommendation is frequently asked for and given weight, but a request for leniency which is not warranted by the pre-sentence investigation is not likely to be followed.

In addition, certain trial court practices make the overt type of plea bargaining characteristic of Michigan and Kansas less important in Wisconsin. The post-plea-of-guilty hearing used extensively in Milwaukee brings to the court's attention the facts of the defendant's criminal conduct and the amount and type of evidence held by the state. The resulting visibility of the relationship between conduct and charge makes what the defendant did rather than what he is charged with of significance in the exercise of the trial judge's sentencing discretion. Overt negotiation does occur in some courts in Wisconsin. The defendant, on his own or through his attorney, makes known to the prosecutor his willingness to plead guilty to a lesser crime than the one charged or to plead as charged if given some reasonable assurance of leniency in sentencing. Whatever bargain is made must be approved by the court if it takes place following the filing of the information. This and the informality of bargaining is illustrated by the following case:

> Defendant was charged with willful neglect of her family, pleaded not guilty, and called a lawyer she knew to represent her. This defense counsel went to the prosecutor and said, "This defendant doesn't have any money and can't raise any so there is no fee for me in this case. What kind of a sentence would you recommend if she pleaded guilty? She needs a good scare and I think she got it. She's not really too bad but she thinks she's a queen and sits around the booze halls all day and before you know it she's loaded and doesn't come home to the children." The district attorney looked up her file and said, "I don't want to monkey around with this case. Let's put her on probation and let the state welfare department worry about her." The defense attorney stated: "O.K., I'll tell her you will recommend probation." The district attorney said, "All right, let's go speak to the judge about this." The judge agreed, the defendant pleaded guilty and was placed on probation.

Not all prosecutor promises to recommend probation are cleared with the judge prior to pleading, but he is made aware of them prior to sentencing.

Charge reductions made after the filing of the information must be approved by the judge.[5] They are almost invariably approved, even on the basis of the prosecutor's most cursory reason, such as "best interests of justice." A number of judges reported that they could not recall ever having failed to go along with a district attorney's recommendation to reduce a charge. Charges reduced by the prosecutor between the issuance of the warrant and the filing of the information, however, do not have to be cleared with the court. In these cases the bargaining situation is similar to that which predominates in Kansas; once the information is filed, however, the pattern is similar to that in Michigan.

Overt negotiation for the plea of guilty in Wisconsin generally takes place when the defendant desires: (a) to avoid mandatory sentencing, as in first degree murder, sex crimes, and traffic charges; (b) to avoid a repugnant conviction label or conviction for a felony; (c) to be convicted of a municipal ordinance violation, which is not a crime in Wisconsin, instead of on a state charge, which does result in a criminal record; (d) to avoid consecutive sentences for multiple offenses; or (e) to be assured in advance of pleading guilty that the prosecutor will recommend a lenient sentence. Where the state's evidence is strong, the charge does not carry a severe mandatory sentence or have a particularly repugnant label, and, because consecutive sentences are rare in any case, most Wisconsin defendants apparently feel it unnecessary to overtly negotiate, preferring instead to rely on the sentencing benefits which accrue from their willingness to plead guilty.

Where there is any bargaining, the trial judge is involved if it takes place after the information is filed. In some courts negotiation takes place in a pretrial conference where the judge may not only agree to a charge reduction but also indicate what the sentence would be with and without a guilty plea. One judge commented, "In these [pretrial] conferences I always make it clear to defense counsel that if his client goes to trial and is convicted, I will impose a sentence pretty close to the maximum permitted by statute and will not consider probation. Under such conditions, a guilty plea can usually be worked out." If a charge reduction is

[5] Judges in Wisconsin evidently retain authority to review the charge reduction decision of the prosecutor under Wis. Stat. §955.17(2) (1963), which requires the district attorney to receive court approval when not filing an information, that is, when exercising their nolle prosequi authority. In effect, the reduction of charge is treated as a nolle prosequi of the original charge but with prosecution desired on the lesser count. In practice, judges do not ordinarily require a charge reduction decision to be in writing, as is required for dismissal, but do question the district attorney in open court about his reasons for the reduction. Conversely, it is expected that the court will seek approval by the prosecutor when it reduces a charge on its own initiative in spite of evidence sufficient to convict. See Memorandum of Authorities in State ex rel. Reynolds v. Proctor (1961, typewritten copy on file in University of Wisconsin Law Library).

agreed upon, either in the pretrial conference or with the prosecutor prior to arraignment, the prosecutor makes a formal motion to reduce the charge contained in the information to a lesser charge. The judge then passes on this motion, almost invariably supporting it, and proceeds with the arraignment.

To summarize, in Wisconsin, in contrast to both Michigan and Kansas, the guilty plea process is characterized by a minimum of plea negotiation primarily because it is not necessary either for the defendant to obtain a lenient sentence or for the court to achieve sentencing discretion. This is true not only in regard to charge reduction, for the sentencing structure is such that downgrading a felony accomplishes little in the way of modifying the sentence, but also in regard to sentence promises. Most Wisconsin judges rely more heavily on the pre-sentence report than on the recommendation of the prosecutor in determining the sentence.

This is not to say that plea bargaining is nonexistent in Wisconsin or even that it is extremely rare. Negotiation occurs regularly when offenses with mandatory sentences are charged. It also occurs when the highest charge has a particularly repugnant label, implying sexual deviation for example, and in cases where there is a chance of avoiding a felony record by pleading to a reduced charge which is a misdemeanor or, better still, pleading to an ordinance violation, which does not result in any criminal record. Likewise, defendants do bargain for prosecutor promises to recommend probation, for while such recommendations are ordinarily given less weight than the results of a pre-sentence investigation, they certainly are considered by the court.

Nevertheless, the over-all picture of the guilty plea process in Wisconsin is one of much less frequent and certainly much less routine plea negotiation. A good deal of the bargaining which occurs is solely a prosecutor's function. Charge reductions prior to the filing of an information and many sentence promises are confined to the prosecutor's office, occurring without any participation or even any awareness on the part of the court. While the judge eventually hears the prosecutor's recommendation as to sentence, and while the court must approve charge reductions made after the information has been filed, these are usually nominal decisions, commonly honored by the judge but not initiated by him.

B. Locus of the Negotiation Decision

The adjudication of guilt, that is, the actual conviction decision, is normally thought of as a judicial function or, in some contested cases, as the shared responsibility of the judge and jury. Where a guilty plea is the result of negotiation over charge or sentence, however, the demarcation of judicial involvement and responsibility is less clear. While the trial judge must accept or reject the plea itself, the bargain on which the plea is based may have been made by the prosecutor or, in some cases, by the police.

Where the prosecutor charges an offense less than the maximum the evidence will support in order to induce a guilty plea, or where police request a warrant for a lesser offense to induce a plea, then in a real sense the conviction decision is made at these stages of the criminal justice process. Judicial concurrence is in most cases routine, although sometimes the judge may be unaware of pre-court negotiation relating to charge reduction or a sentence promise. The prosecutor, or more rarely the police, may "promise" a defendant a lenient sentence if he "cooperates" and pleads guilty, relying on their knowledge of sentencing practices and habits of various judges to honor their promise. In other instances their recommendations may influence the judge or they may withhold from the court certain information which, if known, would result in a higher sentence than the one promised.

Who actually makes the negotiation decision depends upon the type of bargain and traditional procedures for implementing it in each jurisdiction. The type of bargain, charge reduction or sentence promise, is dictated pretty much by the formal sentencing structures of the state. The actual point at which the bargain is made, however, differs somewhat between jurisdictions with roughly comparable sentence structures, such as Michigan and Kansas. These variations are difficult to account for except by the accident of different traditional alternatives to accomplish roughly the same ends. In routine charge reductions, for example, the Michigan procedures contrast with those of Kansas in regard to the stage at which the bargain is made as well as the relative role of the judge in the process. The Michigan procedure typically occurs at or just prior to arraignment on the information. The process is characterized by a prior decision to charge the maximum offense which is reflected in the information, some pre-arraignment hallway bargaining between defense and prosecution, and a visible, open-court procedure of adding the new charge to the records.

In Kansas defendants plead guilty at the arraignment to the charge contained in the information. If the arraignment alone were the basis of comparison between the two states, charge reduction would be clearly visible in Michigan but Kansas would present an illusion of on-the-nose pleas. This is deceptive, because the bargain in Kansas is typically made by the prosecutor, who charges the maximum offense in the warrant but negotiates before filing the information, so that by the time of arraignment the information already contains the agreed-upon lesser count.

The judge in Michigan is more often directly involved in the decision to reduce the charge. It is ordinarily accomplished in open court with the judge initiating the reduction in some cases and in all instances being fully aware of the process and agreeing to it. In Kansas the trial judge is usually confronted with the accomplished fact of a lesser charge at the time of the arraignment. Most judges are fully aware of the practice and support it but report "no alternative but to go along with the county attorney or his deputy" once the bargain has been made. In certain highly publicized cases in Kansas the county attorney will explain to the judge his reasons for reducing a charge, in effect asking the judge's opinion of the reduction decision. One prosecutor explained:

> Under these conditions [publicity], I will tell the judge in open court my reasons for reducing the charge. This way I get my explanation in the court record and give the judge a chance to give his opinion pro or con as to the wisdom of the charge reduction. If he goes along with me, I am taken off the hook if there is any adverse public opinion.

While charge reduction is less common in Wisconsin, when it does occur it follows more closely the Kansas pattern rather than the Michigan pattern; that is, charges are sometimes reduced by the prosecutor on his own initiative and without the knowledge of the court prior to the filing of the information. After the information has been filed, the court must be notified of the reduction and give approval.[6] In practice this works out to be much like the Kansas procedure, where the judge has no alternative but to accept the reduced charge, because Wisconsin judges almost invariably agree with the prosecutor's reduction decision. In contrast to the Michigan situation where the trial judge plays a central role in charge reduction and where he often initiates the reduction, Wisconsin judges ordinarily play a more passive part. There are some exceptions. In some courts, although not in Milwaukee County, negotiation for both charge reduction and sentence promise occurs during a "pretrial conference" of judge, prosecuting attorney, and defense counsel. Here the judge plays a direct and central part in the negotiation process.

The sentence promise without charge reduction as a type of plea bargain is almost solely a prosecutor's function, even though he has only an indirect relationship to the sentencing decision.[7] From

[6] See note 5 *supra*.

[7] One of the complex factors in sentence promises as inducements for guilty pleas

the defendant's point of view a pre-plea sentence promise by the trial judge would be much more desirable, but most judges are reluctant to commit themselves to a specific sentence prior to a plea of guilty, both because such action might be interpreted as an improper inducement of the plea and because there has not been an opportunity to weigh relevant information in a pre-sentence report. Fairly frequently, nonetheless, the defendant's counsel[8] or, in some instances, the defendant's wife or other member of his family will seek out the judge and attempt to influence the sen-

---

is the separation of prosecutor and judicial functions and the extent to which defendants discern this difference. It is not an uncommon practice for the prosecutor to promise probation to a defendant when, of course, he has no authority to actually place anyone on probation. He relies on his knowledge of common sentencing practices of a particular judge to fulfill his promise, but this does not always happen. Appellate courts are split on the question of whether such promises should be honored, either by voiding the guilty plea or, as in Oklahoma, by modifying the sentence in accord with the promise. For this last practice, see Courtney v. State, 341 P.2d 610 (Okla. Crim. App. 1959), and also United States v. Graham, 325 F.2d 922 (6th Cir. 1963), where the defendant was given the option of being sentenced according to the agreement or of withdrawing his plea and entering a plea of not guilty.

Most states and the federal government honor prosecutor promises. See Machibroda v. United States, 368 U.S. 487, 82 Sup. Ct. 510, 7 L. Ed. 2d 473 (1962); Kercheval v. United States, 274 U.S. 220, 47 Sup. Ct. 582, 71 L. Ed. 1009 (1927); Dillon v. United States, 307 F.2d 445 (9th Cir. 1962); Ward v. United States, 116 F.2d 135 (6th Cir. 1940). See also Kansas v. Finch, 128 Kan. 665, 280 Pac. 910, 66 A.L.R. 1369 (1929), and In re Valle, 364 Mich. 471, 110 N.W.2d 673 (1961). *Contra:* People v. Hasenstab, 283 App. Div. 433, 128 N.Y.S.2d 388 (1954); People v. DeMaio, 303 N.Y. 939, 105 N.E.2d 629 (1952); Wight v. Rindskopf, 43 Wis. 344 (1877).

[8] The propriety of defense counsel's approaching a judge to obtain a sentence promise prior to entry of the guilty plea arose in a recent case in Pennsylvania. In Commonwealth v. Scoleri, 415 Pa. 218, 202 A.2d 521 (1964), the defendant, charged with murder, pleaded guilty relying on his defense attorney's statement that one judge sitting in a three-judge court had promised that the defendant would not receive the death penalty. However, the court unanimously sentenced him to death, at which point he sought to withdraw his plea of guilty. At sentencing his attorney said, "I have an unpleasant duty to perform. For the reason that I had a flat promise from [the judge] that he would impose life . . . I must move to withdraw the plea." The defendant also said: "Your honor, it was most reluctantly that I agreed to change my plea. It was only on the assurance that there had been some prior agreement, and I certainly would not have changed my plea if I did not have this assurance." The trial court, refusing withdrawal, commented upon the practice of an attorney's approaching a judge to arrange a sentence prior to his client's guilty plea, calling such conduct "shocking" and "not becoming a member of the Bar." The district attorney commented that this behavior was an attempt to "fix" the case beforehand and was "highly shocking. . . . It is no different to try to fix a juror than to try to fix a judge." The appellate court concluded, "we agree with [the district attorney]. . . . This conduct was indefensible and outrageous and cannot be too strongly condemned." 415 Pa. at 228-229, 202 A.2d at 525-526.

The law partner of the attorney in question, however, who had also approached one of the judges hoping for a commitment to a life sentence rather than the death penalty for Scoleri, testified that there was nothing "dirty" in this procedure and that it was a practice which had been indulged in by district attorneys, assistant district attorneys, and Philadelphia judges for about thirty-five years. 415 Pa. at 236 note ***, 202 A.2d at 530 n.14.

tence. The common result is no more than a vague assurance that the court will "certainly consider" or will take into account the plea itself and whatever mitigating circumstances have been presented. Occasionally the judge may go further and indicate that he is "favorably disposed" toward probation or some other leniency. Rarely will he be more specific. Infrequently, however, a judge will explicitly promise probation or a specified term of years. In a pretrial conference in Wisconsin, for example, the only issue was the prison sentence a defendant would receive if he pleaded guilty: probation or charge reduction was not in question. The prosecuting attorney suggested a ten-year sentence, the maximum for the crime; defense counsel asked for not more than three years; the judge offered the "compromise" of five years, which was agreed upon, and the defendant pleaded guilty.

Usually the sentence promise does not involve the judge at all, except by implication. Most defendants and their counsel are willing to accept the promise of the prosecuting attorney to "recommend" probation or some other leniency. The prosecutor, of course, is not in a position to flatly promise a particular sentence. Nevertheless, knowledge of a judge's sentencing proclivities and that he almost invariably follows the prosecution's recommendation places some prosecuting attorneys in a position to give unqualified assurance of the sentencing outcome. Probation, or in Kansas, bench parole, is the most desirable sentence for most crimes, and, consequently, a prosecutor's promise to recommend probation at the time of sentencing is most likely to induce a guilty plea. A weaker promise, although sometimes sufficient to induce the plea of guilty, is the prosecutor's agreement "not to oppose" probation although not to ask for it either. A variation is the prosecutor's promise to "recommend probation if asked" but not to initiate the consideration.[9]

The prosecutor can also offer to influence sentencing in a number of other ways. He can refrain from filing an information charging the defendant as an habitual criminal; he can drop some charges or consolidate counts; he can recommend concurrent sentences in multiple count convictions; he can bring to the court's attention the cooperation of the defendant, his willingness to make restitution, or other factors which would normally elicit leniency. He can request credit for jail time served or consolidate charges from other jurisdictions or attempt to have detainers dismissed. Generally he is in a position to clear up actions extraneous to the major offense and to present the defendant in a favorable light to the judge at sentencing. In short, the prosecutor can offer an en-

[9] Dillon v. United States, 307 F.2d 445, 449 (9th Cir. 1962).

tire approach to leniency without necessarily making a specific sentence promise. A general pledge of cooperation or assistance at or prior to sentencing may be sufficient inducement of the guilty plea.

The role of the police in influencing the charge complicates the fixing of responsibility for the negotiation process. Police may request a warrant for an offense less than the one reflecting the defendant's actual conduct or, to insure that the more serious offense will not be charged, may withhold some evidence. Where this is done purposely to induce a guilty plea, the conviction decision is functionally if not formally made by the police. In Michigan, for example, police often bargain with minor narcotics sellers to get information about their sources and in return cooperate in having the charge reduced to possession of narcotics, a less serious offense. While this is explained as "trading the little ones for the big ones," other motives, such as avoiding long or inconvenient court appearances, underlie police downgrading in some assault, gambling, and traffic cases. This serves to illustrate the pervasiveness of accommodation techniques and the difficulty of functionally limiting the negotiated plea decision to any single stage or to any single agency. In a way, the division of the process in Michigan into four stages: warrant, information, bargain, and conviction is classic, since the charging and bargaining decisions are neatly separated. Yet the same or roughly comparable results can be obtained by altering the order, as in Kansas: warrant, bargain, information, and conviction. In this sequence the charging and bargain decisions merge. Wisconsin, with an entirely different type of sentencing structure, presents yet another process. The difference between Kansas and Michigan appears little more than fortuitous, but the difference between these two states and Wisconsin can be accounted for by differences in sentencing provisions. Where the judge is limited by statutory maximum sentences or prohibitions against the use of probation, objectives which otherwise would be obtainable in sentencing must be met by charge manipulation.

C. ADVANTAGES AND "BARGAINS" OF THE NEGOTIATED PLEA

The advantages of the guilty plea over trial for the court, the prosecutor, the police, and in some instances for postconviction correctional authorities are many; some apparent, some more indirect. Not only does the guilty plea avoid the time, expense, and work of proving guilt at trial, but most, if not all, complex corollary issues such as the admissibility of evidence or the propriety of police investigation and arrest practices are largely avoided. In most cases, assuming a competent defendant, the plea assures conviction, whereas the result of a trial, no matter how carefully conducted, is an uncertainty, given the vagaries of jury decisions. Furthermore there is or may be a certain psychological satisfaction provided by an offender who admits his guilt. A defendant who continues to protest his innocence even though found guilty "beyond a reasonable doubt" after a full and fair trial may nevertheless leave some doubts about his guilt and the propriety of conviction. Furthermore, from the viewpoint of correctional authorities, rehabilitation can only begin once the person has recognized his problem. The probationer or inmate who steadfastly denies the crime presents a very real dilemma to treatment personnel.

There are also other advantages of a guilty plea. The victim of a crime is often as reluctant to be exposed to the publicity and trauma of a trial as is the perpetrator. The guilty plea is quick and relatively anonymous. Not only are the details of the crime largely kept from public view, but there is ordinarily minimal interference with the daily routines of complainant and witnesses. The guilty plea, even if not preceded by charge reduction, offers the sentencing judge both a rationalization for showing leniency to deserving defendants and an opportunity to do so in a setting ordinarily free from the publicity which attends trial. Furthermore, law enforcement agencies may benefit, directly and indirectly, from a guilty plea. The police may escape the onerous duty of long court appearances and may avoid being challenged by the defense on their grounds for arrest or their apprehension procedures. Indirectly, a defendant pleading guilty may help them solve other crimes by admitting other offenses or may implicate other offenders in his crime. The police of course are under pressure to clear their books of unsolved crimes. A defendant who pleads guilty to one count of an offense is more likely to admit other counts and thereby "solve," to police satisfaction at any rate, a series of burglaries or whatever crime is involved.

These various advantages of conviction by plea of guilty in contrast to conviction by trial provide the incentive for the prosecution to participate in the negotiated plea process. But plea negotiation, like all bargaining, is a two-way street. While some guilty and remorseful defendants may plead guilty without any concessions being made to them, in the aggregate there must be clear advantages for most defendants who waive their right to trial. Apart from such matters as avoiding adverse publicity for themselves and their families and in addition to whatever self-satisfaction confession brings, the defendant who pleads guilty is typically most concerned with what will happen to him following conviction.[10] In pleading guilty most defendants ordinarily expect a break, some leniency either in the seriousness of the offense of which they are convicted or in the sentence or, best of all, in both. Preconviction assurance of such leniency is the defendant's incentive in plea negotiation.

In general the types of concessions offered defendants in exchange for the guilty plea are (a) a reduction in charge to one less serious than the evidence would support, (b) a promise of a sentence that is considered lenient in view of the offender's actual conduct, prior record, and reputation, (c) the dismissal of other charges, or (d) avoidance of prosecution under statutes which compound either the conviction label (sexual psychopath) or sentence (habitual offender) or both. More than one of these concessions may be involved in any given case, but the most prominent and sought after is charge reduction. In general, this is the best allround bargain from the defendant's point of view because it results in a less serious record than is warranted by the defendant's conduct, the avoidance of any mandatory sentencing provisions applicable to the original charge, and whatever intrinsic sentencing benefit is brought by the guilty plea. The sentence promise, assuming it is made and honored by appropriate officials, has the advantage of a lesser sentence but does not lessen defendant's criminal record. The dropping of additional charges or the agreement not to invoke a habitual offender or sex deviate law are certainly important to the defendant, but he still stands convicted of the single, original charge.

Charge reduction as a form of plea bargaining also has a number of advantages from the point of view of both the prosecutor and the judge. In the first place, charge reduction can be rationalized if necessary on grounds of insufficient evidence, and evaluation of evidence is the area of particular competence of both prosecutor and judge. The overt sentence promise raises potentially more difficult questions for the judge who is supposed to accept a plea of guilty only if it is freely entered without threat or promise. Furthermore, responsibility for charge reduction is commonly divided between the prosecutor and court, and if there is any subsequent criticism of the bargain the diffuseness of the decision is a handy

[10] A study of convicted and sentenced defendants, most of whom had engaged in plea bargaining prior to conviction, concluded, "The outcome of the conviction process from the point of view of the offender is satisfactory or unsatisfactory depending upon the actual sentence he receives compared to his expectations of punishment at the time he is arrested." See Newman, Pleading Guilty for Considerations: A Study of Bargain Justice, 46 J. Crim. L., C. & P.S. 780, 783 (1956).

defense. The honored sentence promise, on the other hand, places accountability solely on the judge in his sentencing role. In only the comparatively rare cases of informants or helpful state's witnesses can he easily divert responsibility to recommendations of the prosecutor's office. Finally, to the extent that leniency is desired for defendants who, in the opinion of the court, do not deserve the severe treatment prescribed by legislation, a reduction in charge accompanied by a lesser sentence offers a maximum opportunity to achieve this objective. In this manner charge reduction offers the court an opportunity to individualize justice by distinguishing between technically similar cases in both sentence and conviction label, especially when sentencing discretion is denied by legislatively fixed terms.

In practice there is some reason to believe that many of the bargains gained by defendants in plea negotiation are more apparent than real. To some extent postconviction decisions can at times "equalize" discrepancies between conduct, charge, and sentence which have resulted from plea negotiation. Thus the multiple check forger may plead guilty to only one of a number of possible offenses but may be required to make restitution on all outstanding checks. And the armed robber who pleads guilty to unarmed robbery may be asked by the parole board about the type of gun he used and in general treated about the same as if he were convicted of the greater offense. Judges, too, often consider in sentencing whether the plea is reduced and, if so, use the conduct rather than the charge as the basis of their sentencing decision. Although the defendant avoids any mandatory sentence carried by the greater charge and the stigma of its label, the actual sentence he serves in many cases is not much less, if any, than it would be if he were convicted of the higher charge.

Sentence promises may also be more impressive on paper than in practice. The defendant asks, presumably, what is the most that can happen to him upon conviction. A more realistic basis on which to calculate the value of the bargain, however, would be to determine the usual sentencing practice in similar cases. If a defendant in a particular type of case would ordinarily, even routinely, be granted probation, a prosecutor's promise to recommend probation can hardly be called a bargain; nor can the avoidance of habitual offender laws, multiple charges, or consecutive sentences where they are virtually never invoked. The sentence promise then, with some exceptions, is always open to the allegation that the promise, although kept, was hollow in value as a medium of exchange. The reduced charge, on the other hand, has the benefit of leaving the defendant with a lesser record. Regardless of whatever countercompensations are made in sentencing by the judge or in release by parole or probation authorities, the lesser record is, or may be, of continuing value. Certainly this is so when reduction is from felony to misdemeanor; it is perhaps of less worth when the reduction is from armed robbery to unarmed robbery and all in authority know of this practice and respond to it.

It would take a sophisticated defendant to bargain for more than the usual reduction of charges, and the psychological basis of the bargain remains primarily the offer and acceptance of less than full implementation. The fact that some state "concessions" are actually ordinary and customary practices does not mean, however, that real benefits never accrue to guilty defendants. No such system could operate for long on superficial promises. Some bargains do result in real and substantial record and sentence benefits to particular defendants, especially when mandatory sentences are avoided. In Michigan, for example, charges of sale or possession of narcotics, both felonies with potentially long sentences, are commonly reduced to "user," a misdemeanor. Likewise, felonious assaults are commonly reduced to simple assaults, more serious sex offenses to indecent liberties, and armed robbery to unarmed robbery. A marked benefit results where the reduction is from a nonprobationable to a probationable offense and probation is in fact granted. The rather common statement of judges and prosecutors that reduction makes little difference in the amount of time actually served by a defendant who successfully bargains has limited applicability to cases where incarceration is imposed following conviction on the lesser charge. This is because the maximum length of the sentence can be accommodated by parole practices, and the Michigan judge who has discretion to set the minimum term can consider the bargained plea in sentencing. However, a reduction from a nonprobationable to a probationable offense may have an obvious impact upon the sentence, and a reduction of a mandatory maximum prison sentence may force discharge from the institution at a time prior to the time an offender would ordinarily be released by the parole board.

D. Limits of Plea Bargaining: Illogical Lesser Offenses and Inappropriate Sentence Leniency

In view of the frequency of negotiated pleas and of the effects of plea bargaining not only on the adjudication process itself but on various postconviction correctional stages, a question of particular significance is the range of bargaining or, put another way, the limits, if any, on how far charges are typically downgraded or to what extent sentencing is affected by the willingness of a defendant to plead guilty.

Charge reduction as a concession for the guilty plea was observed in all types of felonies and misdemeanors. Reductions were either to a lesser included offense or to an illogical lesser offense, that is, to some lesser charge not included in the greater offense. Theoretically, it would be possible for a person charged with a crime against a person or a sex crime to plead guilty to some property offense, larceny for example, which is not included in the greater offense and furthermore which is grossly inconsistent with the actual criminal conduct of the defendant. In practice this is rare. There appears to be an unexpressed but commonly followed practice of reduction to a count that bears some categoric similarity to the original charge. In homicide, for example, there may be reduction from murder to manslaughter or negligent homicide or, occasionally, even to assault, but grossly inconsistent offenses such as larceny or possession of narcotics are never arbitrarily used in place of murder unless these offenses were part of the actual conduct involved. The illogical lesser offense, then, is rarely categorically different from the original charge. It is illogical ("inconsistent" would perhaps be a more accurate term) only in the sense that it requires proof of conduct inconsistent with the facts which would have to be established to convict for the offense originally charged. For example, in Michigan breaking and entering in the daytime (a probationable offense with a five-year maximum sentence) is a less severe crime than breaking and entering in the nighttime (a nonprobationable offense with a fifteen-year maximum sentence). If the offense occurred at night the lesser charge of breaking and entering in the daytime would be illogical in relation to the facts.[11] The Michigan practice is illustrated by the following case:

[11] For the distinction between breaking and entering in the nighttime and breaking and entering in the daytime, see Mich. Comp. Laws §§750.110 and 750.111 (1948). As to probation for these offenses, see Mich. Comp. Laws §771.1 (1948).

There is some question of whether breaking and entering in the daytime is included in the offense of breaking and entering in the nighttime. While there are no cases directly in point, the Michigan court held that an information charging breaking and entering a dwelling which failed to allege whether entry was at night or in the day was fatally defective and the sentence following a guilty plea to such information was invalid. In re Rhyndress, 317 Mich. 21, 26 N.W.2d 581 (1947). While this might be interpreted as error because of failure of notice, from the wording of the separate statutes it appears that the lesser offense is not included in the greater, and no prosecutor has yet seen fit to test it when the process of adding a separate count is so much safer and equally simple. At any rate this is one of the most common charge reductions in Michigan, because nighttime breaking and entering is not probationable and carries a maximum penalty three times as severe as that for the same crime committed in the daytime. For a discussion of the problem

Defendant was arrested after having broken into a building at 10:00 P.M. The prosecutor had to decide which of the two facts, the breaking or the time, he was to ignore in adding a lesser count, i.e., whether to charge unlawful entry without breaking or breaking and entering in the daytime. He chose the latter. Although the defendant pleaded guilty to this added count at arraignment, the judge did not immediately accept the plea but took it "under advisement" because "the facts were too inconsistent with the plea." He later accepted the plea, a universal practice, although where obvious inconsistencies are seen, the "under advisement" delay in acceptance for a day or two is also common.

Sometimes the selection of the lesser offense leads to amusing results. A defendant in Wisconsin was originally charged with speeding, an offense which carried sufficient "points" so that, if convicted, he would lose his operator's license. (He had ten previous points, speeding would add three, and a total of twelve points means automatic revocation of license.[12]) In conference with the judge, prosecuting attorney, and his own counsel, the defendant offered to plead guilty to some lesser traffic violation carrying only one point and therefore insufficient to result in revocation. For an unknown reason the lesser, one-point offense chosen was "driving the wrong way on a one-way street." Somehow it was learned, and duly reported in the press, that the small community in which the defendant was arrested had no one-way streets.[13] The impossibility of the lesser offense caused some embarrassment to all involved despite the fact that the type of charge reduction it illustrates is by no means unusual.[14]

---

of what constitutes a necessarily included lesser crime, see Note, 56 Colum. L. Rev. 888 (1956). (In 1964 the Michigan legislature removed the distinction between nighttime and daytime from the breaking and entering statutes. See Mich. Pub. Acts 1964, no. 133. The field data for this study were gathered before this enactment.)

[12] Wis. Stat. §343.32(2) (1963) authorizes the Commissioner of the Motor Vehicle Department to revoke an operator's license when the person has been convicted of a sufficient number of traffic violations in a given period of time. Conviction for each traffic offense carries a certain number of "points," depending upon the seriousness of the offense. A driver who accumulates 12 points in 1 year, 18 points in 2 years, or 24 points in 3 years is subject to revocation of his operator's license. See Wis. Administrative Code §M.V.D. 11 (April, 1963).

[13] See Wrong Way Charge Wrong, So Judge Seeks Right Way, Milwaukee J., Oct. 11, 1961, p. 2, col. 3.

[14] Another ludicrous aspect of plea bargaining was recently reported in California newspapers. A defendant who was being arraigned along with several other persons responded when his name was called and pleaded guilty to a charge of statutory rape. Before he left the courtroom it was discovered that he was in fact charged with grand theft and that another defendant, who happened to have the same name, was charged with rape. When asked why he pleaded guilty to the rape charge, knowing all along that his offense was theft, the defendant replied, "Well, I thought maybe my attorney had made a deal for me." Los Angeles Daily J., May 12, 1964, p. 1, col. 1.

Most reduced charges are inconsistent to some extent with the facts where there is clearly sufficient evidence to convict of the original, more serious charge even though the lesser crime is an included offense. "Swallowing the gun" cases in which armed robbery is reduced to unarmed robbery although the facts clearly show the use of a weapon are an illustration of reduction to an included offense yet with a significant fact ignored. Prosecutors and court personnel commonly refer to all such inconsistent pleas as "illogical," yet retain roughly the same conduct category in deciding upon the lesser charge.

Many prosecutors and judges have no objections to illogical pleas and, in fact, support the practice as both necessary and desirable: necessary to induce the high rate of guilty pleas required to process the daily case load efficiently, and desirable to achieve sentencing flexibility which would otherwise be prevented, in some cases, by mandatory sentences. One judge explained that reduction practices were merely a form of compromise not inconsistent with proper objectives of criminal justice administration and basically similar to the desirable practice in civil cases. Another judge, who said that he is "not at all bothered by illogical lesser offenses," argued that this flexibility enables the court to consider relevant circumstances, such as the possibility of acquittal of guilty defendants by a jury and the fact that conviction on the lesser count gives the court assured control of guilty defendants. In addition, this judge commented, "many defendants are sentenced to and spend the same amounts of time in prison as if they had pleaded guilty or were found guilty of the original offense."

Some judges, however, while accepting pleas to lesser and illogical offenses, show some uncertainty about the propriety of this practice where the reduced charge is too far from the actual conduct.[15] Some Michigan judges take such pleas under advisement

[15] Judicial uncertainty of the propriety of accepting an illogical lesser offense may in part reflect common practices of submitting included offenses to a jury in contested cases. Here the general rule seems to be that judges charge the jury with respect to included offenses only when the evidence makes it appropriate to do so. In the routine situation where a guilty plea is entered to a reduced charge there is ordinarily little doubt that the evidence supports the greater crime. In the reduction from armed to unarmed robbery, for example, the facts may clearly reveal use of a weapon. Likewise, in the typical case of reduction of nighttime breaking and entering to the lesser offense of daytime burglary there is no real doubt about the sufficiency of evidence to prove that the offense occurred in the nighttime. Judges therefore are confronted with a distinction between the standard used in deciding whether an offense should be submitted to a jury and the standard, if it can be called this, controlling the acceptance of a plea. For a discussion of judicial discretion to submit an illogical lesser offense to the jury, see Model Penal Code §1.08 (Tent. Draft No. 5, 1956) and Comments at 42-43. At the general session of the institute in May, 1956, however, it was voted to give the trial judge discretion to

for a few days rather than accept them outright, which is interpreted by prosecutors as an expression of displeasure with the inconsistency between the facts and the offense to which the defendant offers to plead guilty. This expression of judicial concern does seem to act as a check on the range of downgrading, although there were no observed instances where pleas to lesser charges were refused. A judge in Wisconsin, commenting on the acceptance of lesser charges in traffic cases to avoid mandatory penalties, cautioned: "The judge who does this is creating a nice job for himself. He will become known as a ticket fixer. He is getting into a field usually left to what is known as the judicial function of a district attorney."

The sentence promise, particularly agreement to grant or at least strongly recommend probation, also raises questions of desirability, including the question of whether the defendant who is promised probation is in fact an appropriate candidate for field supervision or whether the person who is promised a short prison sentence will be under the control of correctional authorities long enough to accomplish the objectives of incarceration. In general, promises of lenient sentences such as probation or short incarceration are very rarely given to defendants who are clearly not suited for such sentences. The major exceptions are informants and members of criminal gangs who are promised lesser sentences in return for testimony against their co-conspirators. In these cases the justification for leniency is not the record or other characteristics of such offenders but the advantage to the prosecution which results from their testimony. Furthermore, what may appear to be a great bargain at the time of sentencing may in fact prove to be something less than this in the long run. For example, a defendant in Wisconsin with a long felony record was promised probation by the prosecutor if he would testify against his co-defendants in a case involving a series of burglaries. He agreed to this and testified; his partners were convicted and sentenced to prison, and he received a suspended sentence and five years' probation. The prosecutor remarked: "I didn't mind promising him probation because I know he'll never make it. He's a drunk and a chronic burglar. He'll violate probation within a month and be on his way to prison with his friends. I'll bet they will be glad to see him."

While dangerous or otherwise grossly unsuited defendants are not promised probation no matter how hard they bargain, there is

submit an illogical lesser offense when he deems it desirable to do so, presumably when a compromise verdict will, in his view, serve the ends of justice. See 33 A.L.I. Proceedings 143 et seq. (1956). See also State v. Braud, 238 La. 811, 116 So.2d 676 (1959), and Note, 21 La. L. Rev. 818 (1961).

little doubt that numerous defendants who are less than ideal probation risks do receive suspended sentences in exchange for their guilty pleas. In other words, the promise of probation is not limited to those who would probably be placed on probation even if they pleaded not guilty. Probation is a very real concession to many defendants who, without bargaining, would in all probability be imprisoned. The selection of probationers on the basis of bargaining skills rather than supervision risk causes some concern to correctional authorities. However, widespread reliance on the pre-sentence investigation in Wisconsin and, to a lesser degree, in Michigan (because of the focus in these reports on evidence of guilt) acts as a check on the type of guilty plea defendants who are placed on probation. In Kansas, however, the extensive use of bench parole without either an investigation or a pre-sentence hearing permits selection for probation solely on the basis of plea bargaining. At the same time, field supervision in most Kansas courts is typically nominal, if it exists at all, so that the field agent is not overly concerned by the fact that he must give close supervision to a person who is unsuited to be a candidate for probation.

CHAPTER 7

Charge Reduction to Avoid Record of Conviction of Original Offense

A. Importance of Record in the Bargaining Process

From a defendant's point of view most charge reductions are for the purpose of avoiding mandatory sentences or of obtaining a lenient sentence, such as probation, in cases where probation is precluded by legislation if the defendant is convicted of the higher charge. In addition, there are instances where charge reduction serves the important objective of avoiding conviction for an offense which has a very disabling label. Generally concern over the label is important in two categories of offenses, overlapping in some instances: (a) felony cases as contrasted to misdemeanors or ordinance violations or (b) crimes, such as certain sex offenses, which carry particular negative connotations and act to label the offender with the stigma of an especially repugnant stereotype.

It can be argued that the desire to avoid a felony conviction is actually a desire to lessen a mandatory sentence or at least to avoid a severe sentence. This is substantially correct, particularly if the sentence is viewed as more than merely the months or years served. Conviction of a felony carries loss of certain civil rights, such as voting privileges, becomes part of the defendant's permanent record (e.g., fingerprints are placed on file with the F.B.I.), and works certain other hardships such as preventing the defendant from obtaining certain licenses, keeping him out of the armed services, and perhaps preventing him from obtaining some types of employment. Reduction of a felony to a misdemeanor or ordinance violation may not prevent all of these consequences but may affect some, for example, denial of licenses. In addition, misdemeanors are generally viewed in the community as less reprehensible than most felonies, if for no other reason than because descriptions of misdemeanors are often couched in vague and encompassing labels like disorderly conduct while felonies tend to be more descriptive of the actual criminal conduct involved, such as burglary or armed robbery.

Consent of the prosecutor to reduction of the charge to an offense with a less disabling label is, in the first instance, the desire to elicit a guilty plea. This is ordinarily not difficult to accomplish when the defendant is clearly guilty and when the original charge involves a repugnant offense. Apart from this, however, there is awareness on the part of both prosecutors and judges that being labeled as a certain type of offender may be far more damaging to a defendant than imposition of even the maximum sentence. As a result some reductions reflect a desire by the prosecutor or judge to prevent undue hardship to deserving defendants or to defendants whose actual criminal conduct is less serious than the label of the original charge would indicate. A prosecutor remarked: "I want convictions, yes. But I have no desire to ruin a person's whole life by hanging a felony record on some young boy who has made a single mistake."

B. Charge Reduction to Avoid a Repugnant Label

Illustration No. 1: A defendant in Wisconsin entered a small store and at knife point ordered the lone female proprietor into the basement, where he forcibly disrobed her and attempted sexual assault. Failing to complete the crime of rape, he left the store taking some money and goods. He was originally charged with attempted rape but, unwilling to be branded with this label, he bargained to plead guilty to the crime of armed robbery, which carried a longer maximum sentence.[1]

Illustration No. 2: A defendant in Kansas was originally charged with drunk and disorderly conduct. He explained to the court that conviction as a drunk would "ruin his career." He was allowed to plead guilty to disorderly conduct.

Illustration No. 3: A defendant in Michigan was arrested for accosting and soliciting when he made homosexual overtures to a member of the Detroit Police Department vice squad. He was allowed to plead guilty to disorderly conduct because he was known as a respectable businessman, and a conviction based upon

[1] A person convicted of armed robbery may receive a maximum sentence of thirty years. Wis. Stat. §943.32(2) (1963). In contrast, the maximum penalty for attempted rape is fifteen years. Wis. Stat. §§939.32(1) and 944.01 (1963). Of course, if the defendant were found to be "in need of specialized treatment" after a mandatory psychiatric evaluation and still "dangerous" after completion of his maximum term, his sentence could be extended at five-year intervals. See Wis. Stat. §959.15(1), (13), (14), (15) (1963).

homosexuality would be very likely to ruin both his business career and his home life.

While it is true that an otherwise respectable defendant may suffer extensive damage to his reputation by conviction of *any* crime, and that one more conviction of public intoxication makes little difference to the skid row alcoholic with an extensive prior record, some offenses carry such repugnant labels that virtually all defendants seek to avoid conviction of them. Generally these are sex offenses which imply that the defendant is a dangerous psychopath, a homosexual, or some form of bizarre sexual deviant. They also include, however, offenses which tend to label the violator as an alcoholic, a drug addict, or an assaultive and dangerous person. All such labels may damage the offender far beyond the legislative sentencing provisions.[2]

In general the severe consequences of labeling lead both the police and prosecutor to exercise caution in charging such offenses. At the same time, once this type of charge is brought it exerts great pressure on the defendant to bargain for a different charge. A police officer commented: "Quite often we pick up people we could charge with some sex offense, even with rape. Some guy goes out with a floozy who has a bad reputation anyway, they have a disagreement, and he roughs her up. Technically it may be rape, but it doesn't seem right to stick the guy with a charge like that." And a prosecutor commented: "We get these middle-aged ladies in here arrested for shoplifting. They are clearly in menopause and not really criminal in any way. Why should we be a horse and buggy prosecutor's office and put their names in the paper?"

Often, as with these shoplifters, the charges against the respectable defendant are dismissed altogether. An alternative is to reduce the charge to the less descriptive charge of disorderly conduct or disturbing the peace. Which alternative is followed depends in part on the practice in the particular court and prosecutor's office and in part on the consequences of any type of conviction to the defendant's reputation. The respectable lady shoplifter would hardly benefit from conviction for the reduced charge of disorderly conduct.[3]

[2] In fact the arrest record itself, if given sufficient publicity, may do irrevocable damage to a defendant's reputation even if he is eventually acquitted altogether or allowed to plead guilty to a lesser or at least to a less repugnant crime.

[3] A common practice in Wisconsin is to reduce a misdemeanor to an ordinance violation, which is not a crime and does not therefore give the offender a criminal record. In many cases this is really a lateral transfer of the charge rather than a reduction in label, for the ordinance and the state charge may be called by the same name and defined in the same way. For example, disorderly conduct is a

Even less respectable defendants ordinarily desire to avoid certain labels, particularly those connoting sexual deviation. In part this is due to the potentially long sentences which many sex crimes carry, but it also reflects the repugnancy of the label for the offender's own conception of himself and a threat to his family and peer reputation. Conviction as a sex deviate may be as ego damaging to a professional burglar as to a respectable businessman. Furthermore, the family of a most recidivistic thief may offer him support and understanding in spite of continued criminality because the nature of his violations does not affect intra-family relationships. Conviction as a sex deviate, however, may threaten both the conjugal relationship and the relationship of the offender with his children. Finally, the labeled sex deviate ordinarily has a low status even among prison inmates.[4]

The severity of the stigma which attaches upon conviction of certain sex crimes may increase the risk of inaccuracy in the guilty plea process. Serious and flagrant crimes of child molestation or rape may lead to "quick justice" dispositions if public sentiment is sufficiently aroused. The likely consequences of extensive pub-

---

misdemeanor under state law and is also an ordinance violation in most cities. A negotiated plea in this type of case usually involves charging disorderly conduct under "city law" rather than "state law."

A recent case involving just such a situation, with the additional consideration of the consequences of a label such as disorderly conduct on the future reputation of the defendant, occurred in one Wisconsin jurisdiction. The defendant, a university co-ed, was arrested for shoplifting, her first offense. She was charged with petty theft, a misdemeanor, and the judge accepted her plea of guilty to this charge. The type of situation posed by this case raised a number of issues in this jurisdiction, which were reported in the press: "A conflict arose last week among judges, the district attorney's office, and the city attorney, about how to charge young shoplifters arrested in the merchants' crackdown on them.

"[One judge], who hears most of the cases, favored charging them with disorderly conduct under city ordinance — a civil violation — instead of giving them a criminal record with a state charge of petty theft.

"Some members of the district attorney's staff followed [the judge's] suggestion. Others did not. And [the city attorney] said he thought reducing a state petty theft charge to a city disorderly conduct count was invalid.

"In the co-ed's case Friday, [the assistant district attorney] moved for the charge to be changed from petty theft to disorderly conduct under state law — which also is a criminal charge.

"[The judge] denied [the] motion, explaining that if the co-ed was to have a criminal charge on her record, it would be to her benefit to have it be for petty theft rather than disorderly conduct.

" 'Disorderly conduct does carry a connotation of a morals offense which in years to come could be very detrimental to her,' [the judge] said." Wis. S.J., April 3, 1965, §2, p. 3.

4 See Clemmer, The Prison Community (1940); Sykes, The Society of Captives (1958); and Weinberg, Aspects of the Prison's Social Structure, 47 Am. J. Soc. 717 (1942).

licity about the crime may exert pressure on the defendant to waive preliminary hearing in order to forestall publication of details of the offense. Furthermore, a defendant charged with an offense which connotes sexual deviation may hesitate to go to trial on this charge even with a good chance of acquittal, or even when innocent, because the publicity attending a trial would be more damaging to his reputation, even if he is exonerated, than would a guilty plea to some lesser offense with a less repugnant label.

C. Charge Reduction to Avoid a Felony Record

Illustration No. 4: Two seventeen-year-old defendants in Michigan had exploded firecrackers in a restaurant, injuring two people. The prosecutor referred them to the juvenile court (which at this age has overlapping jurisdiction with the criminal courts) saying: "As far as you boys are concerned, it will keep you from getting a record so that when you grow up and have more sense and try to get a job you will not be dogged by this foolish prank. On the other hand, the juvenile judge is no softy. He can do the same things as any other judge."

Illustration No. 5: Two young men in Kansas entered a liquor store and stole some beer. In the process of removing the beer from the store they were spotted by a policeman who chased them. In attempting to hide, one of the boys jumped into a parked automobile and, noticing that the keys had been left in the ignition, drove off. He and his partner were later apprehended and charged with burglary with the additional count in one case of auto theft. The deputy county attorney, however, discovered that neither offender had a prior record and said: "I hate very much giving felony records to these young men. I think they have learned a lesson and there's no point in putting a blight on their whole future." He then reduced the charges to misdemeanors and both defendants pleaded guilty and received bench parole.

Charge reductions to avoid a felony record are common, even when the offense is not particularly repugnant, but the ordinarily shorter sentence for the misdemeanor makes it difficult to know whether the reduction was primarily for the purpose of avoiding a felony record or to obtain a lesser sentence. When the felony record is of direct concern to the prosecutor or the judge it usually reflects the belief that the conduct involved does not deserve the felony label or that the label would excessively harm the particular defendant. These may overlap in many instances, but there are some distinguishable considerations. Certain types of legislatively proscribed conduct are not really considered criminal by most prosecutors and judges. For example, a charge of illicit but consensual adult sex relations such as adultery, if not dismissed outright, is usually reduced to disorderly conduct. Likewise certain borderline violations of serious criminal statutes may be reduced as an alternative to a de minimis acquittal.[5] In general, reductions on these grounds reflect a willingness of the state to modify the charge because of an attitude toward the conduct itself rather than because of the effect of conviction on a particular defendant.

In contrast, charges are also sometimes reduced even when the conduct is viewed as a serious crime because the characteristics of the defendant are such that it is believed the conviction record itself would excessively harm his reputation. Reductions on this basis usually occur with young defendants who deserve another chance and with otherwise respectable persons who, as one judge put it, "engage in an isolated instance of law violation which is in no way a symptom of patterned criminality."

The distinction between a reduction to avoid a criminal record because the conduct is not thought to be sufficiently serious and reduction to avoid undue harm to a particular defendant may be less precise than the above dichotomy suggests, because in many instances the attitude may be that a given type of conduct is not particularly serious unless engaged in by a certain type of defendant such as a professional criminal or a repeater. Thus, the differential leniency shown to Negro gamblers and youthful offenders may well reflect a "lesser criminality" attitude toward certain conduct when engaged in by certain defendants or, as a form of extension of the juvenile delinquency concept, the lesser liability of the young. There is a prevailing attitude that youthful defendants, Negroes, and certain other categories ("hillbillies") are "really not to blame," at least not to the full extent, for their conduct, nor should they be early stigmatized by a criminal record. In a case involving a young thief who stole to make payments on his car, the judge commented that "cars should not be sold to young people"; and in cases of Negro assaults and intraracial sexual promiscuity judges and prosecutors frequently say that the "moral standards of the group" must be taken into consideration. Thus evaluation of the conduct and the effect of conviction on the individual become intertwined; a court rarely excuses or mitigates conduct per se, except in the context of the offender and his cultural base.

[5] For a discussion of de minimis acquittals, see Part IV, Chapter 9. See also A.L.I. Model Penal Code §2.12 (Proposed Official Draft, 1962).

What might be termed differential leniency can be shown in various ways, such as acquittal, downgrading of the charge, or sentencing. Part of the motivation of the first two is not only to eliminate or modify the sentence but, particularly where the young are involved, to avoid or lessen the record.

CHAPTER 8

Charge Reduction to Individualize Criminal Justice

A. Charge Reduction to Avoid Mandatory Sentences

The purpose of the court in reducing charges to avoid mandatory sentences and the pattern these reductions follow rest on one of two objectives. In some types of cases charges are routinely reduced after only token bargaining by the defense and, except in unusual instances, regardless of the traits of the particular defendant or the circumstances of the crime. These routine reductions[1] reflect a judicial dislike of the mandatory penalty for the more serious crime and represent a frank attempt by the judiciary to avoid legislative sentencing mandates. For example, in Michigan in cases involving the sale of narcotics virtually all trial judges feel that the twenty-year mandatory minimum sentence is inappropriate except for the most flagrant professional seller. The only way of avoiding this sentence is by charge reduction. While the reduction is sometimes rationalized on the basis of the inappropriateness of the penalty for a particular defendant, it is clear from the universality of the practice that the purpose is not to individualize the consequences of conviction but to nullify the legislative mandate on the grounds that it is inappropriate in the usual case.

This type of routine, quasi-automatic reduction to avoid "bad law" can be distinguished from charge reduction to obtain a more appropriate sentence for a particular defendant. Most trial judges feel that they are in a better position than the legislature to determine the appropriate sentence in any particular case.[2] The judge knows the facts in the specific case, while the legislature is distant

[1] See Chapter 13.

[2] N.C.C.D. (National Council on Crime and Delinquency) Advisory Council of Judges, Guides for Sentencing (1957); see also N.C.C.D. Model Sentencing Act, 9 Crime and Delinquency 339 (1963); Wyzanski, A Trial Judge's Freedom and Responsibility, 65 Harv. L. Rev. 1281 (1952).

and must necessarily generalize. Unlike the legislator, the trial judge deals with the offense in the total context of the personality of the offender, the circumstances of his life, and his participation in the crime. With appropriate information, the judge may feel able to distinguish between codefendants and to assess the likely effects of leniency or severity on the future conduct of a particular defendant. Most judges want some discretion to select among alternative sentences on the grounds that it is both fairer and more effective to individualize the consequences of conviction. Mandatory sentences, particularly where both minima and maxima are legislatively fixed or where probation is precluded, deny discretion to the judge. Faced with a defendant whose actual conduct or personal characteristics make the mandatory penalty seem inappropriate, the judge can achieve sentencing flexibility only by charge reduction. The case for discretion was illustrated by a trial judge:

> When the public becomes aroused over the prevalence of some crime, like drunken driving, and the inadequate sentences sometimes imposed, the amateur critic has a perfect remedy. Simply fix the sentence, or a minimum sentence, by legislative act, make the imposition of sentence mandatory, and leave judges little or no discretion! That has been tried often, but it has always proved a failure. Cases always arise that do not fit the pattern that the legislature had in mind. I remember a case that came before me, in which the driver of an automobile became "unexpectedly drunk," about two miles from home. Trying to get home, he was hugging the right-hand curb at a rate of speed so slow that his wheels barely turned. His exceeding care was what caused his arrest. True, it would have been wiser for him to get someone to drive him home. But apart from that he was doing his best. It would have been a shame to send him to jail. As the judicial council of Massachusetts has said, "The principle of mandatory sentences is in our opinion wrong." [3]

In addition, the use of charge reduction to obtain sentencing discretion has been recommended by the Model Penal Code of the American Law Institute:

> If, when a person has been convicted of a felony, the Court, having regard to the nature and circumstances of the crime and to the history and character of the defendant, is of the view that it would be unduly harsh to sentence the offender in accordance with the Code, the Court may enter judgment of conviction for a lesser degree of felony or for a misdemeanor and impose sentence accordingly.[4]

[3] Lummus, The Trial Judge 52-53 (1937).
[4] Model Penal Code §6.12 (Proposed Official Draft, 1962).

This is an interesting proposal in that it provides for charge reduction *after* conviction on the greater count, based solely on undue harshness of the greater penalty in view of the traits of a particular defendant. Because it is a postconviction reduction, this section of the code does not serve to induce guilty pleas but rather is a frank attempt to provide statutory authority for sentencing discretion in an otherwise fixed-sentence system.[5] The objective is to give the reduction process visibility by having it take place in open court and to have the decision made by judges rather than by "agencies of prosecution." [6]

An analysis in detail of the merits of legislatively fixed sentences in contrast to judicially fixed terms will be found in another volume of this series.[7] Both Kansas and Michigan are characterized by legislatively fixed sentencing structures. Wisconsin is not, but even in that state there are certain offenses which carry mandatory penalties. Judges and prosecutors in all three states, when confronted with mandatory penalties, typically use charge reduction as a device to obtain what they consider to be desirable sentence flexibility.

B. Charge Reduction When the Characteristics of the Offender Make the Mandatory Sentence of the Original Charge Inappropriate

Characteristics of the offender which somehow mitigate the seriousness of his conduct are a common basis for charge reduction to avoid mandatory sentences. These are not routine, automatic reductions based on a general judicial dislike of the statutory sentence. The prosecutor and judge have no quarrel with sentencing provisions in many, even most, cases, but in some instances certain traits of the defendant, such as youthfulness, respectability, lack of any (or at least any serious) criminal record or reputation, emotional disturbance, low intelligence, ability to make restitution, or being a member of a relatively deprived racial or economic minority, make the mandatory consequences of conviction

[5] See Model Penal Code §6.11, Comment at 28-29 (Tent. Draft No. 2, 1954). See also Ohlin and Remington, Sentencing Structure: Its Effect upon Systems for the Administration of Criminal Justice, 23 Law & Contemp. Prob. 495, 505 (1958).

[6] Model Penal Code §6.11, Comment at 29 (Tent. Draft No. 2, 1954). Opponents of this provision, chiefly the Advisory Council of Judges and other members of the National Council on Crime and Delinquency, counter with the argument that fixed sentences necessarily lead to charge reduction and that with a different type of sentencing structure a proposal for charge reduction would not be necessary. See A.L.I. Proceedings 39 et seq. (1956).

[7] See the volume on Sentencing.

on the original charge seem excessively severe. Consequently, the charge is reduced, in exchange for a guilty plea, of course, in order to individualize the consequences of conviction, to effect a program of rehabilitation not possible under the sentence for the higher crime, or to accomplish some other end, such as restitution, which would be impossible if the defendant were incarcerated.

The entire concept of individualization of justice is a complex one, but most judges feel that discretion is necessary to fit specific cases to abstract categories. Justice Charles Breitel has said:

> [C]riminal conduct must be described in generalized terms. The rules must sweep together identical acts with their markedly different actors amid infinitely variable circumstances. So, as the chancellor and the general verdict of the jury softened the impact of common law rules in the civil law field, so discretion functions to provide the selectivity needed in criminal law enforcement. Thus, the respectable businessman who inadvertently carries a pistol across state lines need not be treated as the gangster who is caught with an unlicensed revolver. Nor need the nurse who technically violates the narcotics law be treated as a criminal because she unwisely administered to a patient in excruciating pain. . . .
>
> [T]here is the much-maligned, but almost universally used, discretion by prosecutors and courts in accepting lesser pleas. . . . It is sometimes a finer adjustment to the particular crime and offender than the straight application of the rules of law would permit.[8]

It is clear that charge reduction in consideration of the defendant's traits and of the consequence of conviction in his particular case is an exercise of trial court discretion. How pure it is, that is, how much it is motivated by this balancing of consequences in the light of the strong desire to elicit a guilty plea regardless of defendant traits, is not quite so clear. It is, of course, no criticism of such discretion that the mechanics of the system are aided at the same time individual differences are considered by prosecutor and court. Nevertheless, the desire to elicit the guilty plea clouds the motives so often expressed when charges are reduced in order to obtain sentencing equity.

1. *The decision to reduce the charge because of the youth and inexperience of the violator.*

> *Illustration No. 1:* Two young men in Michigan were charged with armed robbery. The charge was reduced to larceny from

[8] Breitel, Controls in Criminal Law Enforcement, 27 U. Chi. L. Rev. 427, 431-432 (1960). In fact, discretion itself can be defined as the exercise of "power to consider all circumstances and then determine whether any legal action is to be taken. And if so taken, of what kind and degree, and to what conclusion." Id. at 427.

a person and both received probation. In commenting on the charge reduction the judge said: "Both of you are only 19 years old, you have good records and you both come from fine families. Because of your behavior you are now at the crossroads — one road leading to misery and prison, the other to decency and happiness. I am going to give you another chance; it will be your last chance. You will have to be very careful in the future."

Youthfulness and lack of a criminal record make a prima facie case for charge reduction where the original offense carries a severe sentence or, as in some offenses in Michigan, is not probationable. The excessive consequences of both record and sentence on young violators are undoubtedly the reason most frequently cited by prosecutors and judges for charge reduction to individualize justice in all three states. With young defendants downgrading of the charge becomes virtually automatic; there is little necessity for hard bargaining. Many judges are so reluctant to send a young person to prison that they will refuse a freely entered guilty plea and ignore overwhelming evidence of guilt of the more serious charge. Some Michigan judges make it a practice to assign counsel to defendants under twenty years of age, with specific instructions to work out a plea to a reduced charge when these young defendants are charged with serious crimes. Furthermore the range of charge reduction for youthful offenders, that is, the difference between the lesser and the original charge, is often greater than customarily afforded older, more experienced defendants. For example, a seventeen-year-old Michigan defendant charged with armed robbery, which he freely admitted, was allowed to plead guilty to carrying a concealed weapon whereas the usual reduction is to unarmed robbery. The judge, in placing him on probation, commented: "I don't like to send a 17-year-old boy to Jackson prison if there is any chance for him." There are other ways of avoiding severe charges against youthful violators. In one case jurisdiction was retained by the juvenile court over a sixteen-year-old defendant who was accused of murder when a victim whose purse he had snatched died as a result of the scuffle. The juvenile judge commented: "I do not feel that such a young boy should be tried for so serious a crime under the criminal statutes because it would inevitably mean that he would spend many years in prison."

It is difficult to separate youth and criminal inexperience because they commonly go together. Lack of a criminal record at any age is generally considered justification for charge reduction when a lenient sentence can be achieved only in this way. Judges will often reduce serious charges against young violators, however, even though they have extensive delinquency records but will compensate for this initial leniency by denying probation and, as one judge put it, "give them a taste of bars." This is evidently an attempt to combine leniency of charge, because it is the youth's first criminal court appearance, with relative severity of sentence, because of the prior record of delinquency. For example, a Michigan juvenile court waived jurisdiction over two young men, aged fifteen and sixteen, who were accused of forcible rape. In the criminal court the charge was reduced to carnal knowledge, even though these defendants previously, while juveniles, had committed forcible rape twice. In spite of the youth of the defendants and the reduction of the charge, one received a prison sentence of ten to twenty-five years and the other of seven and a half to twenty-five years. Other cases reveal roughly the same pattern: when the defendant is young but has a bad record, the juvenile court will waive jurisdiction, the charge will be reduced in criminal court in exchange for a guilty plea, but the offender will be given a severe sentence within, of course, the maximum possible sentence for the reduced charge.

2. *The decision to reduce the charge because of the "respectability" of the defendant.*

> *Illustration No. 2:* A forty-five-year-old defendant in Milwaukee was charged with larceny when he was apprehended shoplifting some sports equipment in a department store. He had no prior record, was a reputable businessman, and could only explain his action on the basis of "a sudden impulse." The judge reduced the charge to disorderly conduct because it "carried less onus" and avoided a "period of unnecessary probation supervision."

The decision to reduce a charge because the defendant (or his family) is "respectable" is actually a complex process usually involving more than a single motive. The respectable defendant typically has a minor or no criminal record; this is part of his respectability. Such is not always the case. In some instances, the defendant is a black sheep in an otherwise respectable family. For example, one woman who had been arrested sixty-eight times in four years and had served jail time and been fined was charged with armed robbery (from an eighty-four-year-old man), but the charge was reduced to larceny because her family was respectable and her father was a former deputy sheriff. Her attorney requested probation, but the judge imposed a sentence of one to ten years in prison, remarking that he knew and respected her father but that in accepting her plea to a reduced charge he had already shown "considerable leniency" because if she had gone to trial on the robbery charge, he was "convinced [she] would have been convicted." More typically, however, the respectable offender himself has no prior record, and this may be expressed as the reason for the reduction.

The elements of respectability, apart from the absence of a criminal record, are difficult to specify but include such factors as good and steady employment, stable home life, education, wealth, and location of residence. The reason why respectability is a criterion for reducing charges is not often clearly expressed. For example, in the case of a couple arrested in flagrante delicto the charge of gross indecency was reduced to a breach of the peace followed by a suspended sentence because they were "married" (not to each other), "had families," and had "good reputations." While it is clear that respectability did motivate both the downgrading and the suspended sentence, there was no explanation of the reason. Such decisions appear to be based in part on the assumption that the law should not be fully invoked against otherwise "good" persons; i.e., respectability mitigates criminal conduct. One Detroit prosecutor explained the downgrading principle in shoplifting cases (which he called the "store-owners" bill) as a "good guy–bad guy" decision. He said:

> If a guy is a good guy and takes something out of a store and its value is under $50, it will be reduced to simple larceny under $50, a misdemeanor. On the other hand, if the defendant has a prior record or is the type of guy who has given the police a good deal of trouble and perhaps has done a few crimes which they can't prove but strongly suspect, he'll be charged with larceny from a building, a felony, under the same set of facts.

It is probably also significant that the consequences of conviction are greater for the respectable defendant than for the defendant who does not have a good reputation and who does not lose much prestige by another conviction. Thus jailing a doctor for thirty days on a charge of public intoxication has much more serious negative effects on his career and reputation than would be the case with a chronic skid row alcoholic.

The decision to treat respectable persons more leniently can be criticized as a socioeconomic class bias with attendant discrimination against the poor and downtrodden. When the decision is related to the actual consequences of conviction to the defendant or his family, however, or when respectability is correlated with good record, such bias is not as evident. Differential treatment of "good" and "bad" offenders is clearly within the court's sentencing discretion and, in fact, the authorization to vary the length of prison sentences and to place defendants on probation recognizes the propriety of this kind of individualization. The reduction of charges in cases involving respectable defendants is the application of the same consideration at the adjudication stage, an exercise of judicial discretion which is, however, given less formal recognition than discretion in sentencing. Probation is ordinarily the major sentencing issue in "respectable" downgrading. One judge explained that when probation is denied by statute but he is "faced with a defendant who is eligible in every way for probation and who does not appear to be a risk to society and is worthy of rehabilitation, I will reduce the charge to a lesser offense or to a different offense for which probation is available."

Reducing a charge often creates more sentencing alternatives for a respectable defendant than for a defendant less well placed in the community. The respectable defendant ordinarily has more money and other available resources and, at the same time, has other persons in the community (family, employer, friends) interested in his welfare. Thus the avoidance of a mandatory prison term may make it possible to order restitution, where this is the issue, or payment of medical costs or payments for damage he has done, and may enable him to maintain good employment and effective family support for his rehabilitative efforts. Furthermore, the respectable defendant can be privately treated by psychiatrists, social workers, or other private agencies. For example, one female defendant had a charge of malicious damage to property reduced from damage over $50 (actual damage was $158) to under $50 when her attorney stated she was "contacting a religious organization for the purpose of rehabilitating herself." In another case, a defendant guilty of sexually molesting a child was allowed to plead guilty to gross indecency although the prosecutor had requested a sexual psychopath hearing and commitment. The judge, in placing the defendant on probation, commented that commitment as a sex deviate would be inappropriate because the defendant came "from a good family [who] had requested the chance to place him in a private hospital."

3. *The decision to reduce the charge because of the disrepute of victim, complainant, or witnesses.*

> *Illustration No. 3:* A Wisconsin defendant, a married man, had picked up a juvenile and had had sexual relations with her. He was originally charged with statutory rape but allowed to plead guilty to contributing to the delinquency of a minor when the prosecutor informed the court that "the girl is a little tramp. She has knocked around a great deal, has been with carnivals and circuses. She's more to blame than he is."
>
> *Illustration No. 4:* Two defendants in Kansas were originally

> charged with armed robbery because they had taken a sum of money at knife point from an acquaintance, going so far as to completely undress the victim and tear apart his clothing and shoes looking for more money. They were allowed to plead guilty to assault when it was disclosed that the two defendants and the victim had been companions on a drinking bout that had lasted a number of days. The victim, who actually had quite a bit of money concealed on his person, had pretended poverty and allowed his companions to buy the liquor. The two defendants inadvertently discovered their friend's wealth, and when he refused to share with them they took the money by force.

A variation of charge reduction for respectable defendants is the practice of downgrading the charge when victim, complainant, or witnesses are disreputable. This may be a sort of comparative respectability decision where the defendant by comparison is a "better" person than his victim or it may reflect a feeling that the disrepute of the victim mitigates the criminal conduct of defendant. For example, in a case in which the evidence clearly indicated murder, the defendant was allowed to plead guilty to manslaughter because the victim was a prostitute. In another case the defendant was allowed to plead guilty to indecent liberties rather than to rape (it was clear the woman was forcibly raped) because of the victim's reputation as a semiprostitute. In still another case, armed robbery was reduced to attempted larceny from a person because the victim-complainant was a homosexual.

While comparative respectability may explain these reductions simply because the prosecutor or court feel it inappropriate to fully convict a defendant who has harmed a prostitute or other undesirable, the known difficulty of getting a conviction at trial because of the poor reputation of the victim also plays some part. For example, a charge of aggravated assault was reduced to simple assault in a case where both defendant and victim were deaf mutes and the victim was intoxicated at the time of the assault. A district attorney commented: "What prosecutor would want to try such a case?" In another case, a continuance for further examination (possibly tantamount to dismissal) was ordered when an otherwise respectable defendant was accused of a sex offense and it was brought out that the two state's witnesses (neither a victim) each had convictions for armed robbery and burglary. In a complicated case in which the complainant had mugged and robbed a victim who subsequently died and in turn was robbed by the defendant, the defendant was allowed to plead guilty to simple assault and battery (a misdemeanor) when the trial judge pointed out to the prosecutor that he "didn't have much of a case with his complaining witness a defendant in a murder action." The lack of creditability of some witnesses or victims may thus cause the prosecution to be more willing to settle for a plea to a reduced charge. It also appears, however, that the fear of being unable to convict is less important in disreputable victim cases than is a value judgment on the appropriateness of the reduction considering the "bad guy" traits of the victim or complainant, even if the judgment is an accurate reflection of jury behavior.

4. *The decision to reduce the charge because defendant is of low mentality.*

> *Illustration No. 5:* A seventeen-year-old dishwasher in Kansas was originally charged with forcible rape of a pregnant, thirteen-year-old girl. While it was clear that the defendant used force, he was allowed to plead guilty to contributing to the delinquency of a minor both because the victim was disreputable and because the defendant was of extremely low intelligence. The deputy county attorney said, in reducing the charge: "This boy is so feebleminded he really doesn't know any better. There's no doubt in my mind that she led him on and he merely used more force than was necessary."

Reduction of charges where the defendant alone or both the defendant and the victim are of low mentality appears to be a fairly common practice. Such reductions occur when the defendant is or appears to be of extremely low mentality, on the borderline of feeblemindedness, yet apparently competent enough for the court to accept his plea of guilty to a lesser charge. Whether they are based upon the belief that such a defendant should not be held fully accountable for his criminal conduct or on a desire to avoid the likely confusion should he go to trial, or whether other reasons, pity for example, play a part is not known with any certainty. Usually the judge will merely refer to the factor of low mentality as the basis for reducing the charge. For example, one defendant in Michigan with a reported I.Q. of 52 was allowed to plead guilty to simple larceny, a charge reduced from larceny from a building (which was already a downgraded charge since the facts of the case and the defendant's admissions indicated breaking and entering) simply because defendant was of such low intelligence. As in many such cases he was unemployed. He was on probation, but seemed to be unable to comprehend the rules and was a constant, if inadvertent, violator. Similarly, a charge of armed robbery was reduced to larceny from a person in the case of a defendant with an I.Q. of 69; and an obviously sexually disturbed young offender (charged with window peeking, public masturbation, and assault) was allowed to plead guilty to indecent conduct, a misdemeanor, because of his low I.Q. When such offenders are put on probation, supervision problems are formidable. As one probation agent said, "The judges won't revoke because of low intelligence" and "there's not much I can accomplish except hope he makes it, that is, stays out of trouble until his expiration date."

As the low intelligence of the defendant seems to make reduction likely, so does low intelligence of the complainant, witnesses, or victim. Here the concern is apparently more the desire to avoid trial. A charge of indecent liberties was reduced to simple assault solely to elicit a guilty plea because the victim, a small child, and her mother as well were both of extremely low mentality and the prosecutor feared that if the case went to trial "the jury would become confused and reasonable doubt established and defendant acquitted."

5. *The decision to reduce the charge because the conduct is viewed as normal within the subculture of the defendant.*

> *Illustration No. 6:* Two slum-area Negro defendants in Detroit were arrested for statutory rape involving three juvenile victims, also Negro. The charge was downgraded to disorderly conduct, and an assistant prosecutor explained: "This kind of behavior is so prevalent among these people that we wouldn't have enough courts or jails if they were all charged and convicted. They don't see anything wrong with this behavior; all their friends are doing the same thing."

A prevalent viewpoint of virtually all officials from police to parole boards is that certain cultural subgroups, chiefly Negroes (meaning, presumably, uneducated, lower-class Negroes) and "hillbillies" (white migrant laborers from Kentucky and other southern states) share certain mores somewhat at variance both with the morals of the larger community and with law enforcement standards. Some kinds of behavior, promiscuous sex relations, gambling, bootlegging, and fighting (assault) are considered normal, or at least inevitable, and therefore to be tolerated within these characteristically illiterate and poverty-stricken subcultures. Consequently there is some agreement that offenders who fit within one of these categories should be treated with less severity, if at all, than should offenders who engage in the same conduct but whose racial, educational, ethnic, or income characteristics are such that the conduct represents greater deviancy when measured against the standards of their group.

The attitude that conduct is less serious if engaged in by members of certain subgroups is reflected in differential treatment on three levels: acquittal, if it is thought that the particular subgroup tolerates the conduct; charging a lesser offense than is warranted by the conduct; or leniency in sentencing. This differential treatment is exemplified in various ways, ranging from police reluctance to arrest Negroes for assaults on other Negroes and prosecutor decisions not to charge in certain sex crimes to dismissals or lenient sentences in gambling cases. Various reasons are given for this practice:

(a) Since the conduct is normal in the subculture, perpetrators should not be held to the same degree of criminal responsibility as violators from groups with different standards of morality. One judge put it succinctly when he said, relevant to sexual promiscuity among lower-class Negroes in Detroit, "You must take into account the social standards of the offenders. Particularly among Negroes the sexual mores of their group must be considered."

(b) The kind of conduct involved, gambling for example, is a less serious alternative to other kinds of crimes which persons in these subgroups might commit if proceedings against their traditional behaviors were fully carried out. One judge stated:

> Most Negroes, in terms of the social and cultural group from which they come, actually have very few other sorts of amusements and they really have nothing else to do. I would rather have them doing this than have them out roaming the streets and probably getting into more serious difficulty. I would a lot rather see one of these colored boys shooting craps in a back room than out on the street committing rape, armed robbery or burglary.

(c) Since the conduct is held to be normal to these groups the most that can be done is to hold it to an "irreducible minimum," that is, contain it within the group but make no full effort to eradicate it. This attitude represents a belief that modification of cultural patterns by full implementation of legal procedures is hopeless, and that there should be accommodation to the "inevitable" at all levels of the process. It is reflected in police harassment and "containment" programs (containment of vice within a given precinct), reluctance of the prosecutor to charge persons in certain cases in this category, and court leniency. A basis for this attitude is the belief that certain conduct is so common within these groups that the system could not absorb a full enforcement program. A prosecutor remarked that an offense which technically could have been statutory rape "was so prevalent among Negroes and the moral code in this group is so low to begin with, that if you insisted on prosecuting every offense like this or even more serious, it would soon load up the courts." The hopelessness of eradication is expressed by the police, who in a primarily Negro precinct in Detroit "do not encourage assault victims to file complaints" because they, the police, would "have to spend too much time in court" with little accomplished.

(d) The bloc-voting power of some minority groups is able to influence prosecutor and court appointments. This is a variable of a somewhat different order, but it illustrates a particular difficulty of administering criminal justice without raising the specter of racial discrimination. In many urban areas there is a clear social and political demarcation between Negro and white communities, and virtually any action or failure to act by police, prosecutor, or court can be interpreted in racial terms. This results in sensitivity among administrating officials, so that interracial crimes are carefully screened by special prosecutors, and police and courts alike are pressured to solve the "Negro crime problem" or to "act equally against whites" in all sorts of situations. Furthermore, some districts are composed almost solely of members of one race, while others are biracial. There have been allegations from police and others that prosecutors and judges who find their electorate primarily Negro tend to reflect the cultural patterns of their voters in their decisions. In an assault case involving some Negroes, for example, the perpetrators were eventually arrested not only for assault but for resisting arrest. The police officers were white, the perpetrators Negro, and the event occurred in an all-Negro suburb of a Michigan city. One judge refused to take the case, but said that if he did he would "set the defendants free." Another judge finally took the case and, according to the police, the preliminary hearing "took longer than most criminal trials" because the judge was "playing politics in this one. The Negro community is watching it closely and an unfavorable decision to the defendants would undoubtedly cost the judge many votes in the next election. He's desperately seeking some solution that won't alienate the Negro voters."

Not all judges or other officials view subcultural moral deviation leniently or share the opinion that illiteracy or ignorance should result in acquittal or downgrading. Some judges define their role as one of "social engineering," expressing an obligation to "raise the moral standards" of such minorities by exemplary convictions and sentences when the defendants come before their court. A Detroit judge, who makes a practice of regularly convicting "hillbilly" partners in common law relationships when the more usual practice is to dismiss charges of fornication, adultery, or even assault, if they get before the court at all, explained: "These people have got to learn that their behavior will not be tolerated by the community. This lesson can be taught only by convicting them and passing sentence. If they are going to live in this city they must conform to the moral standards."

C. Charge Reduction Because of Mitigating Circumstances

The totality of circumstances leading to and surrounding the commission of a crime may be such that the prosecutor or court or both feel it would be inappropriate to hold the defendant to full liability. The circumstances of the offense may be confusing, as in assault charges growing out of barroom fights, so that it is difficult to pinpoint clearly the origin of the trouble. In some cases the victim and defendant may have had an unusual prior friendship, such as living in a common law or homosexual relationship, so that their mutually illegal relationship tends to be considered as mitigating when one complains about the other. It is difficult, in many instances, to separate the circumstances of the crime from the personal characteristics of the defendant, with the result that respectability or lack of it, for example, may be considered along with the particular conditions of the offense. This is particularly true in cases where the victim is disreputable and may have contributed to or participated in the crime itself or in another offense ancillary to it.

1. *Assaults or homicides as a result of a fight.*

> *Illustration No. 7:* A defendant was arrested for felonious assault, having beaten his victim seriously about the head and face with a beer bottle in a tavern. The charge was reduced to simple assault and battery when various witnesses told investigating officers that the victim, a much larger man than the defendant, had started the fight and had "pushed and slugged" the defendant as well as having called him obscene names.

Charges are most commonly reduced by the court in cases involving homicide or assault growing out of fights in which the victim has possibly contributed to his own death or beating. Ordinarily these are confusing cases, in that charges and countercharges are leveled, each side has some witnesses who contradict the other's testimony, but the fact remains that the victim is either dead or seriously hurt because of the action of the defendant. The consequences are not denied; the motive and full liability are. While this ordinarily might be a matter to be settled by a jury, more often the court offers lesser charges to both defendant and victim so that trial is avoided, liability for damages established, and the whole matter is thereby settled.[9] These assaults are typically the results of a fight between defendant and victim in which excessive force was used. For example, in one case the charge of assault with intent to murder was reduced when the following facts were established: The defendant, as a landlord, went to evict the victim, his tenant. An argument and a fight ensued in which virtually the entire neighborhood became involved. The eventual result of the fight was that defendant, pulling a pistol, shot and seriously wounded his tenant and a friend of his tenant. On the other hand, it was brought out that the victim was flailing at one and all with an automobile jack at the height of the melee. Faced with all this, the court offered the defendant a lesser charge of felonious assault, which he accepted, and placed him on probation on the condition that he pay the hospital costs of his victims. The judge privately commented that he was not at all sure defendant could have been convicted if he had demanded trial. Acceptance of the plea to a reduced charge was merely a way of forcing payment of medical costs.[10]

Another fairly common circumstance in which assault charges are downgraded involves barroom fights. Here again, determination of the relative liability of victim and complainant is virtually impossible, and a lesser charge is offered as a compromise. This situation also applies in youthful gang fights in which liability or even clear identity of the participants is difficult to establish.

2. *Prior illegal relationship of victim and defendant.*

> *Illustration No. 8:* A defendant was charged with larceny for having stolen clothing, money, a radio, and a record player from an apartment of a friend. When it became apparent to the prosecutor and judge that both the victim and the defendant were homosexual and had lived together for some time, the charge was reduced to disorderly conduct and the defendant ordered to return the stolen property.

Charge reductions or dismissals typically occur where victim and defendant together have participated in some illegal relationship

[9] Cases involving assaults growing out of family disputes are typically shunned by prosecutor and court alike and, as has been described in the volume on Arrest, the Detroit Police Department has developed the Misdemeanor Complaint Bureau with its "peace bond" technique as an alternative to charging, thereby relieving both prosecutor and court from the burden of such cases and the settlement function. For further examples, see the discussion of this in the forthcoming volume on Prosecution.

[10] For a case involving a similar set of facts, but where the judge used acquittal with an order to pay medical costs rather than conviction and probation, see Chapter 12, Illustration No. 6.

out of which the present offense developed. Thus felonious assault, rape, and larceny growing out of a common law relationship are either downgraded or result in no formal charge because, as one prosecutor said: "When the case got before the judge and he found out these people had been living common-law for quite a period of time the chances are this would simply be thrown out. This way (offering a lesser charge where the complaint was rape) we are sure of getting a conviction for assault and battery." Much the same procedure is followed where one homosexual brings a complaint for larceny or assault against another. The attitude seems to be to settle the dispute by offering a lesser count rather than risk dismissal or burden the court with such unsavory characters and circumstances.

Likewise, dismissal or reduction of the charge of confidence game or larceny by trick is common where persons complain they have been rolled by prostitutes, or where the complainant has given money to the defendant to "get a girl" for him but the defendant has absconded with the money. In dismissing or reducing the charge in such cases the judge commonly points out to the victim his own illegal involvement in the crime or his stupidity in getting into such a situation. One judge asked, "Did you really give him money for this purpose [to 'get some girls']? And you gave him this money on Hastings Street? Case dismissed." The assumption seems to be that clients of prostitutes, homosexuals, or assorted con men assume a risk of "being taken," but at the same time there must be some check on the ancillary crimes of these disreputable defendants and some, but not full, protection is given their clients. Thus a reduced charge, primarily the substitution of a misdemeanor for a felony, serves this function. When the larceny itself is small or the defendant particularly gullible, as in the Hastings Street "Murphy game," [11] the case may be dismissed.

Another variation, although rarely reported, occurs when one offender, a robber for example, is in turn robbed or when a gambling game is held up or, in general, where the underworld victimizes itself. It is believed that most of these occurrences are never reported to the police. When such a case is reported, however, the solution seems to be charge reduction or dismissal to settle the dispute short of trial, because of the disreputable characteristics of both victim and complainant or the general attitude that the victim's participation in the present offense or in another crime mitigates the liability of the defendant.

[11] The "Murphy game" is a racket in which prostitutes and their male employers or friends try to trick men who frequent the area out of any funds they may have.

3. *The general "circumstances of the case" criterion for charge reduction.*

> *Illustration No. 9:* A defendant in Milwaukee was charged with turning in a false fire alarm, which carries a mandatory minimum fine of $100. The defendant, however, said he thought the alarm box was a police call station and that he was trying to call the police. The judge reduced the charge to disorderly conduct and fined the defendant $50, saying that "this defendant made a mistake which is partly the fault of the police department for having poorly marked boxes."
>
> *Illustration No. 10:* An alcoholic defendant in Milwaukee took $250 from a cash register and went to Madison, where he voluntarily turned himself in to the police. He was returned to Milwaukee, where he was charged with theft of "less than $100" because both the police and the prosecutor "felt sorry" for him. The prosecutor commented: "After all, he did turn himself in. If we charge him with stealing over a hundred dollars he will almost surely go to prison because he's on probation right now. This way he will probably get probation again since the money was returned."

Most prosecutors and judges, when asked about charge reduction, in particular the matter of illogical lesser offenses, support such practices upon a number of grounds, ranging from the costs saved by avoiding trial to the desirability of providing sentencing flexibility where this is denied by statutory mandate. Among the most common responses to questions about the necessity for or justification of reduction practices is the expression that the "entire circumstances of the case" must be considered if there is to be equity in adjudication. This is such a broad, all-inclusive response, bringing on its face virtually no disagreement, that specific criteria of "circumstances" are hard to uncover. It apparently encompasses virtually all of the factors discussed in previous sections, such as the characteristics of both defendant and victim, whether they are members of racial or class minorities, and the relationship between victim and defendant. In addition to these factors, however, "circumstances of the case" implies other criteria less suited to generalization. Some relate to the motive of the defendant in committing the crime. The police, for example, who typically oppose charge reduction, may qualify their opposition when the defendant steals "because he is really hungry" or "to get food or other necessities for his family." In addition to this, charges are sometimes reduced or dismissed when the defendant is "really emotionally disturbed" or when the motive for the crime is otherwise "understandable." For example, in a family assault case when the character of the shrewish wife was revealed in the hearing the court felt she was really to blame for her own beating. In another situation, a skid row bum arrested for larceny from a store was convicted of simple larceny, a misdemeanor, primarily because it wasn't his usual type of crime; he more typically was a common drunk and petty thief. He needed money for his wine and rather accidentally happened to commit a felony. Since his pattern was of minor crimes, the "old penalty," jail, was good enough to keep him "off the street awhile."

The general position seems to be that there are circumstances either in the background of the offender or in the immediate offense that must be weighed in the adjudication decision. These variables, complex and peculiar to the individual case, make it difficult to fit the offense and the offender into the customary slot where similar offenses are uniformly treated. The range of the mitigating circumstances is about as broad as the types of cases faced by the courts and, in general, is used to bring adjudication close to an equity decision. Such a decision rests upon a rather general but not clearly articulated sense of "fairness" in convicting and sentencing.

Reduction in return for a plea of guilty may also be desirable to avoid the trauma to which the victim would be subjected if the case went to trial. Whereas filing a complaint is reasonably private, trial is public and when the crime is serious or otherwise newsworthy, the limelight of the offense may be equally upon the victim and the offender. This is particularly true in rape and child molesting cases. The guilty plea forestalls the necessity for the victim to give public testimony concerning the embarrassing circumstances involved. In such cases it is common to offer a lesser charge for just this reason. While the victim avoids the problem of testifying at trial, the plea to the lesser offense assures conviction of the defendant, with whatever protection or satisfaction this provides.

Charge reduction may also lead to a more satisfactory way of making restitution. This applies most specifically where downgrading leads to probation for the offender with an accompanying order to make restitution or to pay for damages or medical costs. To the extent that one of the acceptable aims of criminal justice administration is the repayment of losses to victims, the charge reduction process aids substantially in achieving this end. It is an unusual victim of such crimes as embezzlement, forgery, bad checks, larceny, and property damage who presses for incarceration without restitution rather than probation with monetary damages righted. In fact, in some shoplifting, embezzlement, and bad check cases, authorities have difficulty getting victims to complain or testify at all if restitution is made prior to adjudication. Where both conviction and restitution are desired, the reduced charge many times serves this function.

PART IV

The Decision Not to Convict the Guilty

> In commenting on the arrest and possible prosecution of a defendant who was charged with use of unnecessary force in that he shot and wounded a man who was stealing his car, a Federal Circuit Court of Appeals Judge said: "I don't think they will find any judge who would convict this man, if they do prosecute him. If they do, the judge ought to be impeached."
>
> *Chicago Tribune*
> May 1, 1963

> I am satisfied that the trial court, where a jury is waived, has the same inherent power to disregard the law and facts as has a jury. However, I am of the opinion this court has the duty of pointing out that the exercise of such power by a court is more reprehensible than the exercise of such power by a jury.
>
> Majority and concurring
> opinion in *State v. Evjue*
> 254 Wis. 581, 594-595 (1949)

Acquittal of defendants in spite of evidence sufficient to convict is a common practice. Many but by no means all of such acquittals involve cases of minor infractions of the law. Acquittal is used by the judge in some instances to free defendants who would, in his opinion, be excessively harmed by the criminal record or the mandatory sentence following conviction. In other instances, particularly where the defendant appears to be emotionally disturbed (although not insane), the judge may acquit in an effort to separate the "sick" from the "criminal." The motivation for these acquittals is essentially the individualization of justice; the freeing of defendants who, while technically guilty, do not deserve a criminal appellation or a severe sentence or who cannot be effectively treated in a correctional setting.

Appeal of an acquittal of a defendant can be taken in only a very few jurisdictions and then only under limited circumstances. The judge clearly has power to acquit the guilty, but appellate courts have generally denied his right to do so. The American Law Institute Model Penal Code includes an unusual provision authorizing the trial judge to dismiss certain prosecutions for de minimis violations in spite of the existence of evidence sufficient to convict.

Acquittal of the guilty, like some forms of routine and systematic charge reduction, is also used for other, administrative purposes. These acquittals, which are analyzed in a separate part of this volume, rest less on a desire to individualize justice by freeing certain of the guilty than on the use of the judicial acquittal power to control police practices or to prevent undue strains on correctional resources. Discretion in this manner exemplifies the judge's conception of the central role of the trial judiciary in the administrative process, the responsibility of the court to review enforcement methods that have gone before and to limit and control processes which follow conviction. This is the judicial exercise of adjudication power to establish policies throughout the entire system and to achieve administrative balance and propriety of procedures from early police decisions onward.

The use of acquittal under immediate consideration has the more individualized purpose of terminating criminal proceedings against those defendants for whom conviction, for a variety of reasons, seems inappropriate, unfair, or ineffective. This represents judicial discretion to review and to nullify the earlier decisions of the police and prosecutor to invoke the criminal process. While the court may not go so far as to say that a particular defendant should not have been arrested or charged, it does say that, in the final analysis, the defendant should not be convicted of a crime.

This type of acquittal is based upon neither insufficiency of evidence nor impropriety of police methods. Instead, it is an act of forgiveness; an attempt to achieve equity and effectiveness by the use of alternatives to formal conviction and sentencing. As such, it raises the very important question of the propriety of judicial acquittal of defendants who are, in the face of the evidence, guilty of crimes. In sentencing, except where controlled by legislatively fixed terms, the judge may show "mercy" or be severe. In general his discretion to distinguish between defendants or cases in sentencing is widely recognized; it is commonly assumed, however, that the judge's role in the adjudicatory decision is limited to assessment of the sufficiency and propriety of the evidence necessary to convict. The judge also may play a part in discretionary dismissals where it is required that he approve the nolle prosequi requests of the prosecuting attorney. These decisions, however, are initially a part of the broadly recognized prosecutors' discretion, and it is not generally anticipated that dismissals other than for insufficiency of evidence will originate with the court. Nevertheless, observation of current practice indicates that acquittals based upon noneviden-tiary criteria are common and have important consequences for the administration of criminal justice.

CHAPTER 9

Judicial Discretion to Acquit the Guilty

A. Variations in Procedures for Acquittal of the Guilty

The purpose of the court in acquitting guilty defendants is essentially the individualization of justice; an attempt at equity by freeing some defendants for whom conviction seems unfair, inappropriate, or less effective than other alternatives. In general judges acquit the guilty (a) to remove from the formal system those offenders for whom private treatment or control methods are available, particularly when these methods are likely to be as or more effective than conviction and sentencing; (b) to eliminate cases involving minor law infractions from further processing; and (c) to individualize justice by preventing conviction of "worthy" defendants where the consequences of conviction would work excessive hardship on them or their families.

It might be thought that acquittal of the guilty merely involves a statement that the court finds the defendant to be innocent. While this is sometimes so, there are a number of variations in acquittal procedures. In some instances, there is a definite statement by the court that it "finds" the defendant not guilty. In others, the judge "dismisses" the action and, while in most instances this is a final order, the defendant sometimes assumes that the case is being held open with the possibility of future action. In other instances, the defendant is merely ordered "released from custody" or an indefinite "continuance" is ordered. While these cases may be reopened, they rarely are; instead they are allowed to disappear gradually from the records if the defendant is law-abiding in the future.

Ordinarily the decision to acquit occurs at the arraignment on the information in major crimes or at the initial appearance before a magistrate at arraignment on the warrant in minor offenses. Occasionally, however, the judge will dismiss at preliminary hearing or after arraignment and before trial, not because of doubt of the defendant's guilt or because the evidence is insufficient or inadmissible but because of the court's desire not to convict. The reason the judge has for acquitting a guilty defendant affects the procedures which are followed. For example, if a judge wishes a defendant to receive private psychiatric care he may use the device of continuance rather than outright acquittal in order to maintain control over the defendant during his period of treatment. On the other hand, an outright acquittal may reflect a desire to prevent the defendant from having a criminal record. The mechanics of acquittal vary somewhat, even within a single jurisdiction, but in general some distinct procedures can be identified.

1. *Acquittal following a guilty plea.* In some instances the court enters a finding of not guilty, even though the defendant has freely offered a plea of guilty to the charge. These acquittals occur not because the judge has doubt about the consent of the defendant or the accuracy of the plea but because in the individual case he does not feel that conviction is warranted. Many of these are acquittals in which no strings are attached; the defendant is neither ordered nor expected to receive treatment or make restitution. In some instances de minimis violations are involved; more often the court simply feels that conviction would work an excessive hardship on the particular defendant in view of his general community reputation.

An acquittal after a guilty plea has been offered is perhaps the clearest illustration of the exercise of this type of judicial discretion. The more ambiguous "continuance" or "release from custody," while tantamount to acquittal in most cases, is less definite, less clearly a use of judicial authority to make a finding contrary to the evidence. Acquittal in spite of sufficient evidence to establish guilt, particularly with a defendant who is willing to plead guilty, and in spite of a desire on the part of the prosecutor to prosecute, illustrates the full authority and central position of the court in the adjudication process. This final decision by the court has important consequences, not only for the defendants involved but for the entire administrative system including both preadjudication enforcement agencies and postconviction treatment agencies. It is in effect a review of the desirability of prosecution, rather than a review of the sufficiency of evidence.

2. *Dismissal prior to pleading.* The acquittal which occurs before the defendant is asked to plead may, in a given case, reflect doubts regarding the sufficiency of evidence of guilt rather than the undesirability of conviction. This type of acquittal usually occurs

when the defendant is allowed to tell his story or explain his conduct at arraignment prior to entering a plea. After listening to the defendant, the judge then orders the case dismissed. Unless he explains his decision to dismiss, it is never certain whether he has taken the defendant's story as a defense to criminal liability or merely as a set of mitigating circumstances which make conviction undesirable, or whether he is otherwise responding to the personality or circumstances of the offender. Such dismissals occur frequently in minor cases of traffic violations, disorderly conduct, petty gambling, or assaults growing out of barroom fights or domestic disputes.

The common practice of most judges is to demand a plea to the charge before listening to details of the offense. If the plea is not guilty, the defendant is bound over for trial or thereupon summarily tried, if the court has jurisdiction. If the plea is guilty, the court often will listen to the defendant's story and sometimes will set aside the plea. Whether the court first demands the plea and then listens to the defendant or listens to the defendant without demanding commitment to a plea appears fortuitous, a matter of custom and judicial preference.

3. *Continuance with eventual dismissal.* Instead of outright acquittal or dismissal, some courts use the device of an indefinite continuance of the case, with a dismissal eventually recorded if the judge or his clerk happen to think of it. The record-keeping practices of most courts do not include any systematic follow-up of cases on continuance, and it is common for a continuance to be recorded at the time it is granted but thereafter be forgotten unless the judge sets a definite date for a future appearance or the defendant again comes before the court on a new offense. For all practical purposes, the indefinite continuance is tantamount to dismissal. It is used most often in cases where there is no doubt that the defendant is guilty but where the court wishes to give him another chance to conform, keeping the current case open in an attempt to exert pressure and to maintain control over him. It is in effect a "suspended conviction," much the same as a suspended sentence in which the defendant is released from custody without any supervision by probation authorities but with the threat of sentence held over him unless he is law-abiding in the future. In fact, the suspended conviction is sometimes used in Wisconsin because technically the court cannot suspend sentence without placing the defendant under probation supervision.[1] It is less common in Kansas, where the practice is to convict but give bench parole, which ordinarily requires little or no supervision. Except for the fact that the de-

[1] Wis. Stat. §§57.01, 57.02 (1963).

fendant who is given bench parole in Kansas has a record of conviction, the consequences of the Wisconsin continuance and the Kansas bench parole are similar.

Continuance is usually accompanied by an expectation that the defendant will become law-abiding or will make amends to the victim. In cases involving offenses such as nonsupport, conviction is threatened unless the defendant immediately begins to support his dependents. Similarly, where restitution is ordered or the defendant agrees to pay medical costs for his victim, the continuance acts as a threat to insure compliance. In other instances, continuance is used to insure that the defendant will continue to receive psychiatric care or other form of treatment. Whether a judge uses a continuance or an acquittal to allow a defendant to receive outpatient treatment or to make restitution appears fortuitous. Some judges use continuance because they feel it gives them continuing control over the defendant. Other judges acquit outright when the defendant agrees to receive treatment or make amends to the victim. These judges commonly assume the defendant will comply and prefer to "clear the records" of the case by recording an acquittal.

It is difficult to evaluate the relative effectiveness of these alternatives. In neither is there any systematic follow-up by the court to find out if the defendant in fact does what is ordered. Since in both cases the defendant has received a "break," it seems likely that he will comply within reasonable limits. Some police disagree. A police official commented:

> These young punks con the court into dismissing charges by promising to enlist in the service, go to school, or get some kind of medical treatment. They have no intention of doing these things and are back on the street the next day. The judge has no way of knowing if they really do what they say they will and in fact I don't think most judges care. As far as they're concerned, once the kid leaves the court the case is closed and we have it all over again.

4. *Acquittal with provision that defendant will enlist in the military service.* This practice is common enough, particularly in Michigan, to be distinguished from acquittal or continuance upon the condition that the defendant receive treatment or make restitution. The typical defendant in the usual case of acquittal with an expectation of treatment is somewhat more "respectable" than run-of-the-mill defendants; at least he has means to make restitution or to pay for private treatment. The chief criteria for enlistment acquittals are appropriate age and physical fitness.

Many judges see the advantage of military service over conviction and sentencing as avoidance of the harmful effects of a conviction record while at the same time removing the person from his criminal environment into the "healthy discipline" of the military. Furthermore, the term of enlistment is often longer than even the maximum sentence and, as one judge put it, "the community is rid of them for just this much longer." Then, too, the military service provides training in various skills at no direct cost to the community or state. And the army takes over during the "growing-up period," hopefully returning a more mature, less troublesome, and better educated citizen.

With these advantages in mind, many courts will go to great lengths to present young defendants with the choice of military service or conviction and sentencing. Until higher military authorities put a stop to it, there was a recruiting office in a Michigan courthouse so that appropriate young defendants could complete their enlistment without leaving the building. One Michigan judge has developed a "court of no record" in which defendants of enlistment age appear before the judge in a special room (not a courtroom) and are given the choice of enlistment or conviction. In some cases, but not all, the judge requires proof of enlistment before recording an acquittal on the charge. This may be provided by a letter from a recruiting officer that the defendant has applied for enlistment, although some courts require proof that the defendant has passed his physical examination. Many judges, however, ask for no more than an expression of intention to enlist. It is in these cases, where there is no follow-up investigation to insure actual enlistment, that the police feel the court is sometimes "conned."

5. *Summary retrial and acquittal after conviction and sentence.* The purpose of this practice is to expunge the conviction record of defendants who have completed serving their sentences but who now find that the criminal record is working a particular hardship on them. For example, a defendant in Michigan found that he could not receive a civil service promotion because of a record of conviction some eleven years earlier. He had long since served his sentence and had subsequently been completely law-abiding. He petitioned the court for a retrial on the old charge. The judge granted it and without taking evidence found him not guilty and ordered the records of his conviction destroyed.

6. *Acquittal at the option of the defendant.* Giving the defendant an option as to whether he wants to be acquitted or convicted is limited to cases of chronic alcoholic derelicts charged with public intoxication or vagrancy. The court in effect gives them a choice of thirty or sixty days in jail to "dry out" or acquittal and immedi-

ate release. The chronic alcoholic is, of course, a persistent and troublesome concern in all communities. In general there is no effective therapy available for the deteriorated alcoholic, and jail terms at best provide only temporary sobriety. As a sort of extension of the "golden rule" treatment by the police, in which an inebriated person is arrested for his own safety but released without probation, some judges take the position that the alcoholic himself is in the best position to know when he needs the food, warmth, and period of sobriety provided by a jail term. If he does not want to go to jail and has not otherwise caused trouble to the police or in the community, he may request dismissal and it will be granted. Some judges show infinite patience with the alcoholics, many of whom they come to know quite well through literally hundreds of court appearances. This is illustrated by a Michigan case in which a chronic inebriate charged with drunkenness told the court he could not decide whether he wanted to go to jail. He first said he needed sixty days; then changed his mind. When he finally decided that he did not want to go to jail, the judge complied and dismissed the case.

B. Relationship of Acquittal and the Negotiated Plea

Both acquittal of the guilty and charge reduction or sentence promise to elicit guilty pleas represent discretion at the adjudication stage of the criminal process. Acquittal removes some of the guilty from further processing, while the negotiated plea results in less severe treatment of some guilty defendants than would otherwise be the case. In many ways acquittal and reduction of a charge are similar. A major purpose of both is to individualize justice, to be more lenient than technically possible when faced with defendants who, while guilty, do not seem to deserve the full consequences of conviction and sentencing. The situations in which these practices are used are similar. The young, the otherwise respectable, and the ignorant or illiterate all present conviction and sentencing dilemmas to the conscientious judge. All trial courts confront cases which, taken in their totality, do not seem to warrant full implementation of the law. Furthermore, there are also administrative advantages to both acquittal and charge reduction. Negotiation encourages the plea of guilty with its many advantages over trial and enables the judge to use discretion when sentences are fixed by legislation. Acquittal of certain defendants with provision for restitution or private treatment enables the judge to achieve these objectives without burdening postconviction resources. Acquittal also prevents the stigma of conviction for defendants who can be rehabilitated outside the formal system or who have been sufficiently deterred from further criminal activity by the experiences of arrest and prosecution.

The choice of acquittal or downgrading depends in part on the nature of the criminal conduct involved. In general, acquittal is confined to cases involving minor crimes like traffic violations, public intoxication, disorderly conduct, consensual sexual misconduct, and petty gambling. Serious felonies, such as homicide and robbery, while appropriate for plea negotiation, rarely result in summary acquittal. There are exceptions, of course, where the charge involves a serious crime but the conduct is a borderline type of violation. These are traditional de minimis acquittals. In part, too, the choice of acquittal or downgrading rests on the traits of the particular defendant. With the exception of chronic inebriates and defendants from racial and ethnic minorities guilty of one of the "minor vices," acquittal is generally based on a prediction that the defendant will be law-abiding in the future. If he presents a threat of continued criminality, even though his offense is minor, conviction on a reduced charge is more likely than acquittal.

There are also administrative considerations which affect the choice between acquittal and reduction. When dealing with an informant, for example, acquittal is used to conceal his identity when he has future value to police agencies. If, however, his identity has been disclosed by his testimony, a reduced charge may be offered as sufficient reward for his services.

While both acquittal of the guilty and the negotiated plea illustrate discretion at adjudication, there are some important differences between them in objectives and procedures. The negotiated plea rests on a basic decision to convict the defendant, although of a charge less than his conduct could warrant. Acquittal, however, removes the defendant from all further official control. The role of the trial judge differs in each decision. Acquittal is solely a judicial function. In a particular case the prosecutor or police may or may not concur in the decision. Plea bargaining, however, is more likely to involve the dual functioning of prosecutor and court with cooperation and consensus between them. As the term implies, the negotiated plea results from active bargaining between prosecutor and defense. Even the most commonly granted charge reduction must be sought by the defendant or his counsel. Except in the case of some informants, acquittal is not negotiated. It is a spontaneous act of the court, the purpose being either to show leniency to the defendant or to discipline the police. A defendant may tell his story hoping to win dismissal, but there is no prearraignment assurance that dismissal will be granted.

The various discretionary purposes of acquittal of the guilty are detailed in the chapters which follow. They deal with decisions by the court motivated largely by a desire to be fair and humane in the treatment of individual defendants. The use of acquittal to discipline and control the police or systematically to avoid legislative controls on the court's sentencing discretion raises somewhat different issues which are dealt with in later chapters.

C. Controls on the Acquittal Discretion of the Trial Court

Judges have no generally recognized right to acquit guilty defendants, although they clearly have the power to do so. It is normally assumed that the trial judge will acquit only those for whom there is insufficient evidence or evidence improperly obtained and thus inadmissible. The value question of whether a particular defendant deserves the consequences of conviction is a matter left to the sentencing discretion of the court or the generally recognized discretion of the prosecuting attorney. The judge, like the police, is supposed to enforce the law if the evidence is sufficient. It is clear, however, that judges do exercise discretion to acquit in much the same manner as police use discretion not to take a suspect into custody. The question of the limits of such discretion and the availability and effectiveness of controls on the practice arises at the court level in much the same manner as with the police.

1. *Right of the state to appeal from an acquittal.* Most states allow appeals from orders of the court entered before jeopardy attaches but not from a judgment of acquittal.[2] This is true in both

[2] In at least three states there is no right of appeal by the state at all. See Ga. Code Ann. §6-901 (1964); Minn. Stat. Ann. §§632.01 to 632.05 (1961); and Texas Const. art. 5, §26. Some states provide only for a moot appeal by the attorney general on disputed points of law where the determination would not affect the defendant in any way but provide an opinion for future practice. Ark. Stat. Ann. §§43-2720, 43-2722 (Supp. 1964); Neb. Rev. Stat. §29-2316 (Supp. 1963); Ohio Rev. Code Ann. §§2945.67, 2945.70 (1953); and Wyo. Stat. Ann. §§10-1308, 10-1311 (1945). The Model Penal Code bars prosecution for an offense if a former prosecution for the same offense resulted in an acquittal, an acquittal being "a finding of not guilty by the trier of fact or . . . a determination that there was insufficient evidence to warrant a conviction." The drafters recognized that some states, such as Connecticut and Wisconsin, give the prosecution a broad right of appeal. These states are expected to add a clause which would make an acquittal a bar to further prosecution, "unless such acquittal has been set aside because of an error of law prejudicial to the prosecution." Model Penal Code §1.08 (Proposed Official Draft, 1962).

Michigan and Kansas.[3] Wisconsin, on the other hand, allows a much broader statutory basis of state appeal:

> . . . appeal may be taken by the state from any:
> (d) Judgment adverse to the state, upon questions of law arising upon the trial, with the permission of the trial judge, in the same manner and with the same effect as if taken by the defendant. A judgment acquitting the defendant of all or part of the charge shall be deemed adverse to the state.[4]

Even though Wisconsin has this broad right of state appeal, it is clear that it is limited to questions of law and puts out of reach the overturning of a judicial finding or a jury verdict of not guilty. In *State v. Evjue*[5] the court refused to set aside an acquittal by the trial judge which was clearly contrary to the overwhelming evidence of the defendant's guilt. The Wisconsin Supreme Court said, in part: "We consider that this court has no power under the statute or constitution to review the merits of the acquittal or to reverse the judgment." [6]

Many acquittals observed in current practice are not based on disputes about points of law or about the facts or evidence of guilt.[7]

For a general discussion of the right of state appeal see Kronenberg, Right of a State to Appeal in Criminal Cases, 49 J. Crim. L., C. & P.S. 473 (1959); Comment, 1939 Wis. L. Rev. 295; Note, 1950 Wis. L. Rev. 337. See also Palko v. Connecticut, 302 U.S. 319, 58 Sup. Ct. 149, 82 L. Ed. 2d 288 (1937).

[3] Both Michigan and Kansas provide for a narrow right of state appeal, limited to such matters as dismissal of indictments as invalid or the law in question as unconstitutional. Mich. Comp. Laws §770.12 (1948) and Kan. Gen. Stat. Ann. §62-1703 (1949). In neither case is a general right to review an acquittal given (People v. Ballots, 252 Mich. 282, 233 N.W. 229 [1930], and State v. Ramirez, 175 Kan. 301, 263 P.2d 239 [1953]). Michigan has clearly stated that this prohibition includes refusal to hear the people upon appeal from directed verdicts (People v. Hastings, 214 Mich. 363, 183 N.W. 10 [1921]), while the Kansas court stated flatly many years ago that "a verdict of 'not guilty' in a criminal action ends the case" (State v. Crosby, 17 Kan. 396, 401 [1877]).

[4] Wis. Stat. §958.12 (1963). The Wisconsin right of state appeal is similar to provisions in Connecticut and Vermont. Conn. Gen. Stat. Ann. §54-96 (1958); Vt. Stat. Ann., tit. 13, §7403 (1958). Of these three only Wisconsin has an express constitutional provision against double jeopardy (Wis. Const. art. I, §8) but has been able to reconcile the two concepts by holding jeopardy to attach only after a final judgment is rendered and the accused is discharged. An appeal requested immediately upon a verdict of acquittal does not bar subsequent proceedings because jeopardy has not yet attached. State v. Witte, 243 Wis. 423, 10 N.W.2d 117 (1943); State v. King, 262 Wis. 193, 54 N.W.2d 181 (1952).

[5] 254 Wis. 581, 37 N.W.2d 50 (1949).

[6] 254 Wis. at 594, 37 N.W.2d at 56.

[7] It is generally assumed that acquittals rarely get to appellate attention where the state has no recognized right of appeal. However, in cases where a defendant has been charged with a number of counts and the judge decides to exercise his discretion by acquitting on one or more of these counts but convicting on others, the result may be an inconsistent verdict, i.e., the various counts will be so interrelated that it is impossible for the defendant to be guilty of one and not guilty

They reflect a decision by the trial judge that the disadvantages of conviction to the particular defendant outweigh any advantages which conviction would bring. In this respect they are similar to many jury acquittals, which often reflect an unwillingness to enforce the law under the circumstances of the particular case. Like jury decisions, acquittal by the trial judge is a final determination not reviewable under even the broadest right of state appeal.[8] Unlike the jury, which never gives its reasons for an acquittal, the judge may articulate the basis for his decision to acquit. If the reason is his interpretation of the relevant law or his opinion of the admissibility of evidence, then his decision is reviewable under broad state appeal statutes like that in Wisconsin, since it would be a question "of law arising upon the trial." If, however, the reason, expressed or not, is that the judge thinks it unwise to convict the defendant, then his decision is not subject to review even though the judge may clearly be exceeding his lawful authority.

Granting a judge power to acquit for reasons of policy unrelated to the sufficiency of the evidence of guilt would presumably make it possible to provide that the exercise of this authority be subject to appellate review since the trial judge's decision would relate to legal policy rather than to the ultimate question of guilt or innocence. Current nonrecognition of the judge's right to acquit for policy reasons, however, puts all acquittals in the category of ultimate determinations of guilt or innocence and thus makes them immune to the risk of appellate review.[9]

---

of others. This may be the basis of state appeal. See United States v. Maybury, 274 F.2d 899 (2d Cir. 1960).

[8] There is a question of whether the trial judge, in deciding a case without a jury, has in effect all the powers of the jury, particularly those involved in a decision which ignores both facts and law. In distinguishing between the power of a judge and a jury to reach an inconsistent verdict, the court in United States v. Maybury, 274 F.2d 899, 903 (2d Cir. 1960), said, in part: "While the historic position of the jury affords ample ground for tolerating the jury's assumption of the power to insure lenity, the judge is hardly the 'voice of the country,' even when he sits in the jury's place. If he deems an indictment multiplicious, he has only to say so, and the time for him to exercise any 'lenity' that he deems warranted is on sentence. . . . We do not believe we would enhance respect for law or for the courts by recognizing for a judge the same right to indulge in 'vagaries' in the disposition of criminal charges that, for historic reasons, has been granted the jury." In addition, the Wisconsin Supreme Court in State v. Evjue, 254 Wis. 581, 595, 37 N.W.2d 50, 56 (1949), called the exercise of acquittal power by the judge when the evidence indicated guilt "more reprehensible" than the exercise of such power by a jury.

[9] In a California case (People v. Winters, 171 Cal. App. 2d 876, 342 P.2d 538 [App. Div. 1959]) the trial judge dismissed criminal gambling complaints against a number of defendants just as trial was about to begin and without any preliminary motions or requests. He argued, in part: ". . . I also take great exception to what I term a discriminatory pattern of enforcement of the gambling laws of

The experience in Wisconsin with appellate review of the trial court's decisions on matters of law makes possible some generalization of the impact of this authority to review trial court practice. There are relatively few state appeals, and these apparently occur only when there is a decision, participated in by the attorney general, in which a significant issue of continuing importance is involved. There is no reason to believe that the trial judiciary views the right of state appeal with any less sympathy than the right of a defendant to appeal, nor is there any evidence that defense counsel views this as either unusual or as an undue hardship on the defendant. On the contrary, the reaction of bench and bar is much the same as their reaction to the fact that both sides have the right of appeal in a civil case. Moreover, the right of state appeal does have a significant restraining influence on some trial judges who tend to be unsympathetic with some laws and thus tend to construe them very narrowly. Put another way, the appellate process serves

---

this city. It is my opinion that they are enforced mostly against members of the Negro race. . . .

"I take the view in this case, where, in one morning, we have twenty-five defendants that are here are all of one race, that constitutes nothing more, and nothing less, than discriminatory enforcement of the law.

"I am dismissing these cases, and I am dismissing them because of the reason that I believe that it constitutes discriminatory enforcement.

"This, of course, is not to say to these defendants that this Court is granting any license or privilege for you to go out and gamble. Because, I am against gambling in all its forms. But, I hope that the Chief will arrest you again if you go out and repeat your act of gambling. Because, I think that each and everyone of you are guilty of what you are here charged with. But, you are no guiltier than others who go unraided and do the same thing." 171 Cal. App. 2d at 878-879, 342 P.2d at 540-541.

Since California law requires the listing of reasons for dismissal in an order entered upon the minutes of the proceedings (Cal. Pen. Code §1385), and because dismissals of this nature have been held to occur prior to the attachment of jeopardy, the reasons as stated were available to the appellate court. This court, in reversing the dismissal order and ordering trial for defendants, commented in part: "A judge dismissing criminal charges without trial, upon his own motion, must record his reasons so that all may know why this great power was exercised, and such public declaration is indeed a purposeful restraint, lest magistral discretion sweep away the government of laws. . . .

"A dismissal 'in furtherance of justice,' upon review, must show that there has been the exercise of a valid legal discretion, amounting to more than the substitution of the predilections of the judge for the alleged predilections of the peace officers. It is an abuse of discretion for a judge without a hearing to hold there is deliberate or intentional unequal enforcement, since in all cases it is presumed that official duty has been fully and regularly performed by the public authorities until there is judicial proof to the contrary.

"The basic question is, 'Are defendants guilty?', not whether there are other lawbreakers who have escaped detection and punishment." 171 Cal. App. 2d at 882, 342 P.2d at 542-543. Had this judge heard the state's evidence and then entertained a dismissal motion, presumably because of insufficient evidence, or had he made a finding of not guilty after trial, the release of the defendants would have barred further action.

as a check against trial court misconception of the meaning of the law, whether that misconception is adverse to the defendant or to the prosecution.[10]

2. *Use of mandamus to force trial.* Although it has been tried, the writ of mandamus is apparently not a feasible way of challenging an acquittal by a trial judge. In a recent federal case,[11] the circuit court of appeals upheld a writ of mandamus ordering a new trial after the trial judge directed a verdict of acquittal prior to the completion of the government's case. The court characterized the trial judge's action as a "usurpation of power" he did not possess, in that it amounted to a refusal to enforce the criminal law.[12] The United States Supreme Court reversed the court of appeals on the ground that a new trial would result in double jeopardy.[13] "[Double jeopardy] is at the very root of the present case, and we cannot but conclude that the guaranty was violated when the Court of Appeals set aside the judgment of acquittal and directed that the petitioners be tried again for the same offense." [14]

While this seems to be the final answer to the possibility of using mandamus to control arbitrary acquittals in trial courts, it is arguable that this kind of trial judge action should be subject to control. Mr. Justice Clark in a dissent said:

> It is fundamental in our criminal jurisprudence that the public has a right to have a person who stands legally indicted by a grand jury publicly tried on the charge. No judge has the power before hearing the testimony proffered by the Government or at least canvassing the same to enter a judgment of acquittal and thus frustrate the Government in the performance of its duty to prosecute those who violate its law.[15]

The problem is how to enforce such conduct without putting the defendant twice in jeopardy. One possibility is provided in those jurisdictions which allow moot state appeals merely to get an ex-

[10] See Comment, 1939 Wis. L. Rev. 295; Note, 1950 Wis. L. Rev. 337.

[11] In re United States, 286 F.2d 556 (1st Cir. 1961).

[12] Id. at 562-564. See also Comment, 71 Yale L.J. 171 (1961).

The wrongful seizure of such power vitiated any claim of former jeopardy as a bar to ordering a new trial (In re United States at 565. See also Comments, 49 Calif. L. Rev. 751 [1961], 62 Colum. L. Rev. 332 [1962], 36 N.Y.U.L. Rev. 1378 [1961], and 16 Rutgers L. Rev. 181 [1961]). The government rested its assertion on the propriety of using mandamus to challenge such acquittals on the All Writs Statute (28 U.S.C. §1651(a) [1958]) and on two previous United States Supreme Court cases which upheld use of mandamus to vacate an improper suspension of a mandatory sentence (Ex parte United States, 242 U.S. 27, 37 Sup. Ct. 72, 61 L. Ed. 129 [1916]) and to force a judge to issue a bench warrant for a defendant properly indicted (Ex parte United States, 287 U.S. 241, 53 Sup. Ct. 129, 77 L. Ed. 283 [1932]).

[13] Fong Foo v. United States, 369 U.S. 141, 82 Sup. Ct. 671, 7 L. Ed. 2d 629 (1962).

[14] 369 U.S. at 143, 82 Sup. Ct. at 672, 7 L. Ed. 2d at 631.

[15] 369 U.S. at 145, 82 Sup. Ct. at 673, 7 L. Ed. 2d at 632.

pression of appellate opinion and to set limits for future administration without, however, disturbing the current case.[16] This may be a major motivation of the prosecution even where state appeal is permitted. Another possibility occurs when judges occasionally state a general acquittal policy, not specifically limited to a single case, but applicable in future cases as well. This may be controllable through supervision by a higher court.

3. *Controls on an expressed judicial policy of future acquittals.* Occasionally a trial judge will openly express disagreement with some particular legislative proscription or with the mandatory penalty attached to some crime and will state his intention to systematically acquit defendants charged with such offenses. If clearly stated and carried out this policy may translate itself into a practice on the part of the prosecutor not to charge such offenses and in a diminution of police efforts to investigate and arrest in these offense categories. If, on the other hand, the prosecutor or police maintain a continuing interest in enforcing such laws and do arrest and charge, then the judicial policy is necessarily put to visible test in the courtroom. An illustration of this occurred in one Wisconsin court. The trial judge was an outspoken opponent of the motor vehicle "point system," whereby defendants convicted of traffic violations accrue a certain number of points or demerits which, upon sufficient accumulation, result in suspension of the person's driver's license. This judge made a practice of dismissing many traffic violations but assigning "costs" to the defendant, thereby in effect subjecting him to a monetary loss equivalent to a fine but avoiding the conviction record and the mandatory recording of violation points. In some instances the dismissals occurred prior to asking the defendant to enter a plea; in others a dismissal was recorded even though the defendant had pleaded guilty or nolo contendere. The state motor vehicle department appealed to the attorney general for a ruling on the propriety of such action by the court, pointing out that 691 such dismissals had taken place in a one-month period in which the court was studied. It was the opinion of the attorney general that the lower court in question had no express authority for such practice and in fact both statutory law and general public interest required the court to convict upon receiving a guilty plea and to pronounce sentence.[17] The attorney general called for the exercise of "the superintending control of the Circuit

[16] Cf. Kronenberg, Right to State Appeal in Criminal Cases, 49 J. Crim. L., C. & P.S. 473 (1959).

[17] Memorandum of Authorities, State of Wisconsin ex rel. Reynolds v. Proctor (copy on file, University of Wisconsin Law School Library, unreported 1961).

Court" over this lower court.[18] The trial judge, in conference with circuit court judges, agreed to cease the practice.

An expressed policy of acquittals in certain types of cases, or the frequency of this practice even if not expressed, ordinarily becomes translated into enforcement practices by police and prosecutor so that challenge of the policy is rare. For example, many trial judges develop an express or implied "tolerance" in speeding cases, ac-

[18] The Wisconsin Constitution provides in article VII, section 3, that the supreme court of Wisconsin "shall have a general superintending power over all inferior courts; it shall have power to issue . . . original and remedial writs, and to hear and determine the same." Section 8 of the same article grants circuit courts "appellate jurisdiction from all inferior courts and tribunals, and a supervisory power over the same. They shall also have the power to issue writs of habeas corpus . . . and all other writs necessary to carry into effect their orders, judgments and decrees, and give them a general control over inferior courts and jurisdictions."

The supervisory control given to these courts augments and complements their power of review. Generally speaking, a court will not invoke its supervisory power unless it is apparent that appeal will not provide the petitioner with an adequate remedy. Other requirements which have been enumerated by the Wisconsin Supreme Court in the past are a legal right on the part of the applicant and a correspondingly clear duty on the part of the inferior court and an exigency which calls for prompt action to prevent grave hardship on the part of the applicant.

Traditionally, supervisory control has been exercised in matters of jurisdiction. When the inferior court has usurped jurisdiction, the superintending court has prohibited it from doing so and reversed its extrajudicial acts. The supervisory court also has the power to compel the inferior court to act within its jurisdiction where it has a duty to do so.

In Wisconsin, the right to force an inferior court to act within its jurisdiction to prevent severe hardship for the applicant has been somewhat expanded, so that it also allows the court to correct judicial error in the inferior court where an appeal is impossible or will not provide a sufficient remedy. Thus in State ex rel. McGovern v. Williams, 136 Wis. 1, 116 N.W. 225 (1908), the supreme court compelled a circuit court to go on with a criminal prosecution after the court had wrongfully quashed a grand jury indictment due to a minor irregularity in the choosing of the grand jury. This power has only been invoked in deciding preliminary questions since the court has consistently given credence to the maxim that a writ of mandamus is not a substitute for appeal.

The Wisconsin Supreme Court has made a consistent distinction between the nature of its own supervisory power and that of the circuit court. The circuit court's power to supervise inferior courts can be exercised only by the instrumentalities which it was given the power to issue (Potter v. Frohbach, 133 Wis. 1, 112 N.W. 1087 [1907]), while the supreme court has this power independent of any instrumentality necessary for its exercise. The supreme court has asserted its right to create new writs but as yet has not done so, and decisions during this century indicate a tendency to frame the writ to meet the circumstances of a particular case.

A 1920 decision, State ex rel. T. L. Smith Co. v. Superior Court of Dane County, 170 Wis. 385, 388, 175 N.W. 927, 928 (1920), stated that the function of the circuit court's supervisory power was, "(a) to compel inferior tribunals to act within their jurisdiction; (b) to prohibit them from acting outside their jurisdiction; and (c) to reverse their extrajurisdictional acts." A strict adherence to this might cause trouble in a situation where the error sought to be rectified was a judicial error in the preliminary proceedings. For a general discussion of the Wisconsin Supreme Court's supervisory powers see: Wickhem, The Power of Superintending Control of the Wisconsin Supreme Court, 1941 Wis. L. Rev. 153.

quitting defendants who are arrested for exceeding posted speed limits within this tolerance and convicting only those who drive faster than the posted limit plus the tolerance. This ordinarily acts to influence traffic police to modify their speeding arrests accordingly. Some judges, in different types of cases, make it a practice to regularly acquit defendants accused of conduct that the court feels is not really criminal, or at least that should not result in conviction and sentence, such as adultery, petty gambling, or adult consensual homosexuality. Again, this normally acts to modify arrest and charging practices. Occasionally, however, the prosecutor or police will desire full enforcement, including conviction, in these cases and will continue to arrest and charge such offenders. Frustrated by repeated acquittals, and with little or no chance of effective official challenge of these practices, they may turn to the press hoping by an "exposé" to force court compliance with the requirements of law. For example, a police official in a Wisconsin community kept a long and detailed record of all acquittals by a trial judge. He confronted the judge with this log and threatened to submit it to the press unless the judge modified his acquittal practices. In another instance, some members of a police vice squad in Michigan actually published articles castigating a trial judge for dismissing actions against prostitutes and homosexuals. As might be expected, this reliance on public exposure to control court practices is remarkably ineffective. Among other things, exposing a practice of acquitting speeders who go a few miles over the posted limits, or defendants accused of adultery or minor gambling, probably wins as much public support for as against the judge. Unless there is evidence of bribery or corruption, judges are not likely to suffer much from accusations of leniency in minor criminal matters.

D. Proposed Legislative Recognition of Acquittal Discretion

The Model Penal Code of the American Law Institute contains a section which gives to the trial judge discretion to acquit guilty defendants under certain conditions:[19]

> Section 2.12. De Minimis Infractions.
>
> The Court shall dismiss a prosecution if, having regard to the nature of the conduct charged to constitute an offense and the nature of the attendant circumstances, it finds that the defendant's conduct:
>
> (1) was within a customary license or tolerance, neither ex-

[19] Model Penal Code §2.12 (Proposed Official Draft, 1962).

pressly negatived by the person whose interest was infringed nor inconsistent with the purpose of the law defining the offense; or

(2) did not actually cause or threaten the harm or evil sought to be prevented by the law defining the offense or did so only to an extent too trivial to warrant the condemnation of conviction; or

(3) presents such other extenuations that it cannot reasonably be regarded as envisaged by the legislature in forbidding the offense.

The Court shall not dismiss a prosecution under Subsection (3) of this Section without filing a written statement of its reasons.

This is a recognition that trial court judges confront types of cases in which conviction is possible but, in a broad sense of fairness, undesirable. It represents a frank attempt to recognize and give statutory authority for judicial discretion to acquit certain of the guilty, a common but largely unrecognized administrative practice. Its value is in recognizing, making visible, and providing some guidelines for judicial decisions that presently are highly individualized and considered by some to be improper use of judicial authority.

The proposal raises a number of interesting questions. There is no provision for state appeal from a de minimis dismissal, and thus the prosecution cannot effectively challenge such action by the court. The filing of written reasons for dismissal under subsection (3) is presumably to force the court to articulate and justify "extenuations," perhaps in this manner exerting some control on the range of such dismissals, but the reasons apparently are in no way subject to review.

Whether the range of authorized dismissals under the de minimis proposal is broad enough to include all types of acquittal practices currently followed by trial courts is not known with any certainty. Some trial judges make it a practice to dismiss charges of "minor vices" such as gambling and fornication and other acts of sexual immorality when the defendants involved come from lower-class racial, ethnic, or regional minorities where, it is assumed, such conduct, if not "normal" to these groups, is at least tolerated within them. Whether the de minimis criterion of conduct "within a customary license or tolerance" [20] fits this situation, or whether it refers only to customary behavior that exists throughout the entire social spectrum without regard to subcultural variation, is an open question. Likewise, in practice a basic motivation in judicial acquittal of the guilty is to discipline the police and to control prosecutor charging policies. It may be that many de minimis acquittals

[20] Model Penal Code §2.12 (1) (Proposed Official Draft, 1962).

would have this effect, but whether the section will be used by judges to dismiss charges not otherwise de minimis within the proposal, for the purpose of controlling other agencies, is, of course, uncertain.

The issue of whether a given offense is de minimis is to be decided primarily by reference to the intention of the legislature. The difficulty is in knowing what the legislature intended, because it is uncommon for there to be any very helpful legislative history in most states. As a consequence, concepts of de minimis, in practice, may come to depend more on the view of the official involved. What to police may seem to be a significant aspect of a general vice situation may, on the facts of the individual case, seem to the judge to be a very minor incident of gambling. To the extent that the right to acquit for de minimis violations puts the judge in the position of reviewing law enforcement policy, it emphasizes the importance of adequate communication between courts and enforcement agencies.

The Model Penal Code provisions also reflect the important relationship between adjudication and sentencing discretion. There is, in addition to the de minimis provision, an authorization for the trial judge to convict of a lesser offense even though the person is guilty of a more serious crime.[21] This is an effort to introduce flexibility and regularity into the process of reduction of charge.

Traditional concern with sentencing tends to ignore the relationship between adjudication and sentencing discretion. Sentencing is treated as a matter of disposition of convicted offenders; the question of who should not be convicted, although guilty, is not usually considered. Likewise, the negotiated plea, while widely recognized as a common administrative practice, is rarely dealt with as a sentencing matter, yet the primary motivation of both state and accused in plea bargaining is the modification of the sentence.

Separation of the adjudication and the sentencing decision, like fragmentation of the whole criminal justice process in stages or steps such as arrest, charging, conviction, sentencing, and release, is a handy analytical device and undoubtedly a logical demarcation of what is a very complex process. There is, however, danger in treating any one stage as if it were a self-contained system rather than merely one decision in an ongoing process of interrelated decisions and consequences of decisions. An assumption, explicit or implied, that adjudication is in fact a quasi-automatic, nondiscretionary process, turning solely on matters of sufficient evidence, is a gross oversimplification much as is the "full enforcement" myth sometimes assumed at law enforcement stages. One of the major

[21] Model Penal Code §6.12 (Proposed Official Draft, 1962).

contributions of provisions such as the de minimis section of the Model Penal Code is that, in spite of numerous problems created by such proposals, they give overt recognition to the "cushion" of discretionary leniency that is found in operation throughout the criminal justice system, even at those points where, by tradition and sometimes by legislation, such discretion has no express authority.[22]

[22] A major purpose of various sections of the Model Penal Code is to make visible what are now common but covert practices. Professor Herbert Wechsler, Reporter for the Model Penal Code, in commenting on the de minimis proposal said, "Nothing is more common in criminal law enforcement . . . than the exercise on the part of the prosecuting attorney . . . — grand juries where there are grand juries — of a kind of unarticulated authority to mitigate the general provisions of the criminal law to prevent absurd applications, and this is an in camera operation. It doesn't come to court.

"It has been a general purpose of the Code to try to lay a foundation for bringing this general practice in criminal law administration, which we agree is necessary, somewhat further out into the open, and the only way to do that seemed to be to vest in the court a kind of power analogous to the general dispensing power which is now exercised in practice by the organs of administration.

"To that end this section was drafted." A.L.I. 39th Annual Proceedings 105 (1962).

CHAPTER 10

Acquittal of the Guilty Because the Conduct Is Held to Be Not Criminal or Constitutes a Minor Violation

A. Conduct Resulting from Emotional Disturbance

Some judges acquit in cases where the criminal conduct is apparently the symptom of some mental disorder, beyond the control of the defendant, rather than the result of rational criminal intent. These are not cases where a defense of insanity would be appropriate but include certain sexual and compulsive behaviors, clearly short of psychosis, but at the same time not fully "criminal" where volition is implicit in the definition. Homosexual offenders, for example, are often viewed by courts as sick rather than criminal, and police vice squad methods of "enticing" them to solicit plainclothes officers are "repugnant" to some judges. One judge who regularly and systematically acquits homosexuals on the basis of this enticement explained:

> These poor souls who should be pitied and medically treated rather than abused and taken advantage of are deliberately, surreptitiously and unethically enticed into committing acts that they may not have committed for years and years and which they may never commit again were it not for these appalling maneuvers by the vice squad.

Homosexuals, transvestites, window peekers, and similar "mild" sex offenders are at best thorns in the side of most courts and clearly present custodial and treatment problems to postconviction authorities, particularly institutional personnel. If a defendant's only offense is one of these sexual deviations and he is receiving, or agrees to receive, private psychiatric care, most courts will typically acquit.

This concept of "sickness" applies not only to defendants in sex offenses but also to defendants whose criminal conduct is some form of theft but whose motive is apparently neurotic. In cases of kleptomania, for example, which usually involve middle-aged women clearly in menopause, there is typically no charge, but when there is, it is usually dismissed. One assistant prosecutor said:

> Why should we be so stuffy as to follow the law and subject these middle-aged women to embarrassment and great anxiety? Their families also suffer. If these cases did get to court, and even if there were a conviction, it would be quickly followed by a suspended sentence. That may be O.K., but I just don't think that these poor women should have a record of conviction.

Other cases may involve more serious offenses, such as burglary, which are, however, basically motivated by the neurosis of the defendant. In a case involving a series of burglaries by a nineteen-year-old college student who was quite seriously disturbed, though clearly not psychotic, the judge acquitted with the provision that he receive private psychiatric care after a psychiatrist appointed by the court assured the judge that the burglaries "will not be repeated in the future" and recommended a "full reprieve" so that the defendant would not be stigmatized at any time in his future. In acquitting this defendant, the judge commented that the state does not have "enough walls, locks, and bricks for these types of persons" and "something else" has to be done. He went on to say that active participation in private therapy serves the ends of justice as well as or better than formal conviction.

In one Wisconsin city a district attorney issued the following memorandum to his staff:

> It has been the practice in the past to issue warrants for disorderly conduct against those who attempt suicide but this procedure seems undesirable. These people are mentally disturbed and should not have the stigma of being criminals. They do need treatment and it is within the province of the court to have these mentally disturbed people taken to court under the city ordinance; thus they do not have a record of being criminals. Often a knowledge of the fact that they have been declared criminal tends only to unbalance them more. Our obligation to society is to attempt to restore them to mental health, and thus return them to society as normal persons. Thus, in the future do not issue any state warrants for those who attempt suicide.

B. Acquittal Because the Conduct Is a Matter of Private Morality or a De Minimis Violation

Illustration No. 1: A husband and wife, neither having a previous criminal record, were charged with public intoxication after being arrested on the way home from a party. The judge dismissed the charge, commenting: "This type of case should be handled at the precinct level."

Illustration No. 2: A Michigan judge, in acquitting two defendants of petty gambling charges, stated: "Upstairs in the Detroit athletic club more than likely there are members sitting around playing cards for money. In a great many of the houses in the city there are people gambling for money. Many other fraternal and civic organizations are gambling right now also. Why then should I send these petty gamblers to jail when so many of my own friends and associates are committing the same crimes without being charged? The operators who make a racket out of gambling are the ones who should be jailed."

Illustration No. 3: A Michigan trial judge met with a district supervisor of the Federal Narcotics Bureau to discuss a case pending in the judge's court involving a twenty-two-year-old narcotics addict, never previously convicted of possession or sale of drugs, who was charged with sale of narcotics (which carries a mandatory sentence of twenty years to life) because he had sold "a few capsules to another addict." Both judge and supervisor agreed that this was an "instance of the kind of prosecution for which the law had not been intended."

Summary acquittal is sometimes based upon a distinction between "immoral" but not "criminal" behavior (even though legislatively proscribed) and behavior which should be proceeded against by use of criminal sanctions. In this sense the court is acting in review of the prosecutor's charging decision and, in many instances, reviewing police arrest policies as well. In such acquittals the court in effect is actually saying that proceedings should never have been started in the first place. Noncommercial gambling, some kinds of drunkenness, private or family disputes, and illegal carrying of weapons where there is apparently no criminal purpose are types of behavior not considered criminal by the courts, as are certain minor variations (de minimis offenses) of more serious crimes.

It is not always possible to distinguish "noncriminal" conduct from de minimis violations, because it is often unclear precisely which is the standard for acquittal. Adultery, for example, is seldom prosecuted, but when it is, the case typically results in acquittal; occasionally there may be conviction followed by a suspended sentence. It is not clear whether the judge is saying that adultery should not be considered criminal or whether he views the particular case as such a minor infraction of the criminal law that the courts should not be bothered with it. Most cases of family assault and private dispute are screened out at the police level by referring them to a misdemeanor complaint bureau or private agency. This informal handling of such matters is supported by most judges, who feel that these are private matters and not really the concern of the criminal court unless the assault is extremely serious; however, there are few judges who would care to go on record as believing that certain conduct is categorically not criminal regardless of legislative proscription.

Many gambling cases are dismissed on the basis that gambling is not really a very serious offense. Most judges, however, do convict and sentence "ringleaders" in gambling conspiracy cases, at the same time distinguishing these from "most cases" of gambling which are "not serious or vicious like other crimes such as rape or murder." Some serious crimes, such as the carrying of concealed weapons, result in acquittal when it is clear that the particular offense is a very minor one. One judge commented that he dismisses those cases in which the person is "ordinarily a good citizen who was simply carrying a weapon concealed on his person under the misconception he needed a gun for protection or simply forgot to have it registered or was transporting it for other legitimate purposes such as hunting or merely because he is a person interested in firearms."

C. Acquittal Because the Conduct Is Considered Normal to the Subculture of the Defendant

Illustration No. 4: A judge, in dismissing an assault charge against the male partner in a white, "hillbilly" common law relationship, explained: "These people couldn't care less about marriage, divorce or other relationships. They are ignorant and their moral standards are not like ours. They come from the backwoods in the South where even incest is the accepted thing. There is no point in this court acting as a referee in these relationships."

Illustration No. 5: A judge, in commenting on differential treatment of certain sex cases, remarked: "In certain types of cases you must take into consideration the social standards of the offenders. For example, in statutory rape or carnal knowledge cases the man might be just above the legal age and the girl just

> below. Usually in such cases, particularly among the Negroes, there is mutual consent and in the Negro group this type of behavior is not particularly frowned upon and is felt to be normal. You have to take this factor into consideration."

A dilemma faced by many judges is whether the conduct of the defendant before him should be tested against the flat rule of the law which was violated or whether, in justice, he should consider the mores of the subcultural group from which the defendant comes. The decision in practice is not simple nor are the consequences of either alternative minor. It is a difficult choice for many judges to convict and sentence a person who, although he has clearly violated the broader legal and moral code of the community, in no sense feels guilty and may have difficulty comprehending the entire proceedings against him, being in fact convinced that his own behavior is normal and natural and little different from that of most of his friends and associates. If the purpose of conviction is to identify the individual who has engaged in deviant behavior and who therefore needs to be rehabilitated, it becomes particularly difficult and perhaps futile in the case of the offender who conforms to the conduct norms of his particular subgroup and who feels no need for rehabilitation. If, on the other hand, the objective of conviction is the "social engineering" function of uplifting the moral standards of the entire subcultural group, then conviction and treatment of some of its members may serve this end.

The most prominent subgroups involved in this conviction dilemma are the very lower-class Negro slum residents of the large cities and some white "hillbillies" who have recently migrated from the South and border states to work in the industrial centers of the North. These persons are typically uneducated, even illiterate, and retain certain customs strikingly at variance with both the standards of middle-class propriety of most judges and the general mores of the larger communities in which they live. A problem of similar dimensions but involving different categories of persons and different types of conduct exists in some rural areas where "moonshine whisky" is produced and sold in violation of state liquor laws.

In the urban Negro community the problems of divergent mores, real or assumed, and differential legal treatment are perhaps most apparent at the police level. The major issue here is not discrimination against Negroes by arresting them more frequently for many types of crimes ranging from assault to gambling, but rather police inactivity resulting in "underarresting" Negroes for conduct which would likely result in arrest in other precincts. Assaults involving

Negro perpetrators and Negro victims commonly do not result in arrest, unless extremely serious, on the general philosophy that such conduct is normal in this subculture. The police have an informal policy of discouraging Negro assault victims from filing complaints, and it was reported that officers newly assigned to primarily Negro districts quickly adopt this practice regardless of the attitudes and policies they brought with them from primarily white districts. This has prompted a prosecutor to remark, "The major difficulty is getting law enforcement officials, judges, juries, and the Negroes themselves to take Negro crimes of violence with any seriousness." Various respectable elements of the Negro community, including such organizations as the Urban League and the National Association for the Advancement of Colored People, have appealed to the police to enforce more rigidly the laws against Negroes than has been the practice.

It is interesting to note that the policy of underarresting Negroes for such crimes as assault has a deceptive influence on conviction and sentencing statistics. For example, if only assault conviction records were used as the basis for comparing court treatment of the two races, it might appear as if there were a court bias against Negro defendants. Most Negroes charged with assault are convicted while a higher percentage of whites similarly charged are dismissed or acquitted; furthermore, the Negro defendant is more likely to receive a longer or more severe sentence. The difference, of course, is primarily due to differential arrest practices. When assault involving a Negro defendant and a Negro victim does result in arrest and charging, it is almost certain to be more serious than is typical of white assault cases and a stronger case in terms of evidence sufficiency. Both of these variables combine to virtually assure conviction once arrest is made and the charge brought and to result in a somewhat more severe sentence.

The assumption of different mores in the Negro community is not limited to crimes of violence but includes much sexual misconduct and "vice" as well. One assistant prosecutor, in deciding not to charge some Negroes with statutory rape, explained, "This sort of an offense is so prevalent among Negroes and the moral code among this group is so low to begin with that if you insisted upon the prosecution of every offense like this or even more serious offenses than this, it would soon load the courts up. Now if these were whites, they would be treated more severely." A judge explained that there was "no doubt that the sex mores of the Negro are different from the whites" and that this should make a difference in the way they are treated by the court.

These practices reflect an assumption that illegal conduct should be treated differently in different subcultures, provided it is confined within the group. The conduct is treated as serious and is proceeded against only when it spreads outside the subculture. Thus some judges explain that Negro gambling in a Negro neighborhood is all right but that Negro gambling in a white neighborhood is not. The police, primarily by harassment techniques, attempt to limit the operation of Negro prostitutes to the Negro precincts and to Negro clients. Both the Negro streetwalker who operates outside a Negro neighborhood and the Negro prostitute seen with a white client run a higher risk of arrest. Likewise, interracial assaults (or, for that matter, any interracial crime) are viewed as intrinsically more serious than intraracial fights.

The practice of differential enforcement also reflects an assumption that certain criminal conduct within the Negro community is a lesser evil to what might happen if there were vigorous enforcement. Part of this is the attempt to contain the conduct, preventing its spread throughout the city, which might occur if intensive enforcement were the practice. Another part, however, relates to the conception of the natural criminal proclivities of Negroes held by certain judges. One judge, mentioned earlier, commented that rigorous enforcement against petty gambling among Negroes would merely drive them onto the streets, with a consequent rise in rapes, burglaries, and other serious crime.

What seems to be differential enforcement may in some situations not be differential at all. Some judges take the position that certain illegal conduct, normal to the Negro subculture, is also normal behavior among all classes. The major difference is in its visibility and the particular forms that it exhibits in the Negro slums. These judges say, for example, that "public intoxication" is not intrinsically different from "country club" intoxication. It is more visible to the police, has perhaps some "nuisance" element to it, but otherwise "a drunk is a drunk." Strict enforcement against the lower-class drunk is, therefore, a form of discrimination. One judge commented, "Take gambling, for example. You gamble, I gamble, most people we know gamble. Only you and I play bridge for money in our own homes. Negroes shoot crap in the alley for a few nickels and get arrested. Is it really any different?"

Not all judges feel that subcultural moral variation should result in differential court treatment. Instead, they urge that offenders should be convicted not only because the conduct is criminal and repugnant to the community but because the court has a duty to "uplift" the morals of certain classes by exemplary convictions to deter others from engaging in this conduct. For example, one judge, in commenting upon the apparently high rate of "hillbilly" incest, said, "While I recognize that this might be a cultural pattern, I just cannot countenance it and I will sentence these people." Another judge felt that the practice of common law relationships should be proceeded against by charging lewd and lascivious cohabitation or "threatening to charge this" to get this "certain class of citizens to conform to more socially acceptable behavior." Other judges felt they were performing a "duty to the broader Negro community" by convicting and sentencing Negro defendants in assault cases.

The "social engineering" function of conviction is not typically carried very far, however. Most judges prefer to have persistent lower-class and minority group problems such as desertion, nonsupport, intraracial fights, public intoxication, and the like handled at the precinct or prosecutor level. In general they fully support the activities of such agencies as the Detroit Misdemeanor Complaint Bureau and other "adjustment" bureaus, and privately support police harassment programs to contain the problems within certain precincts and to hold them to an "irreducible minimum," so long as such harassment "does not get out of hand and shock the public conscience."

CHAPTER 11

Acquittal of the Guilty Because Conviction Would Be Ineffective and Better Alternatives Exist

A. The Objectives of Restitution and Rehabilitation

In certain cases judges decide that an alternative to conviction is available that will better serve the objectives of the criminal process. In fact, conviction and sentencing would probably forestall these objectives. For example, in some situations a purpose of the criminal law is to force the defendant to make a money payment to his victim. Laws making nonsupport and the issuance of worthless checks criminal are designed to do just this. In these cases, it is not surprising that the judge is commonly willing to acquit a defendant in return for the payment of family support or for restitution to victims of fraudulent checks.

In other situations, a major purpose of conviction and sentencing is to rehabilitate the offender. In certain types of cases in which the defendants are chronic alcoholics, homosexuals, mentally retarded, or neurotic, available methods of treatment are inadequate and conviction and sentencing are not only futile in terms of successful treatment but place great strains on correctional resources. In such cases, the trial judge is ordinarily willing to divert these defendants to private agencies for treatment, if available, by acquitting them of the criminal charge. In addition there are some types of frequently recurring criminal activity, such as assault growing out of family disputes, with which most judges do not wish to be burdened on the general grounds that the very frequency of the offense would overtax their already crowded calendars. These cases are largely handled more informally by court-attached officials and agencies who take all reasonable steps to settle such matters before invoking the criminal process.

B. Avoidance of the Issue: Systematic Use of Alternatives to Charging

Over a period of years some alternatives to the criminal process have been developed to handle certain types of persistent criminal conduct out of court. The Adjustment Division of Recorder's Court in Detroit receives all nonsupport cases directly or on referral from the prosecutor or police and attempts to work out an appropriate settlement before criminal sanctions are used. The office of Friend of the Court does much the same thing with delinquent alimony cases. The Misdemeanor Complaint Bureau of the Detroit Police Department attempts to settle, by peace bond or otherwise, the bulk of family and neighborhood dispute and assault cases. In Kansas, many family desertion cases are placed on "consent" probation. In these cases charges are dismissed when the offender agrees to return to his family and to report regularly to a probation officer. Likewise in Wisconsin many cases of nonsupport and other intrafamily disputes are supervised and "settled" by the prosecutor's office and the probation staff of the court, with no prosecution if the defendant does not commit another violation.

These agencies annually handle hundreds of cases which technically could be proceeded against criminally. Because they greatly reduce the court congestion and, in all but extreme cases, deal as effectively with the problems as would conviction, they are uniformly supported by trial judges. Even such harassment programs as the Detroit practice of arresting prostitutes for Disorderly Persons Investigation (with the requirement of a medical examination) are supported by many judges as more effective than formal prosecution in controlling the problem. In these ways courts avoid much chronic lawbreaking of particularly "fringe" criminal nature and are not called upon, except when these alternatives fail, to convict and sentence such offenders.

C. Acquittal When Private Treatment or Other Alternatives Are Available

Illustration No. 1: A defendant charged with a series of sexual offenses involving window peeking and exhibitionism had all charges dismissed when his family agreed to commit him to a state mental hospital.

Illustration No. 2: A homosexual defendant charged with indecent behavior with two teen-age boys had charges against him dismissed upon pointing out that he was under private psychiatric care and making "progress" in the control of his problem.

Illustration No. 3: Two young men charged with burglary had the charges dismissed because they were about to enter the armed services. The judge commented: "I'm giving you a break. I think the Army will be good for you. They know how to deal with boys like you. If you apply yourselves, you can learn a trade and return as useful citizens."

One of the most widely used alternatives to conviction and sentencing is the pledge of the defendant, or his family, that he will have private treatment by a psychiatrist or a social work agency. Usually these cases involve neurotic or sexually inverted offenders who are unwelcome in the correctional system, which in any case has no effective program for their rehabilitation. There are numerous examples of homosexual violators whose cases are dismissed upon a promise of private treatment. In some cases shoplifting and other types of theft result in acquittal when the defendants agree to submit to private psychiatric treatment. When the offender, although with a record of repeated offenses, is apparently motivated by a deep-seated psychiatric disturbance, and when he or his family agrees to civil commitment in a state mental hospital, dismissal of the charges usually follows. In addition some narcotics addicts have charges against them dismissed upon the condition that they seek voluntary commitment to the federal hospital for addicts at Lexington, Kentucky. In certain cases chronic alcoholics charged with drunk and disorderly conduct are acquitted when representatives of the Salvation Army or Alcoholics Anonymous agree to vouch for the person and to offer him care and treatment. The judge does not necessarily believe that private agency treatment will cure these offenders. Most judges are somewhat pessimistic about the possibility of rehabilitating homosexuals, alcoholics, narcotic addicts, and emotionally disturbed violators. At the same time these judges feel that the criminal process is really not designed for such persons. They tend to disrupt correctional facilities and may become worse problems as a result of conviction than if allowed to remain in the community under the supervision of an agency. Furthermore, private treatment saves state costs. In short, judges tend to see private community treatment for "sick" offenders as an expedient way of dealing with these persons but do not necessarily hold high hopes for their cure.

Whether the judge first convicts and then suspends sentence upon condition of private treatment or whether he acquits outright seems fortuitous in some cases, depending upon customary practice of the particular judge. In other cases the acquittal reflects the effort of the judge to avoid the negative effect which conviction itself might have on the rehabilitation of the offender. One of the major alternatives to conviction and sentencing of young offenders whose crime is of a minor nature (such as auto theft for "joyriding" purposes and drunk and disorderly conduct) is enlistment in the armed services. Where such an alternative is possible, however, the conviction record itself may prevent the armed forces from accepting the defendant or, if he is accepted, may negatively influence his military career. The practice, consequently, is to acquit these young men upon a pledge of enlistment. In certain other cases where a conviction record might jeopardize the person's employment even though sentence is suspended, the practice is to acquit, given reasonable assurance of future conformity. Sometimes it is felt that the trauma of conviction itself might hamper private rehabilitative efforts.

In addition to private treatment and military service, one alternative occasionally used by judges is banishment from the community, commonly referred to as "sundown" or "Greyhound" parole. This occurs when the offender is from out of town and agrees to leave and stay away if acquitted. The offenses involved in such cases are usually vagrancy, minor sex crimes, or gambling violations. Typically the offenders are on either end of the social class continuum: hobos on one extreme, respectable business-class visitors to the city on the other. One judge reported his practice with transient homosexuals to consist of a brief conference before arraignment, at which time he would tell the offender that on the basis of evidence already in hand he would be convicted and sentenced to an institution. He would then release the offender on his own recognizance to await the arraignment. The judge pointed out that this "little talk" invariably caused such "queers" to rapidly leave the city.

D. Acquittal When Restitution Is Made or the Victim Is Otherwise Satisfied

Illustration No 4: A defendant who had written a number of bad checks had criminal charges dropped when he agreed to make full restitution. This was his only bad check offense and the judge commented, "If there is a next time, you will not get off so lightly even if you return double what you have stolen."

Illustration No. 5: A defendant charged with assault had the charges dropped when he agreed to pay the medical and dental costs of his victim and further agreed to give the victim's family twenty-five dollars a week until the victim was once again able to go to work.

Illustration No. 6: A young man was charged with statutory rape when the father of the underage girl, upon discovering that his daughter was pregnant, complained to the prosecuting attorney. The trial judge dismissed the charge when the young man agreed to marry the girl on the grounds that this was "the proper solution to this kind of problem."

Occasionally bad check, minor theft, and property damage cases are dismissed when restitution is made and when the offender is a person whose reputation or that of his family would be excessively harmed by formal conviction and sentencing. Often these cases are handled at the prosecution stage, where the prosecuting attorney will drop the charge when restitution is made. Some prosecutors, however, argue that their office is not a "collection agency" and persist in prosecution even though the defendant has made monetary amends. In these cases the judge is faced by a formal charge for which there is sufficient evidence to convict but at the same time the victim is satisfied and often the violator is an otherwise respectable person. Assuming further court action would serve no useful purpose as far as the individual offender is concerned, acquittal usually follows.

In addition to monetary restitution, there are other alternatives to conviction which may serve to satisfy the victim. Acquittal is the practice in certain cases of sexual misconduct where the girl has become pregnant and the defendant agrees to marry her to legitimize the child. Likewise in nonsupport, family dispute, and abandonment cases which have not been successfully adjusted informally and now face criminal charges, dismissal may follow if a satisfactory solution is worked out between the time the charge is brought and the court appearance. During one year in Detroit, for example, of eighty abandonment charges formally filed, seventy-five were successfully "settled" and resulted in dismissals.

E. Dismissal of the Current Charge upon Revocation of Parole

Illustration No. 7: A defendant, on parole from a burglary sentence, had two charges of bad checks dismissed when the parole agent told the court that his parole would be revoked and he would be returned to prison.

An alternative to convicting and sentencing defendants already on parole or probation for past offenses is revocation and incarceration for whatever the terms remaining under their previous sentences. This not only saves the time, expense, and difficulty of securing a new conviction but may result in as appropriate a term of imprisonment as would conviction for a new offense. The fact that the defendant benefits from such an arrangement, both in terms of a lesser criminal record and perhaps less cumulative time, acts as a deterrent to his challenge of the revocation order. Such dismissals on assurance of revocation usually occur when the remainder of parole or length of the original probation is sufficient to accomplish whatever ends the court feels appropriate in the case. A variation on this acquittal procedure occurs in cases where the defendant is wanted in some other jurisdiction where conviction will be more easily assured or where the punishment is greater or otherwise felt to be more appropriate.

While this practice may benefit both the system and the defendant, it does create certain problems. The use of revocation as an alternative to adjudication raises the matter of relative requirements for sufficient evidence. In the weak case, revocation circumvents the protections inherent in the formal conviction process, yet after revocation, for all practical purposes (except the record), the defendant is treated as if he were convicted. Dismissal of new charges when parole or probation is revoked adds a certain deceptiveness to correctional statistics. This practice is necessary to consider in evaluating revocation statistics which are customarily divided into "new offense" or "rules" violations. For example, it is apparent that many rules violation revocations of probation and parole are actually based upon a belief that the offender committed a new crime while under supervision.[1]

[1] For further analysis of this point see Newman, The Effect of Accommodations in Justice on Criminal Statistics, 46 Sociology and Social Research 144 (1962), also in Applied Sociology: Opportunities and Problems, chap. 12 (Gouldner and Miller ed. 1965).

CHAPTER 12

Acquittal of the Guilty Who Do Not Deserve the Record or Sentence of Conviction

Judges exercise their discretion to acquit certain defendants whom they do not feel deserve conviction in spite of their guilt. In part, these acquittals represent attempts by trial courts to individualize justice by taking account of the consequences of conviction for defendants who differ markedly in background and social characteristics and for whom the effects of conviction would be quite disparate. In these instances, the court is facing the issue of whether it is more just and proper to uniformly apply the criminal process to all who engage in the same proscribed behavior or whether justice is better served by considering the relative effects of conviction on the life of each defendant or on his family. In other instances, the acquittal decision relates not as much to the characteristics of the defendant as to mitigating circumstances in the offense itself. This sometimes occurs in cases where the victim of a crime has in some way induced or contributed to the criminal conduct of the defendant. For example, occasionally a client of a prostitute will complain that the girl has stolen his wallet or in some other way has defrauded him. Acquittal of the prostitute of the larceny or fraud charges may follow on the general theory that the complainant has invited the crime by his own participation in illegal activity.

A. Acquittal of Respectable Defendants

Illustration No. 1: A defendant who was vice-president of a large bank was arrested on a charge of soliciting and accosting on the basis of conduct involving his homosexual overtures to a member of the police vice squad. At his court appearance he admitted both the particular act and his homosexual proclivities. However, he explained that he was presently receiving private psychiatric counseling and pleaded for "mercy" on the grounds that conviction would destroy his family life and would probably cost him his position at the bank. The judge dismissed the charge and admonished the defendant to continue counseling and to control his impulses.

Illustration No. 2: Two codefendants were charged with gross indecency growing out of their sexual misconduct with young girls. The older of the defendants, who had a previous criminal record, was convicted and sentenced to from two to five years in prison. The charge against the other defendant, who was a college student, was dismissed by the judge because the defendant was "otherwise a respectable boy" who came from "a good family" and had merely "fallen under the influence" of the older man.

Illustration No. 3: A seventy-year-old defendant was arrested for drunken driving. He had no prior record. He entered a guilty plea. The judge, however, refused the plea and dismissed the case saying: "Anyone who has reached the honored age of seventy years without so much as a parking ticket should not have his fine record blemished by a single lapse."

Most of the activities of the police, prosecutor, and criminal courts are directed to the control of the chronic criminal element of the community. The majority of persons arrested, charged, and convicted are members of the least educated, most economically depressed classes in both rural and urban settings.[1] The reasons for this are complex and beyond the scope of analysis here but include in part: (a) The types of conduct proscribed by conventional criminal codes are, in large part, forms of crude theft, violence, and vice traditional to the lower classes. The middle and upper classes have neither the need nor the opportunity for such conduct. (b) The deviant conduct of the lower classes is both more visible and of greater immediate threat to general community standards. (c) The lower classes are heavily composed of the least integrated racial and ethnic minorities who often share subcultural values and behavior patterns which are divergent from those of the more established classes. At any rate, the typical law violator apprehended by the police, processed by the prosecutor, and facing the trial court falls far short of common standards of respectability.

Otherwise respectable persons are, however, sometimes arrested, prosecuted, and tried for crimes. In particularly serious offenses,

[1] See, for example, a discussion of Categoric Risks in Crime in Reckless, The Crime Problem 26-42 (2d ed. 1955). See also Berelson and Steiner, Human Behavior: An Inventory of Scientific Findings 488 (1964), and Carlin and Howard, Legal Representation and Class Justice, 12 U.C.L.A.L. Rev. 381 (1965).

such as murder or negligent homicide or sex crimes such as rape, the relative respectability of the defendant apparently makes little difference except, of course, in his economic ability to obtain counsel. However, in such routine offenses as public intoxication, homosexual soliciting, and shoplifting there is differential treatment of the respectable violator by all agencies from the police on. The respectable violator is less likely to be arrested, less likely to be prosecuted if arrested, and less likely to be convicted if prosecuted than a less respectable defendant who engages in the same conduct.[2] There may be many reasons for this, but by and large differential leniency is based upon the fact that (a) respectable violators are "occasional" offenders who do not ordinarily present a threat of continued criminality, (b) the consequences of arrest, prosecution, or conviction may be much more damaging to the respectable defendant in terms of loss of employment or professional standing and family and social degradation than to the less respectable defendant, and (c) the respectable defendant ordinarily has available more resources to obtain treatment, if needed, outside the criminal justice process.

In current administration, respectable defendants are given a "break" by the courts. They are often acquitted in spite of evidence sufficient to convict, and occasionally there is an acquittal even though the defendant has pleaded guilty. In other instances, continuance may be granted under circumstances that make it tantamount to dismissal. The judge ordinarily explains that the case will be continued for a period of months with an eventual acquittal if the defendant does not get into further trouble during this time. An alternative to either acquittal or a continuance is conviction followed by a suspended sentence with no requirement of supervision. The use of any particular alternative depends in part on the historical practice of the particular court and in part on the desirability of avoiding a conviction record for the particular defendant. Some Wisconsin courts use the continuance device because judges cannot give outright suspended sentences without probation supervision, whereas the Michigan practice is more likely outright acquittal; Kansas courts usually convict but place the defendant nominally on bench parole. Conviction followed by suspended sentence occurs in cases where the record of conviction does not cause particular damage to the reputation of the defendant and where the sentence will apparently serve no useful purpose.

[2] Reckless, The Crime Problem 26-42 (2d ed. 1955).

B. Acquittal to Expunge the Conviction Record by Means of a Summary Retrial

Illustration No. 4: A defendant had been convicted of assault some years ago as a young man and had been placed on probation for one year. He successfully completed his probationary period, subsequently served four years in the army, received an honorable discharge, and in general became a respectable citizen. For the past eleven years he had been employed as a state civil servant in Michigan. However, he had been passed over for promotion a number of times because of his prior criminal record. He approached the court and requested a retrial on his old offense. This was granted, whereupon the judge found him not guilty, set aside the old conviction, and ordered the Detroit Police Department and the probation department to destroy their records pertaining to this case.

Illustration No. 5: A young defendant previously convicted of auto theft and currently on probation requested a retrial and acquittal to void his record so that he could enlist in the army. The probation staff of the court sent him to the army recruiter for both physical and psychological tests to determine whether he would be acceptable to army enlistment standards. Following an affirmative reply from the recruiter, the retrial was granted, the defendant found not guilty, and records of his past conviction were destroyed.

The rather unusual practice of a summary retrial and acquittal of formerly convicted defendants is found in some Michigan courts. These retrials ordinarily occur well after the statutory time for appeal by the defendant has passed [3] and, in fact, in about half the instances noted, the retrials occurred a number of years after the defendant had completed his sentence.[4] This is clearly a device for expunging conviction records in deserving cases where the record is working some particular hardship on the defendant. There were ninety-seven retrial acquittals in one year in one Detroit court. In about half, the purpose was to remove the convic-

[3] See Mich. Comp. Laws §770.2 (1948), which states that motions for new trial shall be made within thirty days after verdict and not afterwards. In these cases, the motion for a new trial is not only untimely as far as the statutory provision is concerned but usually occurs some months or years after the defendant has completed serving his sentence.

[4] While it is possible for the court, on its own motion, to order a retrial at any time, the basis for the retrial must be some error in the original proceeding. Mich. Comp. Laws §770.11 (1948). This practice does not fit within the statutory provision on either ground: the defendant, rather than the court, typically moves for retrial and there is ordinarily little doubt that the original conviction was properly made and based upon sufficient evidence of guilt.

tion record so the offender could enlist in the armed forces. In the other half, the reason was to remove the criminal records which continued to prevent otherwise rehabilitated persons from getting employment, promotions, certain types of licenses, and the like. In all of the cases observed, the defendants were on or had been on probation. No observed case involved a defendant who had been incarcerated.

This practice is not limited to a single court or to the Detroit area but is found throughout Michigan. It apparently is not common in Kansas or Wisconsin. One variation is the "court of no record" which is a special proceeding used in one jurisdiction at the point of conviction when defendants are of military age and likely candidates for enlistment in the armed services. Instead of the arraignment in the usual courtroom, the judge meets with these boys in a basement room where, in effect, they are given the option of enlistment or conviction. If they choose enlistment, the case is continued until this is confirmed, at which time an acquittal is recorded. There were no recorded instances of refusal of this option.

Acquittals for purposes other than enlistment are granted to offenders who have subsequently led a respectable life. In general, judges approved of this device in the belief that a person should not have to pay endlessly for the "sins of his youth." Some judges commented on the apparent usurpation of the governor's pardoning power by use of the retrial acquittal. However, they generally resolved any conflict by pointing out that this device is only used in types of cases in which the governor "is not and should not be concerned." They felt that the pardon power should be used only in "more serious" cases and that administrative expediency should give the court discretion to "see that justice is done" in relatively minor cases.

The police expressed discontent with court orders to destroy the fingerprints and records of defendants acquitted on retrial. A practice in some departments is to reproduce the records and retain a copy before turning over the original fingerprint card and other papers to the defendant. One police official explained: "Just because he has been acquitted doesn't mean he's innocent. We know he was guilty and he might be again. We need every record of every criminal we can get. Sure we duplicate them; these are our records. Besides, the record that went to the F.B.I. doesn't come back."

C. Acquittal Where Circumstances of the Case Mitigate the Conduct

Illustration No. 6: A defendant was charged with felonious assault growing out of a fight with his landlord in which he had shot and wounded him. Upon examination by the judge, however, it was revealed that the landlord, in attempting to evict the defendant, had struck the first blow and that the entire neighborhood had somehow become involved in the melee. At the time of the shooting, the victim was swinging at everyone involved with a tire chain. The trial judge, explaining that "it is impossible to get a clear story in this case," dismissed the assault charge but ordered the defendant to pay the victim's medical costs.

Trial judges occasionally acquit defendants when examination of the total context in which the crime occurred reveals circumstances which mitigate the defendant's conduct. In some instances it is because the victim in some way contributed to the crime or because the defendant was otherwise acting understandably, if not wisely, in doing whatever he did. In a number of assault cases, for example, it is apparent that the victim has provoked the attack. In others, particularly assault charges growing out of barroom fights, it is often unclear who initially assaulted whom and the judge may dismiss to get rid of the whole unsavory matter.

In other acquittals, the grounds may be the relative disrepute of both victim and defendant or the prior illegal relationship between them. For example, assault charges involving a victim who is a common law mate of the defendant are commonly dismissed because this type of relationship is considered disreputable, as well as illegal, and the court does not wish to be in the position of enforcing normal standards of conduct between such partners. In other cases involving assaults, fraud, or larceny where both the victim and the defendant are known gamblers or have criminal records, the court may dismiss charges against the defendant on much the same grounds, namely, that the court should not be "a referee for the underworld."

In cases involving an otherwise respectable defendant fleeced by a procurer, prostitute, gambler, or confidence man, the court may dismiss on the general grounds that the defendant has "asked for" such treatment by his attempt to engage in illegal activities. Not all such cases result in dismissal because many judges feel that if established as a policy these acquittals would in effect license the Murphy game, the rolling of clients of prostitutes, and the general swindling of the gullible public. One judge asked: "Can you imagine what would happen when big conventions come to town?" Acquittals are most likely to occur in cases in which the victim is a local citizen who "should have known better" or where the victim was particularly deeply involved in illegal activity with the defendant or was especially gullible in participating in the confidence game.

PART V

Charge Reduction and Acquittal of the Guilty to Control Other Parts of the Criminal Justice Process

There isn't a single judge in this state who likes the narcotics law. Juries don't like it either. Everyone here abhors the idea of sending persons to prison for a minimum of twenty years for what in most cases are really minor crimes. The legislature no doubt had a high purpose in mind but the law is based on a picture of the drug problem that is unrealistic. All that it has accomplished is to increase reduced pleas.

Prosecuting Attorney
in Michigan

It is not a proper police function to go out hunting for homosexuals and for women in bars to entice them into crime. Many of these homosexuals are sick and should be medically treated. Many of the women would remain law-abiding if these affairs were not initiated and staged by the police officers. I refuse to convict persons enticed in this manner.

Trial Judge in Michigan

[The trial judge], under his present powers, . . . is no mean figure. . . . He is, in an extraordinary degree, at the heart of things. With means for getting information, with broader edutional background and with more freedom from political entanglements he can take over much of the power now exercised by the prosecutor and become the master of criminal law enforcement.

Moley, *Our Criminal Courts*
at xix, xx (1930)

Trial judges commonly use the decision of guilt or innocence to control other parts of the criminal justice system and to avoid legislative controls on their own sentencing discretion. Systematic acquittal of guilty defendants is used to discipline and to control the police when they use what the court considers improper enforcement methods. Routine charge reduction, commonly initiated by the court, is used in certain categories of offenses to bypass legislatively fixed mandatory sentences and to modify certain correctional consequences of conviction. Charge reduction acts to limit both the minimum and the maximum length of time an offender will be under correctional supervision and to obtain probation for certain offenders actually guilty of conduct defined as nonprobationable by legislation. These practices are illustrative of judicial discretion, but of a somewhat different order than that exemplified by the court showing leniency to certain deserving defendants. The major distinction lies in the judge's reason for acquitting the defendant or reducing charges against him.

Dismissing charges of drunkenness against a seventy-year-old defendant with no prior record is essentially an attempt at fairness, an assessment of the minor nature of the conduct and the inappropriateness of the consequences of conviction in this particular case. Acquitting a known prostitute of solicitation in an effort to force the police to modify their "enticement" practices is quite another matter. In the latter situation, the question of whether the defendant deserves leniency is secondary to the broader objective of controlling police enforcement practices. Routine downgrading of sale of narcotics charges does not reflect a decision that conviction for sale would be inappropriate under the facts of the particular case. Except for the syndicate criminal, all sale of narcotics charges are reduced to charges of possession, a lesser offense. The purpose is to avoid the severe mandatory sentence because judges consider it an undesirable limitation upon the sentencing flexibility of the court; because mandatory sentences curb desired correctional discretion; and because most judges feel that most mandatory sentences, especially in narcotic cases, are much too severe given the circumstances of the ordinary case which comes before the court for sentencing.

Accommodations of the adjudication decision to avoid legislatively prescribed mandatory sentences or to control the police become routine and systematic. There is little need for plea bargaining on the part of the defendant nor does the decision rest on any intensive search for desirable traits in the defendant or mitigating circumstances in his offense. Who the particular defendant is, is virtually irrelevant to the decision. The judge responds not to deserving defendants but instead to "bad law" or "improper methods."

Judicial acquittal of the guilty as a means of influencing police practice is similar to, but in important respects different from, the judicial role in the exclusion of evidence illegally obtained or the formally recognized defense of entrapment. They are similar in the sense that both represent an effort by the judiciary to control law enforcement practices. They differ in the respect that the exclusionary rule and the defense of entrapment are formal, articulated policies which are frequently the subject of attention by appellate courts. A significant amount of trial court activity designed to affect police conduct is not, however, based upon formally recognized rules or defenses. Instead it reflects a given trial judge's reaction to a particular enforcement practice in the context of a specific case. Commonly an outright dismissal or acquittal is given without any effort to articulate the reason other than a general expression of dissatisfaction with police conduct. Ordinarily there is no attempt to relate these acquittals to the exclusionary rule or to entrapment; in fact, some judges frankly distinguish them and coin terms to describe the basis of their decisions. This is perhaps best illustrated by one trial judge's defense of "enticement," which he acknowledged to be different from the defense of entrapment as it is commonly recognized and defined by appellate decisions.

Manipulation of the decision of guilt or innocence to control other parts of the process raises the important question of the extent to which the trial court performs as an "overseer" of the entire criminal justice system. The issue is whether the actual administrative system is composed of a number of linked but relatively independent agencies, notably the police, the prosecutor, the court, and correctional services, each with its own sphere of activities and influence and more or less equal powers in decision making, or whether among them the trial court occupies a supervisory and controlling position. Many trial judges consider themselves and are considered by others as responsible for and the chief administrators of the entire criminal justice process, at least from arrest through sentencing and perhaps including some postconviction correctional processes as well. Police and prosecutors, and probation officers too, submit a good many of their decisions to the court for final approval. Furthermore, the trial judge is a public figure, usually elected, and more than any other person or agency is symbolic of orderly, reasoned, and dispassionate justice in the community. Other agencies operate from their own perspectives: enforcement efficiency, vigorous prosecution, and selection of appropriate probationers. The judge, legally trained and presumably capable of "neutral" review of contested matters, makes the final decisions and balances delicate issues of community sentiment, police effectiveness, and correctional objectives against the rights of the individual defendant.

The judge's role as arbiter and symbol of justice is one thing; the necessity for him to act as an administrator of the daily routine of criminal justice is another. A great deal of attention has been paid to the function of the judge in criminal trials. As has been seen, there has traditionally been little concern with his parallel role in the much more common guilty plea process and virtually no concern with the informal use of judicial authority to control agencies other than the court itself. Yet the trial court acts very much as an administrative agency in the routine processing of most criminal cases.

The judge has no direct control over many of the other agencies. He neither appoints nor directly supervises police officials. The legislature has clear authority to impose sentencing mandates on the court and any discretion to avoid them is assumed rather than given. By requiring written reasons for nolle prosequi or charge reduction by the prosecuting attorney, as well as by the desirability of an amicable relationship in daily contact, the court can ordinarily exert a more direct control over the activities of the prosecutor. Likewise, where probation agents are officers of the court, the judge can direct probation policies and practices. But prison authorities and parole boards are more distant and independent. Any attempt at control here, as with the police and the legislature, is of necessity less direct and, because adjudication is the intake process for the correctional services, it becomes the focal point of judicial manipulation when this control is desired.

CHAPTER 13

Routine Charge Reduction to Avoid Legislative Controls on Sentencing Discretion

A. Routine Charge Reduction to Avoid Severe Sentence

Faced with certain mandatory sentencing provisions which are thought undesirable, some judges adopt a policy of always reducing the charge to a lesser offense unless the case is an aggravated one. These are routine reductions to avoid the mandatory sentence rather than reduction because of mitigating circumstances in the individual case. An example of an individual case reduction would be reducing burglary to larceny where the defendant is young, has no prior record, and is otherwise respectable. In contrast, an example of routine reduction is provided by sale-of-narcotics cases in Michigan where judges, who "abhor" the twenty-year minimum, have a policy of *always* reducing sale to possession or addiction *unless* defendant is a flagrant violator, a member of a criminal syndicate, or otherwise undeserving of leniency. The case reductions are made *when* defendant is deserving; the routine reductions *unless* defendant is *un*deserving.

In practice it is not always easy to tell when an offense is routinely reduced to avoid a mandatory penalty. When sale of narcotics is reduced to possession, for example, the judge may rationalize the decision on the basis of the youth of the defendant, the de minimis nature of the violation, or perhaps explain only that "justice will be served as well." Only by observing the practice over a period of time (and interviewing the judges) does it become clear that such reductions are routine regardless of circumstances in the individual case. In sale-of-narcotics cases particularly, because of the mandatory minimum incarceration of twenty years, Michigan judges, without exception, not only accept reduced charges but actively participate in making certain that charges are appropriately reduced. As for exceptions, one prosecutor said: "Unless the defendant is flagrant in his violation or has a long criminal record, the case will always be reduced to possession." By "flagrant" is ordinarily meant "the top man in the narcotics racket or where [defendant] has aggravated the offense by pushing, selling and stimulating juveniles into becoming addicts and steady customers."

Routine reductions are an operational response to what is felt to be inadequate legislative sentencing provisions. In this way the "system," meaning here court and prosecutor, can avoid legislative mandate, can retain sentencing discretion at the court level when it is denied by the legislature, and at the same time can obtain all of the administrative benefits of a guilty plea induced by charge reduction. The routine reduction is an illustration of how difficult it is to deny sentencing discretion by requiring the judge to impose high minimum and maximum sentences.

B. Routine Reduction to Avoid the Mandatory Minimum Sentence of the Original Charge

Illustration No. 1: A judge in Detroit, who routinely accepts guilty pleas to the lesser charges of possession or user when defendant is originally charged with sale of narcotics, an offense with a twenty-year mandatory minimum sentence, remarked: "This is a ridiculous law, passed in the heat of passion without any thought of its real consequences. I absolutely refuse to send to prison for twenty years a young boy who has done nothing more than sell a single marijuana cigarette to a buddy. The law was not intended for such cases. I have been accused of usurping commutation and pardon powers. This is not true. I simply will not give excessive sentences and where the legislature leaves me no alternative, I will lower the charge or dismiss altogether."

Illustration No. 2: A lower court judge in Wisconsin expressly disagreed with provisions of the Motor Vehicle Code making revocation of operator's license mandatory upon accumulation of sufficient "points" for convictions of moving violations or upon conviction of drunken driving. He developed a practice of acquitting defendants on payment of costs to avoid "points" and of reducing drunken driving to reckless driving or some lesser offense to avoid mandatory revocation. In one year he dismissed 479 traffic violations and reduced, on his own initiative and without consent of the prosecutor, 26 drunken driving cases.

Mandatory minimum sentences (or mandatory consequences such as license revocation) are almost universally disliked by trial judges because sentencing discretion is denied.[1] Judges feel that mandatory sentences improperly deprive them of the opportunity to take into account the circumstances of the individual case. Long legislative minima also discourage a guilty plea by those charged with these crimes.

The clearest illustration of routine reductions is provided by reduction of sale of narcotics to possession or addiction in narcotic cases in Michigan. This is perhaps a classical illustration of reduction to avoid a judicially unpopular mandatory minimum in the sense that all of the judges involved disliked the twenty-year to life sentence and not only articulated this dissatisfaction with legislative control but actively participated in the charge reduction process to the extent of refusing to accept guilty pleas to sale and "liberally" assigning counsel to "work out" reduced charges. It is difficult to assess accurately the effect of the mandatory sentence provision because prior to its enactment no distinction was made between sale and possession nor did police and court records tabulate these two offenses separately. To demonstrate its infrequent use, however, from the effective date of the revised law (May 8, 1952) to the date of tabulation some four years later (June 30, 1956), only twelve sale-of-narcotics convictions were recorded in Detroit out of 476 defendants originally charged with sale.[2] The remainder (except a handful acquitted altogether) pleaded guilty to reduced charges.

It would be erroneous to assume that the existence of a high mandatory minimum sentence for any crime inevitably leads judges to reduce charges systematically so that the legislative mandate is bypassed. Routine, systematic reduction occurs only when the court feels that the law is bad, that in the majority of cases the minimum term is not deserved. Where the usual case does exhibit serious or dangerous conduct, however, there may be judicial acceptance of the long sentence. For example, first degree murder in all three states carries a long mandatory minimum,[3] yet it is not subject to judicial nullification in most cases. There certainly is no routine practice of avoiding murder convictions.

Judicial nullification of long mandatory minima is generally

1 A.L.I. Proceedings 53 et seq. (1956). See also Lummus, The Trial Judge (1937).

2 These data were collected and tabulated by research teams in the American Bar Foundation project. They are essentially a refinement of statistics reported from the Detroit Recorder's Court and the Detroit Police Department from 1952 to 1956.

3 See Wis. Stat. §940.01 (1963); Mich. Comp. Laws §750.316 (1948); Kan. Gen. Stat. Ann. §21-403 (1949).

supported by correctional authorities, for the mandatory minimum denies discretion to the parole board as well as to the court.[4] Correctional authorities would like to release an inmate at the point in his sentence where he is most likely to make a successful community adjustment. They feel better qualified to make this decision on a case-by-case basis than have it determined by the legislature which, in fixing minimum sentences, in effect assumes that there is little or no difference between offenders convicted of the same statutory offense.

It is likely that the legislative purpose in establishing long minima is primarily one of deterrence and community protection by keeping the offender in prison. Without denying the desirability or propriety of either deterrence or community protection, both judges and correctional authorities are quick to point out that most crimes carrying long minima are not based upon types of conduct easily deterred. While possibly repetition of the crime is prevented (or delayed), it is at the cost of long imprisonment of all persons violating the same law whether the risk of reviolation is high or low, whether the actual conduct is minor and infrequent or serious, persistent, and patterned. In short, a mandatory minimum rests on a crude assumption of similarity of risk, denying to both court and parole board discretion to deal with cases on the basis of a more refined and individualized prognosis.

Confronted by laws which make the sentencing decision mechanical and buttressed by dislike of mandatory minima by correctional authorities, trial court judges frequently use charge reduction or sometimes acquittal of the guilty to nullify the legislative mandate. Routine, systematic charge reduction in these instances acts to telescope the adjudication and sentencing decision. Just as police harassment programs develop in response to such court controls as the exclusionary rule,[5] so systematic reduction is used by courts to avoid legislative controls on sentencing discretion. The relative ease of charge reduction and the obvious willingness of defendants to participate make legislative attempts to control minimum sentences difficult to implement.

[4] See Rubin, Sentencing and Correctional Treatment Under the Law Institute's Model Penal Code, 46 A.B.A.J. 994 (1960); Bennett, The Sentence and Treatment of Offenders, in Of Prisons and Justice 352-354 (1964); Rubin, Weihofen, Edwards, and Rosenzweig, The Law of Criminal Correction, chap. 4, §7 (1963).

[5] LaFave, Arrest: The Decision to Take a Suspect into Custody (1965).

C. Routine Reduction to Avoid the Mandatory Maximum Sentence of the Original Charge

Illustration No. 3: A defendant in Michigan, charged with two counts of armed robbery, appeared at arraignment without counsel. Upon discovering that the defendant was unrepresented, the trial judge, on his own initiative and without request by the defendant, postponed the arraignment and assigned defense counsel to the case. At the next arraignment the defendant entered a guilty plea to one count of unarmed robbery.

Defendants in Michigan who are charged with armed robbery, an offense carrying a maximum term of "life or any term of years," routinely have the charges reduced, in exchange for a guilty plea, to robbery unarmed which carries a fifteen-year maximum sentence. A prosecutor explained:

> Nobody really likes the armed robbery statute. Judges don't like the fact that imprisonment is mandatory and they don't like to send a person up for life unless he is a repeater. Defendants don't like the possibility of life in prison; fifteen years looks better to them. We charge armed robbery for plea leverage, but don't really expect convictions. Sometimes young defendants will plead guilty to it but generally the judge won't accept their plea. He'll send the case back with instructions to work out a lesser charge.

Mandatory minimum terms present the greatest problem to judges who wish to retain sentencing discretion. Mandatory maximum sentences are of somewhat less concern if the court has discretion to set a low minimum or if a statutory minimum is low and probation can be used. On the other hand, maximum sentences are of crucial concern to defendants, who typically ask what is the most that can happen to them, so that, as one prosecutor remarked, "most plea bargaining is a matter of dickering with the maximum." This, along with the promise of probation, is the basis of most negotiated pleas. In most cases it represents charge reduction on a case rather than on a routine basis. The administrative purpose is, of course, to avoid trial but there usually is no systematic attempt by courts to avoid legislative control of maxima as there is with minima, as long as the minimum which accompanies the maximum term is not mandatory and as long as the judge can grant probation when he believes it desirable to do so. Where long maxima are combined with a legislative prohibition against probation, as in a number of serious crimes in Michigan, or where both minimum and maximum terms are fixed by law, as in Kansas, a type of systematic downgrading often results, much as occurs with long fixed minima.

At the same time, long maxima are so feared by defendants that what may begin as a practice of individualized charge reduction becomes routine. The severity of maxima for some crimes, even if the court has discretion to set the minimum or to use probation, is such that no defendant, except perhaps the most remorseful or naive, will plead guilty. The defendant charged with such an offense has little to lose by demanding trial. Consequently, sustained pressure is put on the court to reduce long maxima to achieve a steady flow of guilty pleas. Downgrading comes to rest less on the individual characteristics of the defendant or the peculiar circumstances of his offense than on the avoidance of the maximum sentence. In Michigan conviction of armed robbery or breaking and entering in the nighttime (fifteen-year maximum compared to five years for daytime breaking) is rare. While the defendant must bargain for the reduction (unlike the charge of sale of narcotics with young defendants where even a freely entered guilty plea is customarily refused by the court), the pattern of downgrading is such that it becomes virtually routine, and the bargaining session becomes a ritual. The real issue in such negotiations is not whether the charge will be reduced but how far, that is, to what lesser offense. As has been pointed out, armed robbery is so often downgraded that the Michigan parole board tends to treat a conviction for unarmed robbery as prima facie proof that the defendant had a weapon. And the frequency of altering nighttime burglary to breaking and entering in the daytime led one prosecutor to remark: "You'd think all our burglaries occur at high noon."

Avoidance of severe legislative maxima becomes routine not so much because judges and prosecutors feel that they represent "bad law" in the same sense as long mandatory minima. There is some of this, of course, for any fixed sentence encroaches on judicial discretion to distinguish cases in sentencing. The primary reason, however, is a combination of defendant reluctance to plead guilty to such crimes and an administrative desire by courts to maintain a flow of guilty pleas. Regular, routine charge reduction is the only way this can realistically be achieved.

D. Routine Reduction to Allow Probation

Illustration No. 4: A defendant in Michigan was charged with two counts of breaking and entering in the nighttime, a nonpro-

> bationable offense. His attorney approached the "bargaining" prosecutor and, in arguing for a reduction in charge, pointed out that the defendant was young, had no previous felony convictions, only a minor record as a juvenile, was married, and had steady employment. He requested a "chance to try probation." The prosecutor agreed and reduced the charge to larceny from a building and said he would "not oppose" probation.

In Michigan legislation distinguishes offenses for which probation can be given and those for which it cannot. Even where not precluded by statute, however, courts tend to develop certain sentencing customs in which probation is virtually never given when conviction is recorded for certain offenses. In Wisconsin, for example, judges have authority to grant probation for even such serious crimes as murder in the first degree but never do so. And in Kansas a trial judge explained:

> It is a practice in Kansas courts to consider and where appropriate utilize bench parole in all cases except where the defendant is convicted of murder, rape, or first degree robbery. First offenders charged with these crimes readily have the charges lowered by the county attorney's office, unless the offenses are particularly aggravated, so that parole can be considered. I can conceive of a case, if the facts warranted it, where I might give parole to a person convicted of murder or one of these other crimes. However, I have never done so; young and deserving defendants in these matters usually have the charges reduced by the county attorney.

In Michigan the courts occasionally go so far as to assign counsel with specific instructions to work out a lesser charge in cases involving youthful defendants charged with crimes carrying long sentences. A prosecuting attorney in Detroit commented that no judge will readily accept even a freely entered guilty plea from a young defendant to an offense which is nonprobationable when, in fact, the defendant seems to be a likely candidate for probation. Counsel will be assigned, even if the defendant says he does not want a lawyer, and counsel is told to bring in a plea to a charge that does not preclude probation.

Where the trial judge is confronted by a defendant who seems to be a good probation risk but, as in Michigan, the crime charged has a legislative proscription against probation, charge reduction is the only way to obtain discretion to use probation. Under certain conditions these reductions become so common as to be routine and the court, while responding in part to individual characteristics of the defendant, is also nullifying the legislative effort to preclude probation for a given class of offenders. Charge reduction is particularly routine in cases involving young defendants. There appear to be a number of reasons for this: (a) Youth and lack of criminal record mitigate criminal conduct — a sort of extension of the juvenile delinquency concept. (b) A person who would otherwise be allowed probation should not be arbitrarily denied this opportunity; i.e., young and particularly first offenders deserve consideration for probation whatever the offense (with the possible exception of murder) and legislative proscriptions infringe on this judicial sentencing discretion. (c) The legislative prohibition of probation is assumed to have been directed at habitual and sophisticated violators, not inexperienced youngsters. (d) If youthful defendants were to face a jury which had knowledge of the severe mandatory provisions for incarceration an acquittal would be likely to follow. Thus charge reduction accomplishes the goal of conviction by inducing a plea of guilty yet allows the judge maximum flexibility including the possibility of probation at the relatively small cost of reducing the charge.

E. Routine Decisions to Convict on a Reduced Charge Although the Sentence Will Not Be Reduced

Illustration No. 5: A defendant in Michigan originally charged with armed robbery pleaded guilty to the reduced charge of unarmed robbery. After accepting the plea to the lesser offense, the judge commented: "What difference does it make? He's going to prison in any case and will probably do the same amount of time on the unarmed charge. On the other hand, if I insisted on the armed robbery charge, he would no doubt demand a trial and fight it. This way he thinks he has received a break and is willing to plead to it."

Where the realistic sentencing issue is not a choice of incarceration or probation but only a question of the length of time to be served in prison, judges in Michigan routinely reduce charges, pointing out the actual time served will probably be the same on the lesser as on the greater charge. Michigan judges must impose the statutory maximum but have discretion as to the minimum. The primary concern of a defendant in Michigan is to avoid a long maximum, and judges are willing to comply since they can compensate for this apparent sentencing leniency by setting what they consider an appropriate minimum.

This type of reduction is common, virtually routine, where the charge concession really does not cost anything. As long as the sentencing judge can still give what he feels is an appropriate sentence and as long as parole eligibility remains or can be fixed at about the same time, the lesser charge brings all of the benefits of the guilty plea without interfering with the sentence. This is an interesting example of the dual perspective of judge and defendant in plea negotiation. The defendant responds to the maximum; he seeks to lessen the most that can happen to him. The prosecutor and the court, however, attuned to the processing of hundreds of cases and perhaps more knowledgeable of current parole practices, negotiate from what might be called practice "norms" of sentencing. Furthermore, the defendant is quite understandably concerned with his own case alone. The administrative problems of a crowded court calendar hardly evoke his sympathy and are relevant only to the extent he can use them in negotiation. The judge and the prosecutor, however, while not unconcerned with any individual case, necessarily view it in the context of an ongoing administrative process, an incident in an endless stream of similar cases. Faced with a young, first felony offender where the crime is neither too serious nor bizarre, why not reduce the charge and thus the mandatory maximum? This does not mean that the circumstances of individual cases are unimportant. What happens, though, in crowded metropolitan courts particularly, is that such discretion becomes patterned, predictable, and routine.

F. Routine Charge Reduction When Offender Is Parole Violator or Will Be Sentenced Elsewhere for Other Crimes

Illustration No. 6: A defendant in Michigan charged with felonious assault had the charge reduced to simple assault, a misdemeanor, when it was pointed out to the judge that the defendant, on parole from a robbery sentence, would have his parole revoked.

It is a routine practice to reduce charges when the offender will be returned as a parole violator or will be sentenced elsewhere for other crimes, so that the aggregate of his sentence is approximately equal to or longer than it would be if he were convicted of the more serious offense. This is another variation on the principle that when incarceration is involved and the lesser count will result in the defendant serving a term approximately the same as if he were convicted on the greater charge, the prosecution concession in negotiation is small and charge reduction will be virtually automatic to get the guilty plea. The defendant, in turn, gets a slight reduction in his record and avoids the mandatory maximum of his present offense.

Michigan law prohibits the imposition of a consecutive sentence except for escape or attempted escape from prison or for commission of a new crime while in prison.[6] This latter exception has been interpreted by the attorney general to include the commission of a new crime while on parole:[7] "All sentences for crimes committed while on parole shall be concurrent with each other but consecutive to the sentence upon which such convict was paroled, the test being that the crime was committed while on parole rather than when the sentence was imposed." [8] Because of this, reductions are common where an offense is committed on parole and the parole will be revoked. In one case embezzlement of over $50 was reduced to simple larceny, in spite of police protests, when it was pointed out that the defendant would go back to prison as a parole violator. In another instance, three counts of larceny from a building and receiving stolen property were condensed to one lesser charge of simple larceny when the parole officer pointed out that the defendant would do "about four years for parole violation." Occasionally dismissal of the new count is used instead of charge reduction when the defendant already on parole will be returned as a parole violator, and sometimes new charges are not brought at all.

Roughly the same procedure is followed where the defendant, although not on parole, is wanted in another jurisdiction for a crime of greater severity. This is routine in Michigan in cases in which narcotic addicts are charged in one place, Recorder's Court for example, with some form of larceny while another charge, possession of narcotics, is pending in circuit court. The practice is to reduce the larceny to a misdemeanor and suspend the sentence or impose a fine, relying on the subsequent narcotics conviction for a more appropriate sentence. The same is true where a defendant is wanted in another state or by the federal authorities for a more serious crime. There is some evidence that servicemen can routinely expect a lesser charge if military authorities will take subsequent disciplinary action.

G. Routine Charge Reduction for Informants and State's Witnesses

Illustration No. 7: A Michigan informant who cooperated with the police in making narcotics purchases with marked money and had arranged large (but police-observed) sales of narcotics was allowed to plead guilty to use rather than possession or sale when

[6] Mich. Comp. Laws §768.7(a) (1948).
[7] Ops. Mich. Atty. Gen. 452 (1952-1954).
[8] Ibid.

he was required to reveal his identity and activities by testifying at trial.

One important administrative purpose of charge reduction or outright acquittal is to support police enforcement techniques by showing leniency to informants and to support prosecution efforts by showing similar leniency to those defendants who agree to testify against their co-conspirators.[9] In the case of informants, dismissal of current charges is the common practice if the informant has some potential future value to enforcement authorities. If, however, he has lost future usefulness by being forced to reveal his identity at trial or otherwise, a reduced charge may be offered as a reward for past services and, in effect, as a notice that there will be no future immunity.[10]

Full acquittal is rarely used with defendants who become witnesses for the state, primarily because it is not necessary. The typical state's witness offers no continuing value to the police or prosecutor and is usually only too happy to settle for charge and sentencing leniency which, without such cooperation, would be inappropriate in view of his past record and present involvement. The most common and sought-after reward for a state's witness is probation on the current charge. This may be accomplished by a sentence promise alone or by charge reduction with a promise of probation. Other concessions may involve the dropping of additional pending charges or the dismissal of other counts. This kind of leniency may be illusory. Often defendants who strike such a bargain are persons of confirmed and persistent criminality whose only weapon in negotiation is their willingness to testify against co-defendants. Even if given probation, many of them are unlikely to successfully complete it without violating supervisory conditions or without committing a new offense. Illusory or not, court support of informant and state's witness practices is considered by the police and most prosecutors as necessary and desirable. The actual number of informants who are prosecuted is few. When there is prosecution, it is routine practice for judges to show whatever leniency is necessary to support police and prosecutor efforts.

[9] The United States Supreme Court reversed a holding of a district court judge to the effect that he had no power to permit withdrawal of a plea of guilty because of "extensive cooperation" of the defendant with government agents between the time the defendant pleaded guilty and the time of sentencing. The government consented to withdrawal of the plea because it "planned to dismiss the pending indictment against petitioner and substitute lesser charges." Nagelberg v. United States, 377 U.S. 266, 84 Sup. Ct. 1252, 1253, 12 L. Ed. 2d 290, 291 (1964).

[10] It is more usual for the informant to be acquitted altogether than to be convicted of a lesser charge. For further analysis of this, see Chapter 14, Section C.

C H A P T E R 1 4

Acquittal of the Guilty to Control Police Enforcement Methods

There appears to be a trend in recent years to give the trial judge greater responsibility for controlling police policy and practice. In *Mapp v. Ohio*[1] the Supreme Court of the United States held that state trial judges must exclude evidence obtained by police in violation of the constitutional rights of the defendant. In announcing its decision, the court said that it was convinced that this is the only effective way of controlling police practice.[2] Furthermore, a minority but increasingly common view of the defense of entrapment reiterates the court's responsibility for supervising police practices. Mr. Justice Frankfurter has said with respect to entrapment: "The crucial question . . . is whether the police conduct revealed in the particular case falls below standards, to which common feelings respond, for the proper use of governmental power." [3] This is a position now adopted in the American Law Institute Model Penal Code.[4]

Both the so-called exclusionary rule and the defense of entrapment as well as their respective effects upon police practices are discussed in detail in other volumes in this series.[5] Both are subject to an increasing effort by appellate courts to articulate their purposes and scope.[6]

1 Mapp v. Ohio, 367 U.S. 643, 81 Sup. Ct. 1684, 6 L. Ed. 2d 1081 (1961).

2 367 U.S. at 660, 81 Sup. Ct. at 1694, 6 L. Ed. 2d at 1093.

3 Sherman v. United States, 356 U.S. 369, 382, 78 Sup. Ct. 819, 825, 2 L. Ed. 2d 848, 856 (1958).

4 Model Penal Code §2.13 (Proposed Official Draft, 1962).

5 See LaFave, Arrest: The Decision to Take a Suspect into Custody (1965); the forthcoming volume on Detection of Crime.

6 An interesting example of an attempt by a trial judge to influence appellate court consideration of police practices occurred in a recent case arising in a federal district court. In a trial of a defendant for manslaughter, after both sides had rested, the trial judge denied a motion by the defendant's counsel for acquittal. The judge then learned that the government had a written confession from the defendant which was not introduced in evidence because the prosecutor recognized

The types of acquittals discussed here are based on less formal criteria than those which underlie entrapment proposals as in the Model Penal Code and the exclusionary rule. The court's basic purpose of disciplining the police and of controlling police practices is, however, the same. In effect these informal methods of control represent an extension of the scope of the trial court's customary supervisory responsibility over the police; an extension that depends heavily on the proclivities of particular judges, is often based on unclear criteria, and is not always uniformly applied even in a single court.

In the federal system of criminal justice, the superintending responsibility of the court over police is acknowledged in situations where there are no constitutional issues involved. For example, federal courts will exclude a confession obtained in violation of Rule 5 of the Federal Rules of Criminal Procedure even though Rule 5 has not been declared a mandate of the Constitution.[7] At the state court level, however, there is less recognition of a general responsibility of the trial judge to superintend police practices. Commonly state appellate courts limit the trial court's responsibility to concern with constitutional violations by police. In practice, however, some trial judges do acquit defendants because they have been dealt with by police in ways thought improper by the trial judge even though the impropriety is not of constitutional dimensions. Along with extension of entrapment and the exclusionary rule, it is this informal, seldom-acknowledged, function of the trial judge that underlies the acquittals analyzed here.

A. Acquittal Because the Trial Judge Disagrees with the Intensity of the Law Enforcement Effort

Some trial judges are in obvious disagreement with police as to how active enforcement should be with regard to certain kinds of criminal conduct. This is reflected in some judicial antagonism over current police activity in respect to consensual vice crimes

its dubious status since the conditions under which the statement was obtained would probably not be acceptable under the Mallory Rule. The trial judge stated that the government should use the "signed statement in order to bring a test case . . . because the circuits are at loggerheads as to what constitutes undue delay under the Mallory Rule." Cunningham v. United States, 340 F.2d 787, 788 (D.C. Cir. 1964). The trial judge then announced that unless the statement were offered in evidence, the case would be dismissed despite his earlier ruling to the contrary. The case was reopened and the confession was admitted and read to the jury. The defendant was convicted and appealed. The case was reversed by the circuit court.

[7] Mallory v. United States, 354 U.S. 449, 77 Sup. Ct. 1356, 1 L. Ed. 2d 1479 (1957).

like prostitution and public solicitation by homosexuals. Since trial judges seldom articulate the exact nature of their concern it is not easy to be certain whether it relates primarily to the propriety of the methods being used, the wisdom of devoting a considerable amount of police time and resources to those activities, a disagreement over the meaning of the substantive criminal statute, or a general sense of frustration with the lack of effectiveness of the criminal justice process in dealing with sexual misconduct.

1. *The enticement of prostitutes.*

Illustration No. 1: The court in acquitting a female defendant of charges of accosting and soliciting for immoral purposes commented: "The vice officer purchased dance hall tickets with state funds and deliberately set out to arrest one of the girls. This is going too far; this is deliberate enticement and it will not be tolerated."

An area of conflict between the courts and the police, particularly in Detroit, has to do with the arrest of prostitutes for accosting and soliciting for immoral purposes. Part of this conflict results from differing views of judges and police as to the meaning of the law which makes accosting and soliciting a crime in Michigan. Another part, however, relates to what the courts consider unfair detection techniques, which at least one judge refers to as "enticement," a word chosen to distinguish this from the formal, recognized defense of entrapment. Enticement involves arrests by plainclothes officers of prostitutes who typically are fully aware of the illegality of their conduct and who certainly are not first introduced to such behavior by the police. The objection of the courts to enticement is based squarely on the belief that police methods in these cases are unfair and improper, and acquittals are used in a frank attempt to change these practices. The vice squad, in order to fulfill what they consider their mandate of arresting prostitutes, use plainclothes detectives placed strategically where they may be solicited by both streetwalkers and pick-up prostitutes. Some judges feel that the zealousness of these officers extends beyond merely being in a position to be solicited and includes a number of techniques whereby the original accosting is by the officer, not the defendant.

It is evident that trial judges differ in their reactions to the propriety of these police practices and that there is no systematic communication of the criteria for enticement to persons involved in police administration. Reports of judge's attitudes are sporadic, generally coming from individual officers who were involved in cases which resulted in acquittal, particularly when the officer has been chastised by the judge in open court. As a consequence, extreme cases are told and retold and come to be looked upon by police as typical illustrations of the difficulty they have with the judiciary.

For example, police officers report acquittals in these illustrative cases: An officer spent about twenty minutes in a bar buying drinks for a girl before she made a proposition. The court felt that "too long a time" had elapsed for a true accosting case. In another instance, defendants charged with accosting and soliciting were acquitted when it was revealed that the plainclothes vice officers were in an unmarked Cadillac automobile when the typical vice squad car was an unmarked Ford. In still another case, a waitress was acquitted when she accompanied the officer to a hotel. The court said that "too much time and too much traveling was involved" and that "this is not the type of case the accosting and soliciting law was intended to cover." Analysis of the situation is difficult because it is not clear whether the trial judge is most concerned over the intensity of the police detection efforts on grounds of general policy or whether he reads the "accosting and soliciting" statute as requiring an aggressiveness on the part of the female which is lacking when the officer plays an active role. In all likelihood both are involved. If the substantive ambiguity in the meaning of the crime were resolved legislatively, it would make it possible to deal more accurately with such difference of opinion as exists between judges and the police over enforcement policy in respect to prostitution.

2. *Enticement of homosexuals.*

> *Illustration No. 2:* A psychiatrist who, on court order, has seen many homosexual defendants for diagnosis, notified the court of what he feels is the "typical" operation of the vice squad in such cases: "The arresting officer goes to a public rest room or to some other location which is frequented by homosexuals. Upon seeing a potential defendant, the officer will stare or smile or will even affect feminine mannerisms. While urinating the officer will handle his genitalia in such a manner as to excite or arouse the interested defendant. The defendant then will make an oral proposition which results in his arrest. In my opinion this form of practice is not only entrapment but is harmful to the defendant in that the individual may have succumbed to the officer's enticement while under ordinary circumstances he would not have been aroused enough to make such a solicitation."

When apprised of such techniques by this psychiatrist and being familiar with the use of the peephole in public rest rooms, one judge was moved to remark that such practices are "atrocious," "appalling," "horrible," and "miserable." This judge is convinced that plainclothes officers make a practice of visiting places where homosexuals congregate, such as the rest rooms of large department stores and bus stations, in order to be accosted. When confronted with a homosexual accosting and soliciting case, the judge puts the police officer on the stand and asks him three "key questions." The first is, "Did you go to the bus station rest room due to nature's call or did you go there for the specific purpose of being accosted and solicited by a homosexual?" The second is, "When did you make the arrest — in the rest room or after you got out?" The third is, "How much time elapsed between the initial contact with the defendant and the arrest?" On the basis of answers to these questions, the judge establishes the facts of enticement. He concludes that officers who testify that they went to the rest room to answer nature's call are "obviously lying" because "a police officer driving around town would certainly not go to a department store rest room or to a bus depot rest room. There are many other places available." The questions of when the officer made the arrest and the length of time involved are usually even more narrowly defined in cases of homosexuals than of prostitutes. The judge explained, "If an officer spends over three or four minutes, then there is definitely enticement and I will dismiss the case." About 40 per cent of all accosting and soliciting cases in the Detroit area involve homosexual defendants, and the enticement concept is used by the courts to acquit these persons with perhaps even more regularity than with prostitutes.

3. *Overzealous enforcement.*

> *Illustration No. 3:* A judge in dismissing drunk and disorderly charges against some defendants arrested in a tavern commented that it is "not a proper police function to go into bars to see who is drunk or not. I don't believe this is your duty. The police have plenty of other things to do rather than making the rounds and bothering tavern patrons."

Judges occasionally acquit defendants when it appears to them that the police have been overzealous in enforcement. Such acquittals apparently reflect the judge's opinion that the violation is of a de minimis nature and should be so considered at the enforcement level. In general, courts do not wish to be bothered with cases of minor law infraction and it is easier all around if criminal procedures are not started. In dismissing some minor disorderly conduct charges, for example, one judge commented, "This should have been handled at the precinct level." Another judge called police arrests in minor gambling cases a "fantastic waste" of police manpower. Another judge commented, "It is ridiculous that the vice squad will assign 28 men to investigate a misdemeanor while we have only 22 men on the homicide squad." The prevailing opinion is that intensive, unrelenting enforcement of minor vice, vagrancy, disorderly conduct, and similar laws is an unwise allocation of police resources and perhaps improper where, for example, a disproportionate number of Negro defendants are involved. The assumption is that systematic acquittal of such defendants will be translated into police nonenforcement in de minimis cases or into the informal settling of problems, such as domestic disputes, by methods short of court appearance.

A major difficulty arises in situations where the judge's conception of de minimis differs substantially from the police view. What may appear to the judge as an isolated case of prostitution, for example, may appear to the police as an integral part of organized vice in the community or what to the judge may seem to be an isolated case of solicitation by a homosexual may, to police, be one instance of a general pattern of homosexual activity which has caused a department store or a hotel to exert pressure on the police to clean up an intolerable pattern of solicitation in men's washrooms. Seldom will the judge see the individual case in the context of the larger law enforcement problem which confronts the police, and it is rare for the police to systematically communicate this over-all enforcement picture to the trial judiciary. Undoubtedly communication of such information to the judge would be improper if it were done for the purpose of influencing his evaluation of whether there is sufficient evidence of guilt to convict the defendant, but it would seem most relevant and proper if addressed to the judge's concern with whether the police were "overzealous" given the circumstances of the case and its relationship to the over-all law enforcement problem.

B. Acquittal Because of Disagreement over the Meaning and Purpose of the Law

Illustration No. 4: A Detroit judge, in acquitting two female defendants of charges of accosting and soliciting for immoral purposes, commented: "It is clear that this entire affair was initiated and staged by the police officers who made the arrest and not by the defendants. The officers made the first contacts, they bought the defendants a number of drinks, and they suggested illicit relations. Under such conditions, the charge cannot stand. The crime charged is not prostitution; it is soliciting and accosting."

An acknowledged function of the trial judge is the interpretation of the substantive law relevant to the particular case. In accosting and soliciting cases in Michigan, some trial judges construe the statute[8] to require the female to have engaged in an "accosting," that is, to have been fairly aggressive in solicitation of a male. Where the plainclothes police officer actively encourages solicitation, this may remove the essential "accosting" element of the offense. The difficulty is that trial court opinions seldom attempt to differentiate clearly between an interpretation of the statute defining the crime, an evaluation of the adequacy of the evidence of guilt, or a ruling on the propriety of the police detection methods which were involved. As a consequence, it is seldom apparent to the police or to the prosecutor whether the trial judge is performing his traditional function of law interpretation or his less traditional function of using his acquittal power to control arrest and charging practices.

Since minor offenses, such as prostitution or homosexual offenses, are seldom appealed, there is little opportunity for an appellate court to construe the statute defining the crime; nor, amid this uncertainty, is there any substantial pressure on the legislature to clarify the meaning of the accosting and soliciting statute. In prostitution cases particularly, the courts typically give literal meaning to the "accosting and soliciting" elements of the offense, while the police, on the other hand, broadly interpret the law to be a prohibition against prostitution and prostitutes per se and translate this into a mandate to "clean the streets" of all prostitutes. Since both the courts and the vice squad hold rather tenaciously to each of these different perspectives, the conflict comes to focus on the intensity of the in-court examination in accosting cases to discover who accosted whom and under what circumstances.

C. Acquittal of the Guilty to Support Police Crime Detection Methods

While there is little doubt that acquittal is sometimes used by trial judges as a device to control unfair police practices, it is also used to lend support to certain crime detection methods. This most often involves the freeing of police informants or of co-defendants whose testimony or other assistance has led to the conviction of their co-conspirators or to the solution of other crimes. All metropolitan police departments use informants, with particular frequency in the enforcement of laws relating to narcotics, gambling, and prostitution. It is general practice not to arrest or charge informants, but there are occasional exceptions, particularly when the arrest is made by police for whom the informant does not work. Federal informants, for example, are occasionally

[8] Mich. Comp. Laws §750.448 (1948).

arrested by municipal police. Once their identity is proved, however, it is the practice to dismiss the charges against them.

In general, the courts support the giving of immunity to informants so long as they do not use their status as a "license to expand their own operations." An informant who is arrested for a crime unrelated to his undercover services will ordinarily be charged and convicted, unless he is of exceptional value to future enforcement plans. Furthermore, informants who have lost their usefulness (through being forced to testify or otherwise exposing their identity) will not ordinarily be fully acquitted; instead charges against them are commonly reduced to lesser offenses. Acquittal to support the activities of the police or prosecutor commonly involves the freeing of defendants who turn state's witness. This often means the acquittal of one member of some sort of criminal gang in exchange for his testimony against his co-defendants. Acquittal is also used as an attempt to control organized crime by offering immunity to gambling runners to get information about higher-up criminals or to prostitutes to obtain evidence against their procurers. In fact, Michigan has a statutory provision granting such immunity in prostitution investigations.[9]

D. The Effect of Use of Acquittal to Control Police Conduct

The effect of informal methods of trial court control over police practice is much like the effect of efforts at control by means of the formally recognized exclusionary rule and defense of entrapment. Efforts at informal control by trial judges do, however, create some additional problems. The informality itself results in greater differences in attitude between judges than is true in their interpretation of formally recognized and articulated rules. As a consequence of this trial court disparity in attitude the police vary their enforcement objectives, depending upon who the trial court judge is at a particular time. This is especially noticeable in multi-judge courts where there is rotation of assignment. There is often a noticeable decrease in emphasis on enforcement of certain crimes like prostitution or homosexual solicitation when the cases have to be brought before a judge who opposes an intensive enforcement program. On the other hand, when the assignment is given to a judge more sympathetic to the enforcement program, the intensity of police effort is increased.

Whether the judicial use of acquittal power as an informal means of controlling police practice has a constructive or destruc-

[9] Mich. Comp. Laws §§750.453 and 750.461 (1948).

tive effect upon law enforcement would seem to depend upon several factors: (a) whether the trial judge's decision is based upon adequate understanding, not only of the facts of the particular case but of the law enforcement context out of which the case arises; (b) whether the judge or judges are consistent in their reactions to law enforcement practices; (c) whether the judge's reasons are made clear and effectively communicated to those in the police department who have the authority to change police practice; and (d) whether informal judicial control causes police to re-evaluate their practices rather than to resort to alternatives like harassment, which continues old practices but avoids bringing these matters to the attention of the trial judge.

To the extent that generalization is possible, it is apparent in current administration that there is wide disparity in attitudes of trial judges toward police practices; there is no effective communication between police and judges; and the judges' efforts at control are resisted by police, who do not rethink the propriety of the enforcement program but rather adopt alternative methods of achieving their objectives. The common result is that police harass prostitutes and homosexuals by arresting them for other offenses such as disorderly conduct or vagrancy, taking only selected cases of accosting and soliciting to court. When acquittal results in even these "strong" cases, the only diminution is in the frequency of court appearances; arrests on other grounds continue as long as the police feel a mandate to proceed against vice crimes. This serves once again to illustrate the difficulty of effective control of one part of the criminal justice process by authority elsewhere. Just as trial judges avoid legislative sentencing mandates by systematically downgrading charges, so the police avoid trial court controls by arresting vice offenders for lesser crimes. This not only demonstrates the operational complexity of the process but questions the assumption commonly made that conformity of practice with court decisions is the inevitable result of trial or appellate holdings which are intended to discipline and control other agencies.

PART VI

The Functions of Defense Counsel in Nontrial Adjudication

Our democratic society has an interest in providing representation to every accused person so that the scales of justice can be equally balanced. Citizens want to know that justice is done to all whether rich or poor; their respect for the administration of justice will be increased by treating all defendants fairly and equally. Moreover, there is a greater chance of rehabilitating the guilty if they are prosecuted in such a way that they realize their rights are being respected. Convictions obtained short of this mark often cause resentment in the convicted man, as well as create disturbing doubts in the public. It seems clear that our society has a deeply rooted and legitimate concern about the representation of an accused. This interest should not be lessened simply because a defendant is financially unable to hire his own counsel.

Statement by the Committee
on the Judiciary, U.S. Senate
(October 2, 1962)

No single issue in criminal justice administration is of greater current interest or has potentially wider implications for the entire criminal justice system than the right of accused persons to counsel. Somewhat surprisingly, in the midst of changes affecting the right to counsel from the police station to the appellate court, relatively little attention has been given to the functions of counsel in nontrial adjudication, particularly in the guilty plea process.[1] By

[1] It is apparent that an indigent defendant who pleads guilty has the same right to counsel as one who demands trial. Since Gideon v. Wainwright (372 U.S. 335, 83 Sup. Ct. 792, 9 L. Ed. 2d 799 [1963]), the Supreme Court ruled several times that state courts have denied due process in failing to provide counsel to defendants who have pleaded guilty. See Berry v. New York, 375 U.S. 160, 84 Sup. Ct. 274, 11 L. Ed. 2d 261 (1964); Doughty v. Maxwell, 372 U.S. 781, 83 Sup. Ct. 1106, 10 L. Ed. 2d 139 (1963), and 376 U.S. 202, 84 Sup. Ct. 702, 11 L. Ed. 2d 650 (1964); Vecchiolli

and large matters of right to counsel at the court level have been raised in the context of the contested criminal case or at least in the context of cases which might have resulted in trial if not fatally prejudiced by lack of counsel. The role of a lawyer as an advocate at trial is well understood; the full range of purposes he serves in guilty plea cases is less commonly considered.

The question of whether counsel serves a useful purpose in guilty plea cases can be only partially answered by considering what direct services counsel performs for his client. The broader issue of the importance of representation to the conviction system itself has to be determined by looking at the effect of counsel on various objectives of the conviction process. The functions which a defense attorney performs for a guilty plea client fall roughly into two broad categories: expert evaluation of the appropriateness of the guilty plea and aid in obtaining charge and sentence leniency by plea negotiation. Both of these are very important to guilty defendants and, as a matter of fact, successful representation of the guilty requires knowledge and skills no less demanding than representation at trial.

While both of these functions can be viewed as client services, it is also important to look at them as they affect the entire conviction system. For example, while assuring the defendant that the charge is not too high and that the guilty plea is an appropriate decision, the lawyer also serves the objective of assuring the court that the guilty plea is accurate. In addition, while charge reduction as a result of negotiation from the client's point of view is a "break," in another sense it serves to assure consistent and equitable treatment for defendants in jurisdictions where charge reduction is a common practice and where only the unsophisticated defendant pleads guilty to the maximum offense.

Furthermore, by the mere fact of competent representation, the lawyer contributes to other objectives of the conviction system, in

---

v. Maroney, 372 U.S. 768, 83 Sup. Ct. 1105, 10 L. Ed. 2d 138 (1963); Garner v. Pennsylvania, 372 U.S. 768, 83 Sup. Ct. 1105, 10 L. Ed. 2d 138 (1963); Weigner v. Russell, 372 U.S. 767, 83 Sup. Ct. 1104, 10 L. Ed. 2d 138 (1963).

The Doughty case is conclusive. The court originally remanded it for further consideration in light of Gideon. On remand the Supreme Court of Ohio reaffirmed its decision by distinguishing Gideon from the facts of the case. Upon reaching the Supreme Court a second time, the judgment of the lower court was reversed.

Whether this right is retroactive to guilty plea cases preceding Gideon has not been expressly determined by the Supreme Court but by its application in Doughty, *supra,* and its nonintervention in cases which have repeatedly applied Gideon retroactively, it appears the court favors such an approach. See Palumbo v. New Jersey, 334 F.2d 524 (3d Cir. 1964); United States v. LaVallee, 330 F.2d 303 (2d Cir. 1964); Craig v. Meyers, 329 F.2d 856 (3d Cir. 1964); Striker v. Pancher, 317 F.2d 780 (6th Cir. 1963).

many cases with no specific intent to serve these ends. No lawyer in the study said that his value to his clients was to give them a sense of full and fair treatment so that correctional rehabilitation could be more effective, yet it is difficult to ignore this when correctional personnel express it as an important consideration. No lawyer said that one of his important functions was to provide a record of proper conviction for appellate court or correctional agency use, yet their need for adequate records is apparent.

The chapters which follow attempt to interpret the data beyond the lawyer-client relationship itself. The role of defense counsel is analyzed in terms of four major objectives of conviction: the accuracy of guilty pleas, the fairness and consistency of the guilty plea process, the necessity for accurate and detailed records of conviction by plea, and the consequences of the guilty plea process for correctional objectives. This approach is not intended to make a case for or against representation in guilty plea cases; it is, however, designed to present the full implications, to defendants and to the entire conviction system, of defense counsel in the guilty plea process.

CHAPTER 15

The Function of Counsel in Assuring the Accuracy of Guilty Pleas

A. Trial Court Reliance on Defense Counsel to Ascertain the Factual Basis of the Guilty Plea

The fact that a defendant is represented by counsel in even the most routine guilty plea case offers some assurance to the judge who must accept the plea that the defendant's rights have been observed and that his plea is truthful and is based on consent. In current administration, conscientious trial judges are very much concerned that defendants who enter guilty pleas are in fact guilty and know the significance of their pleas. Various devices are used by courts to insure an adequate basis for the guilty plea. In Wisconsin some judges regularly use a post-plea-of-guilty hearing to take testimony and other evidence of the crime. In Michigan the pre-sentence investigation is largely focused on just these same points. Judges in Kansas rely most heavily on any information they can elicit at the arraignment itself.

In all three states, the presence of defense counsel is commonly taken as an appropriate substitute for other methods of assuring the accuracy of the plea. The fact that a defendant is represented by competent counsel is presumed by most judges to indicate that in all probability the plea is truly consensual, that is, it is not the result of coercion, trickery, or ignorance of rights; the defendant is guilty of the conduct charged or is guilty of more serious criminal conduct if the plea is to a reduced charge; and the defendant is competent to plead, fully understands his rights including his right to trial, knows his chances for acquittal, and comprehends the likely consequences of pleading guilty. In Wisconsin, even though the defendant has been represented by a lawyer, a post-plea hearing is sometimes held for reasons of added assurance and to provide a record of the hearings to protect both the court and defense counsel. With or without the post-plea hearing, however, the trial judge generally rests easier in accepting a guilty plea if he knows that the defendant has a lawyer. This reliance on counsel as a check on the accuracy of the plea is based on an assumption that the lawyer thoroughly researches the case and brings his professional competence to bear on the appropriateness of the plea decision. Implicit in this is a certain image of the lawyer-client relationship in which the defendant and his counsel, together and sharing common objectives, weigh the evidence in the case and, perhaps reluctantly, come to the conclusion that a plea of guilty is a proper decision. While there is no doubt that some guilty pleas do result from such a detailed, shared analysis of the case, the quality of representation in routine guilty plea cases and the conditions under which representation occurs raise some questions about whether this image is generally true.

B. Pretrial Functions of Counsel with Guilty Plea Defendants

The traditional and important pretrial function of a defense lawyer is to assess the convictability of his client and to advise him as to the type of plea he should enter at arraignment. Except for the conclusion as to plea, this service is supposedly much the same whether the case goes to trial or terminates by a guilty plea. On the surface the pretrial problems which counsel confront in guilty plea cases are very little different from those in cases which go to trial. All defense lawyers face the issue of pretrial discovery of state's evidence, and lawyers appointed for indigent defendants often face the disadvantage of entering the case late and discovering that their client has made premature damaging admissions. Again, particularly in cases of indigents, lawyers must cope with the economic imbalance between the resources of the prosecutor and the resources of the defense. Within these limits, however, the functions of the lawyer in assessing the accuracy of the charge and the convictability of the defendant are similar in theory, at least, whether or not the case is tried.

One of the difficulties with this theory, and relevant to the question of whether in the typical guilty plea case the defense lawyer really does substantially increase the probability of the accuracy of the plea, is that the conditions preceding a guilty plea are often different from conditions preceding trial. The defendants in the two types of cases commonly move somewhat differently through the pretrial stages, and they begin this whole process with a different set of expectations and commitments. For example, defendants who eventually plead guilty often make it known very early that they are willing to so plead. In Michigan, for example, defendants are asked to plead at their initial appearance before a magistrate at a time when most, including all indigents, are unrepresented. While a plea of guilty at this point is not binding as the final plea at arraignment on the information and is used administratively only as an indication that the defendant wishes to waive preliminary hearing,[1] it does involve an early express commitment to the guilty plea.[2] Whether a defendant is likely to rethink his plea after this early commitment, whether he is likely even to request counsel or to assess the effectiveness of counsel's services regarding the plea decision remains speculative, but certainly the early psychological set in the typical guilty plea case is quite different from that in the usual case which proceeds to trial.[3]

Likewise, the lawyer in the guilty plea case often confronts a defendant who not only has made an early commitment to the plea but who is actually eager to get on to the formal pleading so that he can start serving his sentence and hasten his release from jail. In Kansas, for example, defendants held in custody who indicate a willingness to plead guilty have their cases moved forward, since in comparison to trial the guilty plea process takes little court time. If a defendant is willing to plead guilty and is at all hopeful of receiving bench parole, it is to his advantage to enter his plea as promptly as possible and thereby be released from custody. There are other differences. Defendants who have decided to plead guilty usually waive the preliminary hearing, while it is more common for defendants who have decided to go to trial or who are undecided as to plea early in the process to demand a preliminary hearing. In this way, counsel for the guilty plea defendant, if in-

1 A plea of guilty to the warrant, in Michigan, has been held to be a waiver of the preliminary examination. See People v. Harris, 266 Mich. 317, 253 N.W. 312 (1934); People v. Sanford, 233 Mich. 112, 206 N.W. 370 (1925).

2 A point which is not known with any certainty but which deserves further investigation is the relationship between in-custody interrogation practices of the police and early commitment to a plea of guilty. It might be fairly assumed that suspects who make incriminating statements very early in the process are much more likely to plead guilty at arraignment. If this is so, then any modification of in-custody interrogation practices or policies, suggested by the Escobedo decision for example, may well affect the percentage of guilty pleas or at least the percentage of early commitments to guilty pleas.

3 The Wisconsin Supreme Court, in considering the question of whether an indigent defendant is constitutionally entitled to appointment of counsel at the preliminary hearing, while reserving judgment on this question, adopted a prospective rule which stressed one advantage of counsel to be "the avoidance of the adverse psychological factors affecting an unrepresented defendant." Sparkman v. State, 27 Wis. 2d 92, 99, 133 N.W.2d 776, 780 (1965).

deed there is one, ordinarily functions without the discovery aid of the preliminary hearing.[4] This pattern involving early commitment to the plea, waiver of the preliminary hearing, and a desire to get out of jail as soon as possible provides a common setting in which defense counsel for the guilty plea defendant must function. Under these conditions the lawyer really cannot do a great deal to accurately assess the plea decision unless he goes beyond what his client says and desires to do.

Not all guilty plea cases begin with a commitment to the plea, of course, and in these cases, where the client is undecided or initially unwilling to plead guilty, the pretrial functions of counsel come closer to those typical of trial cases. There is little doubt in guilty plea cases where the defense counsel is engaged in active search and assessment that the final decision in regard to the plea is a studied one, more likely to be accurate than if the defendant were left to his own devices. Perhaps even in cases where counsel enters late in the process and where the defendant has intended to plead guilty all along a brief consultation adds a measure of sureness to the decision. Certainly counsel can screen out grossly inappropriate guilty pleas with only a fairly quick assessment of the charge and of the defendant. Across-the-board reliance on counsel alone to insure accurate convictions, however, ignores great differences in defendants and in the way they proceed through the process. It also ignores the quality of representation, for practicing in all courts are lawyers of varying degrees of skill and experience.

Many, perhaps most, guilty plea defendants waive counsel,[5] but some do not. In these cases, as indeed in most criminal matters, defendants are likely to be indigent and must rely on counsel provided by public funds.[6] Regardless of the system of assignment of

[4] For a discussion of pretrial discovery in relation to defendants who plead guilty see Fletcher, Pretrial Discovery in State Criminal Cases, 12 Stan. L. Rev. 293 (1960). See also Goldstein, The State and the Accused: Balance of Advantage in Criminal Procedure, 69 Yale L.J. 1149 (1960), and Louisell, Criminal Discovery: Dilemma Real or Apparent? 49 Calif. L. Rev. 56 (1961).

In general, appellate courts have been unsympathetic to arguments that the accused has a right to use the preliminary hearing as a discovery device. See United States ex rel. Parker v. Meyers, 233 F. Supp. 563 (E.D. Pa. 1964); United States ex rel. Cooper v. Reincke, 333 F.2d 608 (2d Cir. 1964); Ronzzo v. Sigler, 235 F. Supp. 839 (D. Neb. 1964); Detoro v. Pepersack, 332 F.2d 341 (4th Cir. 1964). But also see Washington v. Clemmer, 339 F.2d 715 (D.C. Cir. 1964), for a statement of the value of the preliminary hearing as a discovery source.

[5] For an analysis of waiver of counsel see Silverstein, Defense of the Poor 91-104 (1965).

[6] In cases where there is statutory provision for counsel or where, because of recent Supreme Court decisions, the defendant otherwise has a clear right to assigned counsel, trial judges uniformly ask the defendant, if he is unrepresented at arraignment on the information, if he wants a lawyer, at state expense if necessary. There

counsel, a general distinction is made by many trial judges between cases involving defendants charged with serious crimes or where there is some initial doubt about the actual guilt or convictability of the defendant and routine cases where the offense charged is less serious or where the actual guilt of the defendant is less in doubt. In the serious or doubtful cases, trial judges ordinarily assign counsel with great care, where possible selecting "good" lawyers, obviously competent and respectable members of the bar. In the less serious, more clear-cut cases, however, many trial judges are content to assign one of the customary "hangers-on" in the courthouse, often a lawyer of dubious ability. Often, too, the total representation in these minor cases involves no more than a short, in-court conference with the client a few minutes before he enters his guilty plea. The contribution of this type of representation in insuring accurate guilty pleas is minimal if it makes much difference at all.

All of these variables combined form a caveat concerning generalizations about the importance of counsel in insuring accurate guilty pleas. This is not to say that counsel performs no function in this regard; commonly the guilty plea defendant is no more capable of assessing the technical requirements of guilt than is his counterpart who goes to trial.[7] The lawyer-client relationship in the pretrial processes of the guilty plea case, however, is typically less an intense, shared search for an appropriate plea than a sort of cursory checkup by counsel of a plea already decided upon by the defendant. Knowing this, many trial judges still prefer to conduct an independent investigation of the factual basis for the plea, even with defendants who are represented by counsel.

The function of counsel in assessing the appropriateness of the

---

is, however, evidence that some defendants really do not know what this means. See, for example, Remington, Defense of the Indigent in Wisconsin, 37 Wis. B. Bull. 40 (1964), and Elison, Assigned Counsel in Montana: The Law and the Practice, 26 Mont. L. Rev. 1 (1965). Furthermore some defendants observed in practice apparently interpret the question of whether they want a lawyer to be another way of asking how they intend to plead. If guilty, then they waive counsel. Judges typically do not explain to defendants that they may have counsel even if they wish to enter a guilty plea, evidently assuming that defendants are aware of this.

7 See, for example, Moore v. Michigan, 355 U.S. 155, 78 Sup. Ct. 191, 2 L. Ed. 2d 167 (1957), for a Michigan case involving a defendant who pleaded guilty to murder and where, had the defendant had counsel, certain defenses or mitigating circumstances might have been raised. The Michigan Supreme Court held that the defendant did not intelligently and understandingly waive his right to counsel.

The United States Supreme Court has said in regard to the defendant's right to counsel at the arraignment, "Only the presence of counsel could have enabled this accused to know all the defenses available to him and to plead intelligently." Hamilton v. Alabama, 368 U.S. 52, 55, 82 Sup. Ct. 157, 159, 7 L. Ed. 2d 114, 117 (1961).

guilty plea decision, whether it is an intense, balanced assessment or only a quick in-court conference, is only one part of representation, one aspect of the defense lawyer's role. In greater or lesser degree, the presence of defense counsel in a guilty plea case affects other objectives of the conviction process which are dealt with in the chapters which follow.

CHAPTER 16

The Functions of Counsel in Assuring Fair and Equitable Guilty Plea Convictions

A. Defense Counsel and Fairness of Guilty Plea Convictions

Just as defense counsel serves a dual objective to his client and to the court in helping to insure accurate convictions by plea, so his function in regard to the fairness of the proceedings acts to the benefit of both the defendant and the court and other agencies of the conviction process. Fairness of the process is no less an objective in guilty plea cases than in cases which are tried, but the dimensions and the significance of fair procedures in the guilty plea process have received less attention than the matter of fair trial. In general, fairness in guilty plea cases involves three major concerns: (a) the plea should be "understandingly" entered by a competent defendant, (b) the process should be deliberate and reflective rather than overly swift, and (c) the process should be regular and consistent to reduce disparity in both convictions and subsequent sentences.

The first of these, the understanding of the defendant, is commonly interpreted by appellate courts to mean that the defendant must understand the nature of the charges against him and the sentencing consequences of his guilty plea as well.[1] In practice, concern for understanding includes both of these but goes somewhat beyond them to include an awareness on the part of the defendant of the procedures of pleading, what he can expect in the

[1] For a discussion of the court's duty to warn defendants of the consequences of their plea see Annot., Court's duty to advise or admonish accused as to consequence of plea of guilty, or to determine that he is advised thereof, 97 A.L.R.2d 549 (1964). For a discussion of a "knowing plea," see Comment, 32 U. Chi. L. Rev. 167, 168 (1964).

courtroom, and what his sentence will actually mean to him. In practice, a defendant is usually fully apprised of the charges against him[2] and of the maximum penalty provided by law but often remains confused by procedures and not fully cognizant of what he is doing, what alternatives there are, or what the actual consequences of his conviction will be. In this regard, the defense lawyer plays an important role as an "explainer" of the process, including realistic assessment of the consequences of conviction.[3]

Concern for the speed of the guilty plea process, exemplified by appellate court reversals in quick justice cases,[4] is a dimension of fairness which is the mirror image of concern for delay in the trial system. The objective is a studied guilty plea, with ample time for the defendant to consider the charge and to assess his alternatives and for the court to dispassionately consider the appropriateness of the plea.[5] In practice, delay to allow defendants to confer with counsel provides both a cooling-off period and greater assurance that the plea decision is a considered one.

Concern for equal and consistent treatment in the guilty plea process in practice means equal opportunity for all defendants to

[2] The defendant cannot always understand the nature of the charges against him merely by hearing the charge contained in the information read. While in a general way he may know what the charge means, specific words and phrases, beyond his ability to comprehend or evaluate, may assume great importance. For example, in one Wisconsin case three defendants pleaded guilty to having "unlawfully, willfully and maliciously" set fire to lands. All three subsequently made motions for a new trial on the grounds that they did not understand the nature of the charge, specifically that they did not realize that the words "willfully" and "maliciously" made their offense a felony while at the same time another statute made the setting of fire without malice a misdemeanor. The convictions of two of the defendants were upheld but a new trial was ordered for the third defendant on the grounds that he was only nineteen years of age and appeared without counsel. Ailport v. State, 9 Wis. 2d 409, 411, 100 N.W.2d 812, 813 (1960).

[3] It does not always work this way. In Hampton v. Tinsley, 240 F. Supp. 213 (D. Colo. 1965), a defendant, through his counsel, pleaded guilty to a crime while under the misapprehension that he had been adjudged not guilty because insane and was being committed to a mental hospital. His lawyer had failed to explain to him the meaning of the procedure whereby he had been previously committed for observation and the consequences of the arraignment proceedings at which the guilty plea was entered.

[4] See, for example, DeMeerleer v. Michigan, 329 U.S. 663, 67 Sup. Ct. 596, 91 L. Ed. 584 (1947); State v. Oberst, 127 Kan. 412, 273 Pac. 490 (1929); People v. Crandell, 270 Mich. 124, 258 N.W. 224 (1935); State ex rel. Burnett v. Burke, 22 Wis. 2d 486, 126 N.W.2d 91 (1964).

[5] See State v. Lane, 258 N.C. 349, 128 S.E.2d 389 (1962), where counsel was appointed at 9:30 A.M. and the trial began at 2:30 P.M. It was held that in the light of all the circumstances of the case, the allowance of only five hours to investigate and prepare a defense resulted in a denial of the defendant's right to counsel. See also Perkins v. North Carolina, 234 F. Supp. 333, 339 (W.D.N.C. 1964), where, although counsel was appointed at 4:00 P.M. of one day and the trial began at 9:00 A.M. the following morning, the court held that since only "two daytime business hours" were allowed for preparation the defendant was denied the effective aid and assistance of counsel.

obtain whatever sentence leniency is customary in guilty plea cases, whether by plea bargaining or otherwise. Counsel in this role is the equalizer of leniency, a source of particular assistance to ignorant and unsophisticated defendants, and insurance of consistency in treatment to the court and the correctional agency.

B. Function of Defense Counsel in Respect to the Consequences of the Guilty Plea

In practice, before accepting a plea, trial judges routinely explain the maximum sentence possible for a particular charge. This is the minimal fairness requirement, but to many defendants and to many conscientious trial judges this routine, letter-of-the-law practice is less than fully adequate for a number of reasons. In the first place, warning of consequences comes late in the sequence; it is usually the very last thing said by the judge before requesting the plea. If the objective is to give fair warning of consequences to the defendant and if implicit in this is a desire to have the consequences carefully considered, a last-minute warning hardly gives time for mature reflection. From the points of view of both defendant and judge, an important function of defense counsel is to thoroughly discuss the sentence possibilities prior to the arraignment.

Second, the warning of consequences goes only to the maximum possible sentence. Judges ordinarily do not indicate what the actual sentence will be because they do not wish to get into a position of actually inducing or being accused of inducing guilty pleas. Furthermore, announcement of a specific sentence at arraignment would be premature in those cases where the judge relies heavily on a presentence report in making his sentence determination. In serious cases, particularly, the judge is rarely in a position to pass appropriate sentence at the time of arraignment. Nevertheless, the warning of maximum consequences is somewhat deceptive in terms of the reality of practice. Except where mandatory sentences are involved, the trial court rarely gives the highest possible term of years and in most cases the judge can consider probation as an alternative to incarceration. Furthermore, sentencing norms for particular offenses and types of offenders develop in many courts so that from the defendant's perspective a realistic consideration of sentence includes assessment of his probable sentence rather than merely the most severe sentence possible. In this respect, advice of counsel is of particular importance both to the defendant and to the trial judge who wishes to give fair warning but feels it inappropriate to do more than admonish the defendant of the statutory maximum sentence for the offense.

Third, the actual consequences of any sentence for a defendant and his family are usually more complex than expressed by the recitation of statutory sentencing provisions. In some instances there are civil consequences of conviction, such as loss of a license, which are not usually mentioned by the court.[6] Some sentences, for certain sex offenders for example, are predicated on the existence of treatment facilities while in other situations no specific therapy is provided. The nature of imprisonment, the conditions of probation, eligibility for release, and the consequences of these for himself and for his family are all primary concerns of the defendant. In practice, these matters are explained to the defendant by his defense counsel, if they are explained at all. Neither the judge nor the prosecutor usually feels called upon to go into specific, individual consequences of conviction and sentencing; they rely on counsel to relate these details to his client and to his client's family.

Effective counseling regarding the likely consequences of the guilty plea requires the lawyer to have intimate knowledge of sentencing provisions and procedures, correctional programs, and parole procedures as well as of common criteria used by judges in selecting types and lengths of sentences. Such knowledge is traditionally less a part of formal law training than is preparation for defense at trial and calls for additional skills on the part of lawyers in guilty plea cases. A lawyer, no matter how inexperienced in criminal matters, ordinarily has sufficient training and professional skills to evaluate a charge in terms of the relationship of conduct and statutory requirements, but a knowledge of probation, or a sex deviate treatment program, or parole practices, if these are relevant, is another matter.[7] To the extent that effective representa-

[6] For a discussion of the civil consequences of felony conviction see Note, 12 Drake L. Rev. 141 (1962). In a Wisconsin case a defendant, as a result of a felony conviction, was forced to vacate his seat on the city council, was prevented from officiating at sporting events, which was one of his part-time jobs, and was threatened with loss of a liquor license at his tavern. He sought to withdraw his plea on the grounds that he did not understand these actions to be part of the consequences of his pleading nolo contendere. His motion to withdraw was denied by the trial court and the trial court's decision was upheld on appeal. See State v. Payne, 24 Wis. 2d 603, 129 N.W.2d 250 (1964).

[7] A common allegation by convicted defendants is that their counsel were incompetent in regard to explaining or predicting the sentencing outcomes of the guilty pleas. Although this is a frequent basis for later appeal, such appeals are rarely successful. See Annot., Incompetency of counsel chosen by accused as affecting validity of conviction, 74 A.L.R.2d 1390, 1436 (1961). See also Hampton v. Tinsley, 240 F. Supp. 213 (D. Colo. 1965).

tion in guilty plea cases is desired, it is important that counsel have sufficient understanding of the whole nontrial process, including sentencing, in order to advise his clients adequately.

C. Functions of Counsel in Assuring Consistent and Equitable Treatment in the Guilty Plea Process

Most defense attorneys can, if necessary, conduct an active and vigorous defense of an obviously guilty defendant and can justify this on the ground that our system of justice assumes it to be proper to give even the most guilty defendant the "best possible defense."[8] There is less basis in tradition for knowing whether the guilty plea system assumes a like responsibility of counsel to get his client the "best possible deal."[9] For the defendant, the best possible deal ordinarily means a reduction of the charge to one less serious than his conduct actually indicates and a more lenient sentence than he normally could expect without the intervention of an attorney. From the perspective of the trial judge and of correctional authorities, the best possible deal for a single client may be nothing more than achieving an equitable charge and sentence and the consistent treatment of defendants in the bargaining process who, without counsel, would probably plead guilty to severe charges disparate with customary practice. Court assignment of counsel to certain defendants is regularly made so that the prosecutor can have someone to bargain with in reducing the charge. This occurs primarily in those cases in which the defendant is young or ignorant and, while he may be technically guilty of a higher charge, the judge or prosecutor or both are reluctant to accept a plea to the maximum offense.

Where the issue is charge reduction, or where it involves entering a client's guilty plea without overt negotiation, a knowledge of court practices and policies is very important if counsel is to be effective. One function of defense counsel in guilty plea cases is to steer his client through the pretrial maze, maximizing his knowledge of the substantive law and of court practices not only to determine to *what* his client pleads guilty but *when* and before *which*

[8] See Canon 5, The Defense or Prosecution of Those Accused of Crime, American Bar Association, Canons of Professional Ethics. See also Schwartz, Cases and Materials on Professional Responsibility and the Administration of Criminal Justice (1961) and Orkin, The Defense of One Known to Be Guilty, 1 Crim. L.Q. 170 (1958).

[9] For a discussion by a trial attorney on bargaining see Steinberg and Paulsen, A Conversation with Defense Counsel on Problems of a Criminal Defense, 7 Prac. Law. 25, 31 (1961). See also Polstein, How to "Settle" a Criminal Case, 8 Prac. Law. 35 (1962).

judge, if a choice is available, in order to effectuate the most favorable consequences of the plea. In the metropolitan court system of Detroit, for example, where there are a number of judges, skillful defense counsel pay close attention to arranging the timing of the guilty plea. A Detroit defense lawyer commented on his techniques of maneuvering or "steering" cases to judges who are likely to impose a light sentence. He also stated that such steering is practiced by most defense lawyers, there being nothing surreptitious about the techniques. He outlined three major methods of controlling the timing of the plea:

(1) Adjournments. Maneuvering takes place to avoid "unfavorable" judges who are near the end of their terms, either as presiding judge (who customarily receives guilty pleas) or as Early Sessions judge. (There are ten judges in Recorder's Court in Detroit who rotate assignments monthly.) Each defendant has an "automatic" right of one adjournment, although more may be granted, and should his case occur near the end of a particular judge's term, he can get his case put over to the succeeding judge.

(2) Steering a case to a particular judge. Defense counsel approach the clerk who assists the presiding judge in assigning cases for trial and inform him that if the case is sent to a particular judge, a jury trial will be waived. The assignment clerk must know with some accuracy how many cases will result in pleas of guilty and how many will require a trial in order to avoid assigning too many trials to one judge. The predictive variables usually used by the clerk are the nature of the crime (virtually all narcotic sale cases result in pleas of guilty to reduced charges); the identity and reputation of the attorney (some lawyers are known as "trial" counsel, others "settle everything"); and whether the accused had pleaded guilty at arraignment on the warrant. The clerk keeps a record of the number of pleas of guilty accepted by each of the judges over the past few years. Knowledge of a judge's prior practices, such as the frequency of his use of probation, also adds to the clerk's ability to predict the number of guilty pleas. Obviously significant is a statement by defense counsel that the defendant will plead guilty if the case is assigned to a certain judge. This virtually assures the clerk of the outcome and, assuming the particular judge is not already overburdened, his practice is to grant the defense counsel's request.

(3) Pleading not guilty before a severe judge to get bound over for trial to a sympathetic judge, at which time the plea is changed to guilty. This occurs when adjournment or reassignment is not likely to achieve the defense counsel's objective. If a judge trying contested cases is felt to be more satisfactory from a defense point

of view, counsel may actually take the case to trial. However, after the first witness for the prosecution has testified, defense counsel will announce to the court that his client is willing to plead guilty. The first witness is permitted to testify merely to "demonstrate to all parties . . . that a request to go to trial while before the presiding judge is not merely for the purpose of getting another judge [before whom] to plead guilty."

If all else fails, counsel will file an affidavit of prejudice against a particular judge, thus forcing a transfer of the case. From all sources, judges, prosecutors, and defense attorneys themselves, come indications that a fundamental skill of competent defense attorneys in guilty plea cases is knowledge of judicial biases regarding offenses and offenders, knowledge of variations in customary practices of the courts in accepting pleas and sentencing thereafter, and attendant skills in arranging the steering of a case to a suitable judge. The decision of which judge to plead before is about as important a function of defense counsel as what offense is agreed upon as the basis of the guilty plea.

Perhaps the major factor influencing defense counsel's selection of an appropriate judge before whom to plead is the judge's philosophy regarding the use of probation. Whatever the reduction in charge and whatever other concessions may be made by the prosecutor, the most sought-after bargain in the negotiation process is probation. Judges who are "believers" in probation also tend to use it freely and are sought as plea recipients whenever probation is at all possible. This, as much as anything, accounts for the considerable variation in the number of guilty pleas offered and accepted before different judges.

In addition to steering a guilty plea to a sympathetic judge, counsel also has a major role in conducting the bargaining in the negotiated plea process. To the defendant who is actually guilty and who decides to so plead, the most important considerations become the particular label which will attach upon conviction and the sentence which follows. From his point of view, if he cannot beat the rap altogether, he ordinarily wishes to have the charge reduced and to otherwise maximize his willingness to plead guilty to obtain label and sentence leniency. Again, from his point of view, his lawyer is effective if he can contribute to this end. Even where plea negotiation is a common practice it is not automatic, that is, charge and sentencing concessions are not given to a defendant unless he actually negotiates for them. This gives an advantage to the sophisticated defendant who knows of the possibility of bargaining and can carry it out. Ignorant and more naïve defendants often plead guilty to charges where minimal negotiation would have resulted in downgrading.

A major purpose of extending the right to counsel to indigent defendants in the trial system is so that they will be on equal footing with their more affluent counterparts. This type of balanced advantage has been held to be a matter of fundamental fairness where a trial is involved. Much the same conditions apply when it comes to pleading guilty.[10] Where plea bargaining occurs the issue is not typically the winning of differential, excessive leniency for a particular defendant, but rather the obtaining of charge and sentencing concessions that are commonly, even routinely, distributed to like defendants accused of similar crimes. In practice the attorney who bargains for a charge reduction for his client commonly rests his argument on precedent, on the pattern of charge reduction which has developed in the jurisdiction; he is seeking equal treatment for his client, not inappropriate leniency. This is important, for to the extent that lawyers are effective in obtaining equal treatment, the function of counsel in guilty plea cases assumes a somewhat different aspect than if viewed solely as winning leniency for guilty defendants. In commenting on the bargaining function of counsel a prominent defense lawyer said:

> If a man is guilty, and the prosecution has a good case, there is little satisfaction to the lawyer or his client in trying conclusions, and getting the maximum punishment. A great deal of good can be done in the plodding, everyday routine of the defense lawyer, by mitigating punishment in this manner. Anyone who has ever spent a day in a prison and experienced, even vicariously, the indignity and suffering that incarceration entails realizes full well that the difference between a three-year sentence and a five-year sentence is tremendous, not only for the wrongdoer who is being punished, but for the innocent members of his family who love

[10] It is an interesting question whether plea bargaining is a "critical stage" of criminal proceedings and, if so, whether counsel is necessary at this point. In Anderson v. North Carolina, 221 F. Supp. 930, 935 (W.D.N.C. 1963), the court so held: "It is idle to speculate whether petitioner's counsel could have, if present, worked out a better deal with the Solicitor. The point is that Anderson was entitled to have him *try*. For lack of effective counsel at a 'critical stage' of the proceedings against him, those proceedings are constitutionally defective." *Accord:* Shupe v. Sigler, 230 F. Supp. 601 (D. Neb. 1964). *Contra:* United States ex rel. Cooper v. Reincke, 333 F.2d 608 (2d Cir. 1964). In this case the court, unimpressed with indigent petitioner's argument that lack of counsel at preliminary hearing denied him opportunity, enjoyed by defendants with privately retained counsel, to bargain for a reduced charge and to obtain a shorter sentence, commented: "[H]ad he chosen to change his plea to guilty after weighing the chances with his counsel [who was appointed later], he was perfectly free to do so. He neither waived nor lost any of these bargaining possibilities." Id. at 613.

> him, and who suffer humiliation and worse while he is away. This is something that the criminal lawyer can rightfully and usefully do for the "guilty" man. In this regard, the criminal lawyer is daily fulfilling a useful function in our society.[11]

The role of the lawyer in assuring some sort of consistency of treatment of guilty defendants has meaning to others in the system beside the defendant. Courts commonly support manipulation of adjudication to obtain sentencing discretion when this is denied by legislative mandate. The same trial judge has both adjudicatory and sentencing functions which are commonly merged in the guilty plea case. That is, in accepting the plea the typical trial judge is not only concerned with the provident nature of the plea itself but with the appropriateness of whatever sentences are prescribed for the conduct. Judges are occasionally confronted with clearly guilty defendants willing to plead to a charge which carries a mandatory punishment which seems to the court excessively severe in view of the actual criminal conduct involved or the traits of the particular defendant. Faced with this, the only alternative short of outright acquittal is to convict the defendant of a lesser charge to avoid the mandatory sentence. In order to do this, judges assign counsel to such defendants to work out a plea to a reduced charge.

Besides avoiding what is considered the unwarranted harshness of mandatory sentences, the lawyer's function in bargaining for his client serves the purpose of correcting sentence disparity, of significance both to the court and to correctional agencies which will receive the convicted offender. Disparate sentences, which involve differences in types or lengths of sentences among defendants who have been convicted of the same crime and who are alike in personal traits, background and record, risk of future violation, and degree of involvement in the present offense, are a major problem of current concern in postconviction treatment of the offender.[12] Both judges and correctional authorities are bothered by sentence differentials which are apparently unrelated to the nature of the crimes or the circumstances of cases. Proper sentencing differences, in the view of most judges and correctional personnel, should relate to meaningful distinctions between offenders in their degree of criminal involvement, both past and present, and to other personal traits which relate to the risk of reviolation and chances for successful rehabilitation. Where differences occur that

11 Steinberg, The Responsibility of the Defense Lawyer in Criminal Cases, 12 Syracuse L. Rev. 442, 447 (1961).

12 See Remington and Newman, The Highland Park Institute on Sentence Disparity, 26 Fed. Prob. 3 (March, 1962); Seminar and Institute on Disparity of Sentences, 30 F.R.D. 401 (1962).

are not based upon appropriate criteria, the problem of sentence disparity becomes acute. Judges are concerned with this because they have a basic commitment to both fairness and consistency in their adjudication and sentencing determinations. Correctional authorities are concerned because disparity infinitely complicates their objectives of rehabilitation. It is extremely difficult to convince an inmate who has been sentenced to ten years' imprisonment for a certain crime that he has been fairly treated and should bend his efforts to rehabilitation when other inmates, guilty of the same offense and not distinguishable in either prior record or future dangerousness, are serving two-year maximum terms.

Sentence disparity is usually accounted for by individual idiosyncrasies in sentencing between judges or by lack of consistency in a single judge from case to case. It is commonly viewed solely as a sentencing problem and is not ordinarily thought related to adjudication itself, yet it is obvious that such disparity is the inevitable result of a system in which plea bargaining is common but where not all defendants have or take advantage of equal opportunity for charge and sentencing concessions in exchange for their guilty pleas. This, of course, is particularly true where mandatory sentences are involved. In Michigan, for example, any defendant who pleads guilty to armed robbery finds himself in prison on a mandatory sentence with many other inmates guilty of the same conduct but serving considerably shorter terms for unarmed robbery, a commonly arranged lesser charge in Michigan. This presents a type of sentence disparity that has nothing to do with the judge's sentencing function as such, but is solely dependent upon plea negotiation at adjudication. In this sense the negotiation function of counsel is directly relevant to the disparity problem. While, seen from one perspective, he is winning leniency for his client, from another he is adding an element of consistency and fairness to the whole process.

D. The Importance of Counsel in Plea Bargaining

A question can be properly raised as to whether defense counsel is really necessary in the negotiated plea process. After all, even where successful, the lawyer does not ordinarily win any great amount of leniency for his client; he merely obtains for him the usual reduction in charge or sentence promise. Successful plea bargaining usually implies nothing more than that the defendant has achieved the norm established in practice and quasi-routine in operation.

Certain defendants, those sophisticated in the ways of prosecutors and courts, feel that defense counsel is as likely to be a liability as an asset in the negotiation process.[13] These are ordinarily recidivists who, by experience, are personally familiar with prosecutors, judges, and the procedures of the system and who at the same time are so vulnerable to severe sentences that their only hope for leniency is a maximum show of cooperation with all authorities. They feel that a request for counsel would be taken as an indication of troublemaking and might hurt their chances for concessions by the court. Perhaps they are right; there is some indication that sentences reflect the amount of trouble caused to all in authority by the obviously guilty defendant.[14] Even with such defendants, however, the mechanics of plea bargaining are such that counsel can effectuate negotiation with more ease than the defendant locked in his cell. There is a question of whether even the most informed recidivist is as skillful in negotiation as he likes to think. A charge reduction or sentence promise is not ordinarily a result of personal influence of the lawyer with the prosecutor or judge. The strength of a lawyer's argument for a charge reduction depends in good part on how strong a professional case he can make for the appropriateness of the lesser charge and doubtful convictability on the higher count. This requires no less skillful legal ability to evaluate alternatives than is required for other decisions where evidence and convictability are involved. The arguments most likely to win a sentence promise of probation must stress those characteristics of the client which lead to this conclusion and, to be effective, must be cast in terms of an entire plan for living and working in the community as an alternative to imprisonment. In short, the full-blown negotiated plea is not merely an appeal for mercy; it is an adversary process and the lawyer serves the function of the guilty defendant's advocate.[15]

Even granting, however, that some defendants are perfectly capable of conducting negotiation in their own behalf, the function of counsel in this process is hardly lessened. There are, no doubt, defendants capable of conducting their own defense at trial but this is not currently a sufficient reason to deny counsel to defendants who plead not guilty to serious crimes. The common prob-

[13] Newman, Pleading Guilty for Considerations: A Study of Bargain Justice, 46 J. Crim. L., C. & P.S. 780, 783-784 (1956).

[14] Pilot Institute on Sentencing, 26 F.R.D. 231, 285-289 (1960).

[15] Silverstein, who analyzed the relationship of guilty pleas to reduced charges and the waiver or retention of counsel, concluded that defendants without counsel were much more likely to plead guilty to the original rather than to a lesser offense. He commented: "This suggests the possibility that a defendant without counsel is in a poor position to bargain with the prosecutor for a plea to a lesser offense." Silverstein, Defense of the Poor 91, 93 (1965).

lem of counsel in negotiation, as at trial, does not revolve around the sophisticated defendant, personally capable of conducting his own bargaining or defense. In both trial and plea systems the issue typically comes to focus on the helpless and ill-informed who are incapable of representing themselves and who are at a disadvantage in seeking equitable and consistent treatment. The lawyer in such cases is the equalizer, the factor that balances opportunity between the most fortunate and the least skilled among the accused. In the adjudication process itself the fear is that without adequate representation certain of the accused will be wrongly convicted. In plea negotiation, the risk is that without representation certain of the guilty will receive unwarranted, disparate treatment.

CHAPTER 17

Significance of Defense Counsel in Providing a Record of Proper Conviction by Plea of Guilty

A. The Importance of a Record of Representation in Preventing Later Allegations of Unfair Treatment

Court transcripts of arraignments in guilty plea cases are, in the main, sparse and contain little helpful information for adequate appellate review. They are of equally little help to correctional authorities who occasionally confront inmates or probationers who claim to have been "bumrapped" in the guilty plea process. A record of a typical arraignment at which an unrepresented defendant pleads guilty and where a post-plea hearing is not held ordinarily contains little more than a few routine questions asked by the judge and the affirmative response of the defendant when he is asked to plead to the charge. While this question and answer sequence currently fulfills minimal requirements for proper conviction in most jurisdictions, when transcribed it is far less than an adequate record of the accuracy and fairness of the process, particularly when the defendant alleges misunderstanding of the procedures or some unhonored informal arrangement such as a sentence promise not reflected in the transcript.

Unless a post-plea-of-guilty hearing is held, the presence of defense counsel does not usually affect the substance of questions and answers in the transcript primarily because counsel seldom views the clarification of the plea of guilty record by the introduction of firm evidence of guilt as a significant contribution to his clients' future interests. The result is that the ordinary transcript itself will still not reveal a coerced plea, an unhonored bargain, or lack of understanding of the consequences of the plea. The only additional fact in the record which is of importance for the appellate court and the correctional agency is that the defendant was represented by a lawyer. Considering the intellectual and personality characteristics of many offenders, it is perfectly possible that at the time they plead guilty they are confused, uncertain, or basically ignorant of their rights. Where the transcript indicates representation by counsel, even though the attorney is silent, doubts about the propriety of conviction are usually more easily resolved, unless, of course, counsel substantiates any later claim of improper conviction by the defendant.

This is not a foolproof method of interpreting the record to indicate proper conviction, but it adds an additional measure of assurance. The fact that a record of representation exists serves to prevent fraudulent claims of improper conviction where offenders are merely unsatisfied with their sentence and wish to withdraw their pleas. The fact that a lawyer appeared for the defendant at the pleading, let it proceed, and, if only by his silence, acquiesced in the defendant's decision to plead guilty requires more than a simple allegation of unfairness to upset the conviction.

A record that a defendant is represented by counsel not only offers some assurance that the defendant's rights have been properly looked after, that the process has been adequately explained to him, and that he is actually guilty but also provides a corroborative source for allegations of unkept plea bargains. This is a common claim of defendants, but reviewing courts and agencies ordinarily have little to go on except the word of the defendant. If there is a defense counsel in the case, such allegations can be checked. In this regard, the process of bargaining, particularly in regard to sentence promises, becomes more visible, more easily a question of fact when a defendant is represented. In fact it has been proposed in one bar association code that prosecutors should bargain with a defendant only through his counsel and that "no representation or promise should be made by a prosecutor to the defendant except in the presence of counsel." [1]

[1] Schwartz, Cases and Materials on Professional Responsibility and the Administration of Criminal Justice 24 (1961). In Shupe v. Sigler, 230 F. Supp. 601, 606 (D. Neb. 1964), the court held: "The court concludes that for a prosecuting attorney to talk with the defendant in the absence of his counsel and attempt to have him change a plea of not guilty to a plea of guilty and in the absence of counsel to reach an agreement as to the length of his sentence, whether made with or without authority of the court, is to deprive the defendant of the effective assistance of counsel at a time when it was needed."

See also Garnick v. Miller, — Nev. —, 403 P.2d 850 (1965), where the defendant agreed to change her plea from not guilty to guilty during an informal conference with the prosecutor and the judge at which defense counsel was not present. The prosecution claimed that defendant had waived counsel during this hearing, but the appellate court reversed the conviction, commenting: "It is suggested that the sparse court record [of the pleading following the informal hearing] may be sup-

A record of representation also protects the court from possible later allegations of denial of counsel and prevents appeals based on lack of counsel. Since the *Gideon*[2] case particularly, and consistent with a memorandum from the state attorney general,[3] some trial judges in Wisconsin are currently assigning counsel to guilty plea defendants who say they do not want or need attorneys.[4] In one case an indigent defendant, on parole, was charged with writing worthless checks, a misdemeanor, but in view of his past record and the amount of the checks, he faced, and eventually received, a prison sentence. In making the assignment over the protests of the defendant and postponing the case for a month to enable the lawyer to investigate the charge and confer with his client, the judge commented that, "by providing [the defendant] public counsel now, it will eliminate his later request for a new hearing such as many Waupun state prison inmates are filing on grounds that they were not properly advised by attorneys of their constitutional rights before sentencing." [5]

Wisconsin trial judges are increasingly using a post-plea-of-guilty

---

plemented by the affidavits which were given by the participants in the preceding informal conference, to aid us in deciding the question of waiver. We reject this suggestion. A waiver must appear from the court record." — Nev. at —, 403 P.2d at 853, and "The mechanical, routine questions of the court, the defendant's responses — the total failure of the court to discharge its duty as delineated by the Von Moltke decision [Von Moltke v. Gillies, 332 U.S. 708, 723-724, 68 Sup. Ct. 316, 323, 92 L. Ed. 309 (1948)] — compel the conclusion that the defendant's constitutional right to counsel was ignored." — Nev. at —, 403 P.2d at 853.

One appellate judge, while concurring in the decision, expressed concern over the possible implications of this holding for informal settlement of criminal cases: "My concern is for the future, that trial judges will refuse to consider change of pleas in chambers because of a natural apprehension of later accusations that negligent or false conduct misled the person accused and caused him to change his plea, or that he did not get what he was promised, or that he was threatened and coerced in the judge's chambers and ad infinitum. The only safe course would be a formal proceeding in open court, hardly conducive to a pre-trial conference. . . . If the trial court cannot safely accept change of plea opportunities the number of costly time consuming criminal trials will be multiplied immeasurably." — Nev. at —, 403 P.2d at 854.

2 Gideon v. Wainwright, 372 U.S. 335, 83 Sup. Ct. 792, 9 L. Ed. 2d 799 (1963).

3 Memorandum to All District Atorneys and Judges of the Courts of Record from the Attorney General of Wisconsin, Sept. 5, 1963.

4 One consequence of this practice in cases of defendants who are placed on probation and, as is the customary practice of some judges, required to pay attorneys' fees as a condition of the probation, is that a defendant finds himself obligated to pay an attorney he did not want in the first place and who, as one defendant put it, "did nothing but cop me out." Such defendants are twice blessed: not only do they find themselves paying for lawyers they did not want, but they also may find many routes to appeal closed simply because they were represented by counsel at arraignment. Appellate courts commonly resolve many doubtful issues in favor of the state if the record shows that the appellant was represented at the earlier proceeding.

5 Wis. S.J., Feb. 11, 1965, §2, p. 1.

hearing, a recommended procedure in all criminal cases, not only because this device allows them to investigate the factual basis of the plea but also because it provides a detailed record of guilty plea proceedings.[6] One judge commented that a major purpose of this hearing is to protect both public officials, such as the police, prosecutor, and judge, and the defense counsel from later allegations of unfairness or inadequate representation. Thus even though many trial judges are satisfied that there is a factual basis for the plea when a defendant has been adequately represented by counsel, the post-plea hearing is often still conducted so that an adequate record of the conviction and of the participation of counsel is preserved.

B. The Importance of Adequate Records for the Future Interests of the Guilty Plea Defendant

A simple record of the fact of representation and, where possible, of the details of a lawyer's services for his client, is, in itself, important to appellate courts and to correctional agencies who are often called on to review some aspect of the conviction. The record of adequate representation also protects the prosecutor, court, and defense counsel from later allegations of unfair treatment.[7] This is essentially a service to the conviction system rather than to the defendant. It acts as a curb on frivolous, unwarranted appeals. The contribution of defense counsel to the record keeping of the guilty plea process, however, goes beyond the mere fact of representation. To the extent that the trial judge questions the attorney about the appropriateness of the charge or the willingness of the defendant to plead guilty, or to the extent defense counsel volunteers this information, the record becomes this much more complete and informative. But most lawyers, on their own initiative, do not try to insure that the record adequately corroborates

[6] An interesting variation in guilty plea procedures supposedly for the purpose of providing a record to protect the defendant was reported in a West Virginia court. This was described in Beckett v. Boles, 218 F. Supp. 692, 694 (N.D. W. Va. 1963): "The Judge . . . has a uniform practice of not accepting pleas of guilty, but of insisting that not guilty pleas be entered; that a jury be empaneled, and that one witness be partially examined, before the accused is permitted to withdraw the not guilty plea and enter the guilty plea. The explanation for this bizarre procedure, as given by the Judge, is that it is for the defendant's protection, so that the record will clearly show that the defendant has been placed in jeopardy and can never be prosecuted again for the same offense. The explanation does not appeal to reason, and the practice has the pernicious effect of giving the appearance that an accused, wanting to assert his innocence and stand trial, has been rushed into a jury trial without adequate preparation and with no real opportunity to defend himself — thus forcing his change of plea."

[7] See United States ex rel. Kenney v. Fay, 232 F. Supp. 899 (S.D.N.Y. 1964).

the fact of the defendant's guilt of an offense at least as serious as the one to which he pleaded guilty, or the fact that the defendant understood the nature of the proceedings and intelligently decided to admit his guilt. It is not apparent to them that this would be a very significant contribution to the welfare of their clients. Yet, careful observation of correctional processes discloses that convicted offenders sometimes change perspective and later deny their guilt or the propriety of the process used in their case. The lack of an adequate record with which to confront the person who does this often makes it impossible to convince him to accept his guilt. The consequence may be a failure on his part to participate in institutional therapy programs and a denial of parole on the part of correctional authorities with the result that he serves a prison term significantly longer than would have resulted if an adequate record of guilt had been made by counsel.[8] Inconsistent though it seems, counsel can, but seldom does, render a service to his client by making an adequate record of the fact that he is indeed guilty of the offense to which he pleads guilty.

Records of the conviction process at arraignment, of the post-plea hearing if one is held, and of the pre-sentence investigation report all become critical documents in the postconviction treatment of the defendant. A transcript which merely records a plea of guilty to a particular statutory charge is not particularly revealing either about the circumstances of the actual offense or about the offender. Pre-sentence reports, which ordinarily give a detailed social history of the offender, sometimes contain a cryptic statement of the offense or some circumstance of the offense that, unless further

[8] Parole boards face a real problem with the offender who maintains he is innocent of the crime and was "railroaded" or tricked into pleading guilty. Without adequate records of the court stages of the process, correctional authorities have no way of independently evaluating the inmates' allegations. Some inmates are very convincing and do cause board members to speculate about the accuracy or fairness of conviction procedures. This creates a dilemma: If the inmate is telling the truth and is indeed innocent (or perhaps not as guilty as his record makes him look) then he should be released; if, however, his story is a complete fabrication, then it is clear that he has not taken responsibility for his own criminal behavior and has not likely benefited from the rehabilitative programs in the institution and therefore should be denied parole until he has recognized his problem and has taken steps to do something about it. Parole boards have sometimes been accused of making prisoners "plead guilty all over again" and of not releasing them unless they do admit their guilt. It is precisely here, however, and in correctional counseling prior to parole, where adequate records of arraignment or a post-plea hearing are of greatest value not only to the parole board but to the inmate himself. If indeed he was not properly convicted, this can be corrected early in his sentence. If he was convicted properly and is in fact guilty, and there are records which substantiate these facts, these records can be properly employed in correctional counseling so that frivolous claims of innocence, or claims based on misunderstanding, can be corrected before the inmate reaches the stage where release must be determined.

clarified, is apt to be misleading and to affect the offender negatively in correctional determinations. For example, a pre-sentence report on a sex offender in Wisconsin contained a statement that the offender "had a knife" when he committed the offense. At his parole hearing some years later this statement assumed great importance and parole was deferred until it could be investigated. As it turned out, the offender indeed "had a knife," but it was a pocketknife which he customarily carried and it was in no way used to commit the offense.

The lawyer's role in the clarification of such matters is particularly important in jurisdictions where the pre-sentence investigation is treated as a confidential document and its contents not revealed to the defendant or his attorney. Under these conditions the attorney is not given an opportunity to correct official records at the time of sentencing. In anticipation, at arraignment or during a post-plea hearing he can often enter factual details of the offense into the official records. This is an important function from the point of view of his client, and it is also important for the judge who must determine the sentence. It is also an important service to correctional authorities who rely heavily on records and who, no less than the court, wish these records to be accurate, fair, and complete.

CHAPTER 18

The Significance of Counsel in Guilty Plea Convictions for Correctional Objectives

There is indication that professional leaders in corrections support widespread participation of lawyers in the early stages of the criminal process not so much because there is something intrinsically valuable in representation of the accused as because representation gives a stronger sense of fairness to the offender, which makes treatment easier once he is received in the prison or on probation. A Wisconsin correctional administrator remarked that he would favor counsel for all defendants, even those most clearly guilty and convicted by the most cursory guilty plea. A prison administrator commented that he would favor the right of inmates to have counsel at parole hearings. These expressions may not represent the opinion of all professional correctional administrators, but they do give some indication of how they look at the functions which lawyers serve in the criminal process. James V. Bennett, former director of the Federal Bureau of Prisons, summed up the correctional significance of defense counsel:

> The defendant who is unable to obtain competent counsel is swept rapidly through the machinery of our courts and begins his imprisonment in a bitter and uncompromising frame of mind. Any feeling he might have had that society is against him is reinforced, and he fights back in those ways that remain available to him. He declines to improve his education in the prison school, he refuses to undertake vocational training, and he is unapproachable to his counselors. Indeed, he may become violent to his fellow prisoners and his keepers or even psychotic after brooding night after night in the loneliness of his cell over the injustice that he is convinced has been inflicted upon him. . . .
>
> In my opinion, the readiness of prisoners to become rehabilitated would be considerably enhanced if they emerged from their

court experience satisfied that their side of the story had been fully, energetically, and capably presented to the court.[1]

In general, correctional support of defense counsel is for stages in the process prior to postsentencing determinations or later only when such objectives as earlier parole can be achieved. It would be erroneous to conclude that correctional personnel favor the participation of counsel at all stages of the criminal process, including the postsentencing stages, or that counsel is commonly viewed as having some abstract merit apart from correctional purposes. Generally speaking, correctional support of widespread representation by lawyers in the conviction process proceeds from a number of premises about the way lawyers assist certain correctional objectives, whether these are the purposes of the lawyers themselves or of the appellate courts which speak to the right of counsel.

A. Defense Counsel Assures More Accurate Convictions

Like the court itself, correctional authorities are interested in the accuracy of guilty pleas. They wish to receive for treatment only those persons who are actually guilty of criminal conduct. In the guilty plea process, particularly, there is always a chance that innocent persons will end up in prison or on probation. Voluntary false pleas, quick justice, and similar matters concern the prison administrator as much as anyone else. Correctional authorities have no proprietary interest in conviction as such; the entire postconviction system rests on the assumption that only the actually guilty are being treated, but in any prison there are usually some doubtful cases which present dilemmas to the professional staff. The inmate who quite possibly should not be there because he is actually innocent, as well as the inmate who probably would not be there if only he had had counsel, create numerous treatment and release problems. This is not to imply that erroneous convictions are commonplace or are by any means a major correctional problem, nor does it mean that prison administrators are naïve enough to believe any prisoner who claims to be innocent. But on the record, at least, there are always some prisoners who, upon close examination, appear to be innocent or at least not convictable by trial standards.

The problems posed by an actually innocent inmate are obvious. Somewhat less obvious are the difficulties in attempting to treat an offender who could have quite possibly "beaten the rap" if he

[1] Bennett, Of Prisons and Justice 364-365 (1964).

were represented by counsel. While the conviction and sentencing of such a person, assuming he is in fact guilty of criminal conduct, is not at all inconsistent with the correctional objective of treating criminality, this type of situation offers opportunity for the offender to blame the system rather than himself for his difficulties. If an offender finds himself in prison as the result of a guilty plea based on evidence which, had he had counsel's advice, would probably have been excluded at trial, he is more likely to be embittered by his poor defense than repentant of his conduct. The lawyer thus lessens the number of such offenders, because he is a factor adding greater certainty to the accuracy of conviction. In this sense he is of value to correctional purposes.

Correctional administrators are, of course, interested in receiving for treatment persons who are actually guilty of criminal conduct, and, in general, their programs are designed to treat persons whose basic problem is criminality in contrast to those whose problem can be better defined as mental illness. In this regard, the function of defense counsel in assessing the competency of guilty plea defendants and in diverting the "sick" from the correctional process is important to postconviction objectives. A defendant's lawyer, more often than any other person in the system, has sufficient contact with him to make at least a preliminary assessment of his intellectual and emotional competence to plead guilty. As a challenge to maximum correctional efficiency, the problem of the incompetent guilty plea defendant is not far behind the problem of inaccurate convictions by plea.

The defense lawyer also contributes to correctional objectives to the extent that he can help insure an accurate and complete record of the conviction process. It is a common correctional experience, particularly with unrepresented guilty plea defendants, to find that court records are of little value in assessing exactly how appropriately defendants were treated in the conviction process. In this respect accurate and detailed transcripts of earlier proceedings, including a record of the active participation of defense counsel, are welcome additions to a defendant's correctional file.

B. Defense Counsel Adds Fairness to Early Proceedings

One major contribution which lawyers can make to the conviction process is the introduction of a sense of fairness in the whole proceeding. The defense lawyer has the opportunity not only to search for possible defenses but to act as interpreter and evaluator of the process to his clients. If nothing more, defense counsel balances the system,[2] giving advice and assistance to his clients and by his mere presence symbolizing to both the defendant and the court the equal legal advantage of the accused. From a correctional point of view it is important not only that offenders are fairly convicted but that they feel fairly treated. This is not meant to imply that penal institutions need or expect only happy and contented inmates or that lawyers can produce this result. As a matter of fact, if defendants were pleased to be convicted, the deterrent and rehabilitative objectives of sentencing would be jeopardized. If a defendant comes through the conviction process confused, not fully aware of what happened to him, or embittered and convinced that he could have beaten the rap if only he had had advantages equal to those of the prosecutor, rehabilitation is very difficult if possible at all. What is needed for rehabilitative progress is an awareness on the part of the offender that his criminal conduct is his own problem, that it will not be tolerated in society, and that during his sentence he can take steps to improve himself and prepare for a law-abiding future. A feeling of remorse may be too much to hope for; but at a minimum rehabilitation requires acceptance on the part of the offender that he has a problem about which he ought to be concerned and which can be lessened, if not fully corrected, by his cooperation in treatment efforts. There is a tendency, certainly not restricted to criminal offenders, to rationalize difficulties, to project blame onto external conditions. It is particularly easy for an offender who was hurried through a guilty plea, unrepresented by counsel, and confused and embittered by the whole process not to regret his criminal conduct but to resent the system which put him in prison. The correctional task increases in difficulty in direct proportion to the extent offenders can legitimately blame their present plight on what they believe to be unfair, unequal treatment in the conviction process itself.

No one would claim that representation by counsel would totally alleviate rationalization by the offender, but common complaints of prisoners relate not so much to unequal treatment in society at large as to disadvantage with the police, the prosecutor, and the judge. Offenders often claim that they did not know what they were doing, what was happening to them, or that so much officialdom was stacked against them that their voice was never heard and their side of the story was not understood.

All offenders have some conception, naïve by lawyers' standards perhaps, of what justice is supposed to be like. From the perspective of the typical, unrepresented guilty plea offender, his own

[2] See Goldstein, The State and the Accused: Balance of Advantage in Criminal Procedure, 69 Yale L.J. 1149 (1960).

treatment may be far from this conception. After arrest and police interrogation, many, if not most, defendants remain in jail because they cannot make bail until they are required to plead in what is ordinarily a very brief, pro forma ceremony. After the guilty plea, to a charge worded in language certainly not common to the vocabulary of most defendants, they are either sentenced or returned to jail to await the results of a pre-sentence investigation. To even the most practiced recidivist, this whole process undoubtedly appears amazingly one-sided, quite different from textbook justice. The typical guilty plea offender spends a few hours in a police station, perhaps two or three months in jail, and about ten minutes in the courtroom. Unrepresented and alone, it is little wonder that many offenders do not emerge from the process praising its fairness and objectivity.

In this setting, representation by counsel becomes important for correctional objectives to the extent that the lawyer is able and willing to take the time to impart a sense of fair treatment to the offender. If the lawyer can impress upon his client that the ten-minute arraignment is his day in court, that his interests are being looked after with the same care and skill as is applied by the prosecutor, then it becomes more difficult for him to rationalize his problem as an inability to obtain just and fair treatment in the conviction system. The job of corrections is made easier if the lawyer gives full service, providing both competent representation and adequate explanation of the whole process, including sentencing. In current administration, counsel seldom make an adequate effort to insure that their clients fully understand the guilty plea process. As a consequence, many guilty plea defendants presently enter the correctional process confused and feeling a sense of injustice which could have been at least minimized were counsel more sensitive to the importance of being certain that his representation of the client has included an adequate explanation.[3]

[3] This is not meant to imply that it is necessary or desirable for counsel to convince his client that this is the best of all possible worlds, to offer false assurance that all is well when, in fact, the person stands convicted of a crime and is possibly on the way to prison. It does mean, however, that misunderstandings and anxiety can be reduced to the extent defense counsel not only explains the steps in the process to his client but actively involves him in confronting alternatives and in making decisions. There is a tendency among many professional persons, physicians as well as attorneys, to compound the mystery of their services by concealing from clients their professional evaluations, decisions, and proposals on the rather dubious grounds that "laymen" could not possibly understand the technical factors involved and are, in any case, interested only in results, not process. This type of representation led an inmate in Wisconsin to comment that he felt like a "spectator" at his day in court until he finally realized it was he being sentenced.

Some preliminary data from an experiment which involves placing law students in correctional facilities (see Footnote 10, Conclusion) indicate that defendants who

C. Defense Counsel Will Press for Leniency

There is a rather general opinion among correctional authorities that sentences are too long, both by legislative mandate and by practices of various judges. The National Council on Crime and Delinquency, representing the majority of correctional social workers, has proposed in their Model Sentencing Act a provision for a five-year maximum limit on most sentences. Most correctional leaders oppose the minimum terms of the American Law Institute's Model Penal Code and the long maximum provisions as well.[4] Furthermore, there is consensus that in many jurisdictions probation can be more widely and effectively used by courts than is now the case.[5] And some prison administrators, confronted with conservative parole boards, feel that certain inmates are being held in institutions longer than desirable for their maximum rehabilitation. In general, there is agreement among professional correctional administrators that maximum effectiveness could better be achieved by shorter sentences and more liberal use of probation. In addition, certain administrative problems, such as prison overcrowding, could be alleviated by earlier and more frequent parole.

From such a position many correctional authorities advocate participation of defense counsel in adjudication, at sentencing, and at parole on the premise that lawyers in the process will lead to more lenient sentences or earlier paroles. Whether this is so is open to speculation, and there are undoubtedly specific cases involving dangerous persons, for example, where if a lawyer did

---

were represented by assigned counsel are particularly disdainful of their lawyers' services and commonly doubt their state-paid attorneys' primary loyalties. One inmate said, "When I pay a lawyer he must work for me. If I get a lawyer from the court, he gets paid no matter what happens." Regardless of the competence of the services of assigned counsel, there may be something to support this attitude. In usual practice, a privately retained counsel must do more than give the client competent service. He usually feels an obligation to justify his actions, or his inaction, to his client and to convince him that he is receiving full value for his fee. Assigned counsel, on the other hand, often defines his job solely in terms of proper representation; too often he feels no obligation whatsoever to rationalize his activities or to offer even minimal explanation of procedure and tactics.

[4] See, for example, Rubin, Sentencing and Correctional Treatment Under the Law Institute's Model Penal Code, 46 A.B.A.J. 994 (1960); Rubin, Weihofen, Edwards, and Rosenzweig, The Law of Criminal Correction, Chap. 4, §7 (1963); Bennett, The Sentence and Treatment of Offenders, in Of Prisons and Justice 352-354 (1964); Proceedings, A.L.I. 54 et seq. (Mimeo. 1956).

[5] This is illustrated by the provisions in the Model Penal Code and Model Sentencing Act which place a presumption on probation rather than on incarceration. See Model Penal Code §7.01 (Proposed Official Draft, 1962) and Model Sentencing Act §9 (1963).

serve to obtain leniency, correctional objectives would be hindered rather than aided. But, overall, the general assumption is that the activities of lawyers will suit the correctional objectives of shorter sentences and greater use of probation.

D. Defense Counsel Will Reduce Sentence Disparity

While correctional authorities want more lenient sentences, they also desire consistent sentences, even when not lenient, for like defendants. In fact this may be even more important; disparate sentences defeat correctional objectives in two ways: by convincing defendants treated leniently that they are lucky or smart and in no need of treatment and by embittering those sentenced severely. To the extent that defense lawyers act to insure consistent treatment, their activities serve an important correctional objective.[6]

One of the bases for sentence disparity is differential opportunity to engage in plea negotiation. In jurisdictions where bargaining is common, equal opportunity for counsel means in large part equal opportunity for consistent treatment. A parole board member in Michigan pointed to the effects of differential opportunity to bargain as making some defendants "smug" at "partially outwitting" authorities while others think of themselves as "suckers" for accepting full liability for their conduct. He went on to point out that differences in bargaining success are commonly attributed to some defendants' being able to retain counsel while others are not. In this regard, sentence disparity appears to the inmate to be economic discrimination, which hardly prepares him for successful therapy.

As it now stands, correctional personnel, especially parole boards, expend a good deal of effort attempting to "equalize" disparate sentences. Where they have wide discretion to parole, as in Wisconsin, this is done with some success. Even at its best, however, correctional equalization is extremely limited. Parole boards can effect release only from institutions; they can do nothing about differentials between prison and probation, nor can they make conviction labels equal. From the correctional point of view, the major attack on sentence disparity must be at the court level, and, to the extent counsel function to insure consistency of treatment, they will be supported by correctional administrators.

[6] For a general discussion of the participation of defense counsel in sentencing and in later correctional determinations see Kadish, The Advocate and the Expert — Counsel in the Peno-Correctional Process, 45 Minn. L. Rev. 803 (1961).

CONCLUSION

Important Unresolved Issues in the Nontrial Conviction Process

Most criminal cases, from very serious felonies to minor, common misdemeanors, are processed through the court stages of the criminal justice system without formal contest, without the procedures of an open, adversary trial. It is fair to say that the major forms of nontrial adjudication — the guilty plea, the negotiated plea, and summary acquittal of certain guilty defendants by the trial judge — together form one of the most important processes in day-by-day criminal justice administration, and yet one that has been largely neglected in professional literature, by researchers, and by lawmaking bodies. Most informed and even general public attention has turned to the trial, particularly the jury trial, as a means of determining guilt or innocence in criminal matters. Perhaps this is as it should be: the nature and conduct of a criminal trial is vitally important in a democratic society. The philosophy, the objectives, the procedures, and the protections of the trial set standards of criminal justice administration that influence all other stages of the process from arrest to correctional treatment.

Yet this strong focus on trial has resulted in relative neglect of the other forms of adjudication. The guilty plea process, frequently occurring and of great administrative significance, has grown without much formal attention, with very little legislative or appellate court guidance. Plea bargaining, while long known to those familiar with criminal courts, has remained largely unrecognized at the legislative and appellate court levels and generally invisible to all but direct participants. Likewise the trial judge's exercise of discretion in acquitting certain of the guilty has been mainly ignored until such recent developments as the American Law Institute's Model Penal Code.[1]

Because observation of current practice demonstrates the great

[1] Model Penal Code §2.12 (Proposed Official Draft, 1962).

significance of nontrial conviction processes, they are given major attention in this volume. Preceding chapters have described guilty plea and acquittal practices and have attempted to analyze certain significant aspects of these practices. But this investigation is by no means intended as a final answer to the study of nontrial processes, nor is it claimed that the descriptions are definitive or complete. Like all preliminary investigations, it tends more to raise questions than to provide answers.

One important conclusion of this analysis, which on the surface is certainly not profound, is that the whole process of nontrial adjudication is more complex than is commonly supposed. The guilty plea, for example, is superficially very simple: it is quick, definite, and administratively efficient. About ten minutes of court time and a defendant willing to waive trial and to plead guilty are all that are commonly required to process even the most complicated, serious charge through adjudication. Yet the same objectives of conviction by trial are applicable in the guilty plea process, and the same basic concerns, such as the accuracy and fairness of the procedures, arise in both systems. Even the problem of the speed of justice occurs in both systems, but with reversed concerns: delay in the trial system, quick justice with guilty pleas. And the matter of equal opportunity for defendants to have a fair trial becomes translated in the negotiated plea to equal opportunity for leniency, for the concessions which the state customarily makes to accused persons in exchange for their guilty pleas. In these and in other ways, issues important to the trial of contested cases arise and demand consideration in nontrial adjudication. These issues are not exactly the same in both systems, of course, but there are a number of very significant parallels which are hidden but not dispelled by the simplicity of traditional guilty plea procedures.

There are also some significant, unique differences between the systems. For example, the guilty plea process, much more than the trial, encapsulates the steps immediately preceding and following conviction. Both the charging decision and sentencing merge into the conviction decision, particularly in the negotiated plea, so that concerns at this stage are not uniquely those of adjudication, of final guilt or innocence, but are intertwined with the prosecutor's discretion and the sentencing discretion of the trial judge. One consequence of this is that representation by defense counsel in guilty plea cases, when it occurs at all, demands knowledge and skills and a whole approach to representation somewhat different than necessary for effective defense of a defendant at trial.

This study of practices in nontrial adjudication has been built around these issues, some common to both the trial and the non-trial systems, some unique to the guilty plea process. The basic approach, indicated by the organization of the material, represents an attempt to go beyond the description of practice to analysis of the research data as they relate to major issues at the court level of criminal justice administration. But when all is said and done, there clearly remain a number of major unresolved issues about nontrial adjudication, each of which is of current importance and each of which deserves continuing attention:

1. *The extent to which the guilty plea procedure should be more formal and more consistently focused on the factual basis of the plea.* There is little doubt from observation of practice and from recent changes in court rules and recommended trial court procedures that the whole process of pleading guilty is undergoing change. Trial judges in all three states are increasingly inquiring into the factual basis for guilty pleas: by and large they are not content to rely on the brief and cursory question and answer sequence that has traditionally characterized the arraignment. In general, judges conduct a more detailed inquiry at the arraignment itself regarding the conduct of the defendant, use a post-guilty plea hearing to view evidence of the crime, or, as in some Michigan courts, direct that the pre-sentence investigation be focused on the facts surrounding the crime to which the defendant has pleaded guilty. This kind of trial court inquiry, currently left largely to the discretion of the individual judge, has recently been reflected in a proposed revision to require such factual inquiry in federal court rules[2] and in a recommendation in Wisconsin that the post-plea hearing become standard procedure.[3]

The innovative practices of judges and the trend in recommended procedures result largely from the vagueness and uncertainty which has surrounded the requirements for proper conviction by plea. The primary concern of trial judges, and, for that matter, of all persons in the criminal justice system, is that guilty pleas be accurate, that defendants convicted by their own pleas be actually guilty. The common requirement that a plea is proper if it is "voluntary" offers little guidance for judicial procedure, and it has been frequently interpreted to mean that the defendant must freely consent to plead guilty. While the consent of the defendant is important in guilty plea cases, concern for accuracy is not dispelled even if willingness to plead is established. Conscientious

[2] Rule 11. Pleas, Second Preliminary Draft of Proposed Amendments to Rules of Criminal Procedure for the United States District Courts 5 (March, 1964).

[3] Recommended Questions to Be Used When the Court Is Determining Whether to Appoint Counsel and Acceptance of Plea of Guilty or of Nolo Contendere (Proposed Mimeo., Aug. 1964).

trial judges, by the use of informal techniques of viewing evidence, are searching for ways to satisfy themselves that guilty pleas are accurate and consensual, and that procedures are fair in the sense that the defendant has understanding of the charges against him and an awareness of the consequences of his plea decision.

The result of the practices developed to meet these concerns is that the total guilty plea process is becoming more elaborate, more focused on evidence of the defendant's guilt, than has been true in the past.[4] There is, in some instances, administrative cost to this, notably the quick processing of cases is slowed down. When a post-plea hearing is held, for example, a procedure that formerly took ten minutes now may take an hour or more. But raw administrative efficiency is not and has never been a mark of proper justice administration. Most judges who now spend more time at arraignment or who use a post-plea hearing or other evidence-viewing device feel that the extra trouble is worth it. Others in the criminal justice system agree. Correctional authorities, for example, wish to receive only persons who are actually guilty and who have had full and fair processing by the court. Both for correctional purposes and for use by appellate courts, a more formal, detailed investigation into the factual basis of a guilty plea and into the circumstances of pleading guilty provides a much more complete record of the conviction process than has normally been the case. On the ground that records of the court process have important later significance, some trial judges use a post-plea hearing or investigate thoroughly at arraignment even in cases where the defendant is represented by counsel and where the court needs no further assurance that the defendant is actually guilty.

[4] A federal judge, a member of the Advisory Committee on Criminal Rules, commenting on the proposed modification of Rule 11, said: "Diverse practices exist throughout the United States in handling guilty pleas. True, the submission of the plea of guilty carries with it the legal significance that the defendant's conduct falls within the charge. Some federal courts hear no evidence or summarization of what transpired. Others permit the United States Attorney to read excerpts from his file, or to listen to the testimony of a government agent, all following the acceptance of the guilty plea. In rare instances, but too numerous for comfort, an inquiry develops that the defendant has committed no federal crime. With the 'bootlegger' caught at the still, it is not unusual for this defendant to say, 'I *pleads* guilty to being near the still,' which, standing alone, is no crime. The advisory committee feels that a more uniform practice of making a brief inquiry into the factual basis of the charge will tend to prevent post-conviction attacks upon sentences which, in past years, either have been successful or have required extensive hearings. The inquiry required is not to be restricted by rules of evidence and probably requires no more information than is already in the pre-sentence report or the file of the attorney for the government. Whether the suggested change, inquiring into the factual basis of the charge, is adopted or rejected, it is likely that many federal courts will continue this already existing practice." Hoffman, What Next in Federal Criminal Rules? 21 Wash. & Lee L. Rev. 1, 10-11 (1964).

These informal devices and the trend toward requiring more thorough investigation are sporadic and localized. A criminal trial, in contrast, is uniformly conducted according to standard operating procedures, at least in serious cases, so that there are only minor differences, if any, between jurisdictions or from one trial to another. This is especially so now that the right to counsel has been expanded on constitutional grounds. But the practices in guilty plea cases are far from uniform, and the requirements for proper conviction by plea remain clouded and uncertain. The form and content of a proper and effective guilty plea process are currently left largely to the discretion of the individual trial judge.

2. *The extent to which the trial judge should have administrative responsibility for the over-all criminal justice system.* In looking over the entire criminal justice system, it becomes apparent that the trial court judge occupies an important, pivotal position in the sequence of steps from arrest to parole. The court stage of the process is the dividing point between concern with proof of guilt and concern with treating proved criminals. In his own right the judge is largely responsible for two major decisions: conviction or acquittal and sentencing those who are convicted. The pretrial processes lead up to the court and postconviction processes away from it and, in merely a physical sense, the judge is a central figure in the flow of this system.

The issue of current, major importance is not whether the judge has a significant role in this process, nor whether he physically occupies a central position, but whether he is the director, the overseer, of the whole system from police stages to correctional determinations. In the guilty plea, as at trial, it is clear that the judge is chief administrator of his own court, that his policies and practices determine the nature and characteristics of court business. What is not so clear is the extent of his sphere of influence outward in both directions from the court itself. There are some formal precedents for such extended influence. The exclusionary rule of evidence, for example, is a formal device for action at the court level designed to control police practices. Legislative authority for judicial sentencing discretion gives the trial judge opportunity to set limits on the length of time an offender will spend under correctional control and, in many cases, to choose which offenders will be incarcerated and which will be placed on probation. But in practice the issue becomes more complex than this; the authority of the court is expanded beyond these formally recognized controls to include a number of practices not specifically authorized by either legislation or appellate case law. Trial judges commonly acquit certain guilty defendants in frank discipline of the police when they believe certain police enforcement methods to be improper. Trial judges often systematically downgrade charges in certain cases when they disagree with and wish to avoid legislative sentencing mandates. In these informal ways and along with the various types of formal authority provided the trial court, judges, in practice, commonly assume a responsibility for the functioning of the over-all criminal justice system, rather than limiting their activities solely to the direct, immediate business of the court.

The propriety and the effectiveness of this judicial role have not been resolved.[5] Current debates about the usefulness and consequences of the exclusionary rule and continuing concern about the proper role of the trial judiciary in limiting or controlling correctional determinations attest to this. This whole matter is probably more complicated in nontrial adjudication than it is where trial is held because the criteria for judicial exercise of this type of discretion are less visible, less often explained in the informal processes of the guilty plea and in summary acquittals of certain defendants. And in many guilty plea cases particularly, where the steps of charging, adjudication, and sentencing overlap or merge altogether, it is difficult to assess the controlling purpose of the court without a detailed study of daily practice.

3. *Whether bargaining for guilty pleas is a proper form of criminal justice administration.* Observation of practice indicates that downgrading charges and promising lenient sentences in exchange for guilty pleas are common and are widely supported by both prosecutors and trial judges as necessary to maintain the guilty plea system. This practice of plea negotiation, while quasi-routine

[5] Professor Francis A. Allen recently addressed this question of the central role of the trial judge: "Why this extraordinary judicial intervention in the administration of criminal justice in the United States? And why the modern emphasis on the adversary process? There is no single or simple answer to these questions. One reason, I believe, inheres in the very structure of American Criminal Justice. Our system of policing, prosecution, and law enforcement is fragmented and decentralized to a remarkable degree. As a result, political responsibility for the decency and effectiveness of the system is widely diffused if it may be said to exist at all. In probably no other advanced nation is this true to the extent that it obtains in the United States. In England, police abuses, or irregularities falling well below what we in this country would conceive as abuse, may result in questions being asked in Parliament. The absence of genuine political and administrative responsibility for the system of criminal justice in the United States has resulted in the substitution of judicial supervision. And judicial supervision has been marked by an attempt to recast all aspects of the criminal process into the adversary mold, perhaps in part to render judicial supervision of the system easier and more effective. Whether this effort can be made to succeed or whether it can made to succeed without serious losses to the security of the community are among the principal domestic issues of our time. But whatever the problems, no one can complain that life with the modern court is dull. It is not dull at all." Allen, The Challenge of the Impoverished Accused in the Administration of Criminal Justice 52, A Symposium on the Criminal Law (University of Illinois, Feb. 1965).

in certain cases, is basically an active bargaining process in which both sides, the state and the accused, make explicit concessions in order to "settle" a case without going to trial. Because the bargaining process is informal, commonly without a record of any agreements, there are often misunderstandings about whether promises were really made, and accusations by defendants of unfilled bargains and of unkept promises by the prosecutor or court. These are essentially problems of the application of plea bargaining, of the internal workings of a process that is otherwise accepted as common practice. However, a major unresolved question in regard to plea bargaining is simply whether such bartering in criminal cases is a proper form of criminal justice administration in a democratic society. This is not a question of the shortcomings of bargaining procedures but of the appropriateness of this practice even assuming that concessions are made in honorable fashion by the prosecutor or judge, that bargains are kept, and that only the actually guilty trade their pleas for leniency. Neither is this a question of unequal bargaining opportunities or of deception by failing to honor agreements or even of fear of inducing the actually innocent to plead guilty. It is instead an issue of informality versus formal and fixed procedures, of an open adversary test of guilt versus out of court settlement of criminal cases, of discretion versus full enforcement.

This practice of bargaining for guilty pleas and the basic question of its propriety are receiving increasing attention by appellate courts. A number of recent cases in which bargains have been made and kept have reached the appellate level, an unusual occurrence because, in effect, there is no truly injured party in such actions. In these cases the propriety of bargaining as a practice in and of itself has come under consideration and, although with some strong dissent, it has been upheld as proper and administratively realistic. These cases by no means provide the final answer to the question, and no doubt the propriety of this practice will be considered and reconsidered in the future.

Whatever the final outcome of the propriety question, whether plea bargaining is eventually forbidden or is given formal recognition, at present it is clearly a major characteristic of nontrial adjudication. Currently informal and sporadic, it raises a number of problems of application and consequences that deserve further attention. Charge reduction as one form of plea negotiation, for example, is directly related to the problem of sentence disparity, a matter of current concern to defendants, trial judges, and corrections personnel. Disparity has traditionally been viewed as solely a sentencing problem, yet it is apparent that downgrading at adjudication not only is closely related to sentencing differentials but is determinative of whatever disparity exists in fixed sentence jurisdictions.

Plea negotiation has consequences for correctional determinations that go beyond disparity as such. There has traditionally been a keen interest on the part of correctional personnel with sentencing practices of judges and on the part of judges with correctional programs and alternatives. Virtually no attention has been paid, however, to the relationship between postconviction processes and adjudication practices of trial courts. Sentencing in its own right, as a joint responsibility of legislature, court, and correctional agency, has been called a "numbers game" because legislative maximum and minimum sentences can be and are commonly modified by the judge, and in turn his sentence can be and is modified by parole practices or reduced time for good behavior provisions of the law. Plea bargaining infinitely complicates this whole process, and where charge reduction is common it makes sentencing a "labeling game" as well as a manipulation of numbers. Sophisticated interpretation is needed not only for the formal sentence of an offender to determine its actual value but also for an official conviction record to determine the offender's actual criminality.

The process of plea negotiation affects both the length of correctional control and the determination of who is incarcerated and who placed on probation. To the extent that a major correctional objective is the treatment and rehabilitation of criminal offenders, the existence of plea bargaining makes the selection for major treatment alternatives and the time under correctional control a matter of skill in negotiation rather than solely a function of the treatment needs of the offender. While there is some evidence of correctional compensation for leniency or label changes as a result of negotiation, this is also largely sporadic and informal. This relationship of adjudication and correctional programs has not received much attention on the part of either correctional authorities or judges.

4. *The extent to which trial judges should have discretion to acquit guilty defendants.* The exercise of discretion by agencies which apply the law is a characteristic common to all stages in the criminal justice process. This is also true at the adjudication stage, where trial judges frequently acquit certain obviously guilty defendants in an effort to individualize justice, to introduce an element of equity in what otherwise would be a quasi-automatic, unfeeling process. But discretion exercised here, as at all stages of the

process, raises questions of its propriety, of its dimensions and consequences, and of controls on it.

In theory and in common expectation, the proper function of the judge in his adjudicatory capacity is to evaluate evidence of guilt or innocence, to make an impartial finding as his assessment of the evidence leads him. Here, as at the police level of the process, discretion is neither traditional nor specifically delegated as it is with the prosecutor in the charging decision, the judge at sentencing, and correctional authorities in postconviction determinations. A judge's desire to distinguish degrees of criminality and individualize the consequences of conviction is customarily provided by sentencing alternatives, by his ability to set variable lengths of incarceration or to place certain defendants on probation. In practice, however, judges commonly confront cases where guilt is clear but in which it seems to them conviction itself and any sentence whatsoever would be unduly harsh, unnecessary, or ineffective. In these cases, usually minor crimes or minor variations of more serious crimes, judges ignore evidence of guilt and order the defendants acquitted.

Judicial power to acquit in this manner is obvious; double jeopardy protections prevent appellate reversal of these cases even in those states, like Wisconsin, with a broad right of state appeal. But, in general, the practice has been viewed as inconsistent with the traditional stress on evidentiary requirements in the guilt or innocence decision, and as improper, even "reprehensible," [6] in certain cases. There is, however, some current recognition of both the frequency and the desirability of this practice in cases of minor law violation. The American Law Institute's Model Penal Code proposes authority for the trial judge to acquit in certain cases of de minimis law infraction in spite of evidence sufficient to convict. The propriety of this practice, the basic nature of the trial judge's adjudicatory role, however, remains in dispute. Appropriate criteria for such acquittals, including the question of which types of conduct constitute de minimis violations, remain worthy of further study and analysis. Likewise the question of whether formal controls on the acquittal practices of trial courts are possible and, if so, how effective such controls can be, also deserves more attention than has been the case.

Too little is presently known about the consequences of judicial acquittal practices on other stages of the criminal justice process. On the one hand, these acquittals keep certain of the guilty, primarily those who are viewed as sick rather than criminal, from cor-

[6] State v. Evjue, 254 Wis. 581, 595, 37 N.W.2d 50, 56 (1949).

rectional agencies. In general this type of screening is supported by postconviction agencies on the grounds that the alternative of conviction and sentencing would flood correctional agencies with minor offenders, many of whom are chronically disturbed and largely untreatable. On the other hand, acquittal of the guilty in effect acts in review of prior arrest and charging decisions. Because the judge views a case with a certain perspective which is quite possibly different from that of the police and prosecutor, and yet, because he rarely adequately communicates his reasons for acquittal to these agencies or fully considers their purposes in bringing the case to court, uncertainty about the purpose of the practice is common. In some cases, acquittal is used in frank discipline of the police, but in others it in no way reflects an opinion that earlier stages were improperly handled. The difference between these is not always clear. There is no doubt, however, that in both instances repetitive acquittal of guilty defendants has an impact on both police and prosecutor practices. This points up the continuing need to view the exercise of judicial discretion in nontrial adjudication in the context of the over-all criminal justice process.

5. *The extent to which defense counsel can make significant contributions to the nontrial conviction process.*[7] A major issue in American criminal justice, still to be resolved, is the importance of counsel in nontrial adjudication, particularly in the guilty plea process. Certainly there is room for the lawyer here. There is little doubt that he can contribute to certain major objectives of the guilty plea system if he is aware of his own potential and sufficiently informed and skilled to do so. A capable defense counsel can help make the guilty plea process more accurate and fair, can assist by providing full and complete records of court proceedings, can help in achieving correctional treatment objectives, and at the same time can serve the best interests of his client by advice in regard to the plea decision and by negotiating the plea. The basic question is whether most lawyers are sufficiently aware of the importance of these contributions and sufficiently informed to carry them out.

By both traditional formal training and by public acclaim a law-

[7] There is currently a good deal of interest in the participation of counsel in judicial and administrative processes where lawyers have traditionally played a minor role or have not functioned at all to any substantial degree. See, for example, Allen, The Borderland of the Criminal Law: Problems of "Socializing" Criminal Justice, 32 Social Serv. Rev. 107 (1958); Kadish, The Advocate and the Expert — Counsel in the Peno-Correctional Process, 45 Minn. L. Rev. 803 (1961); Pharr, On Sentencing: What a Judge Expects from Defense Counsel, 1 Prac. Law. 76 (Oct. 1955); Schinitsky, The Role of the Lawyer in Children's Court, 17 Record 10 (1962); Tappan, The Role of Counsel in Parole Matters, 3 Prac. Law. 21 (Feb. 1957).

yer is prepared to be an advocate at trial of a contested case. While many of the skills and most of the knowledge which make a good trial lawyer are also applicable in the guilty plea process, the ground rules are different, the client's needs are different, and some additional knowledge and skills are required for effective representation in this largely informal process. In bringing his professional competence to bear on the guilty plea decision, the attorney's knowledge of the substantive law, of defenses to criminal liability, and of evidence and standards of proof is comparable to knowledge required to go to trial. But in the case of a guilty plea, if the lawyer is to achieve maximum effectiveness he must also be familiar with informal procedures and with bargaining possibilities and avenues,[8] must be able to explain the whole process to his client, including an accurate assessment of likely sentencing consequences, and must have awareness of the importance of records not only for immediate purposes but for the future needs of his client as well. In this respect, he must know court practices and common plea bargaining patterns. He must be familiar with sentencing structure and sentencing practices and with correctional programs, policies, and practices. In short, he must have knowledge and skills that relate the conviction process to other stages in the total system of criminal justice, to the informal, discretionary handling of cases from the prosecutor's level onward to the correctional stage.

The problem is that many lawyers lack the knowledge and skills

[8] In Cortez v. United States, 337 F.2d 699, 701 (9th Cir. 1964), the court, taking judicial notice that "the vast majority of those who are indicted for federal crimes plead guilty," commented: "In a sense, it can be said that most guilty pleas are the result of a 'bargain' with the prosecutor. But this, standing alone, does not vitiate such pleas. A guilty defendant must always weigh the possibility of his conviction on all counts, and the possibility of his getting the maximum sentence, against the possibility that he can plead to fewer, or lesser, offenses, and perhaps receive a lighter sentence. The latter possibility exists if he pleads guilty, as Cortez did, to the whole charge against him.

"No competent lawyer, discussing a possible guilty plea with a client, could fail to canvass these possible alternatives with him. Nor would he fail to ascertain the willingness of the prosecutor to 'go along.' Moreover, if a co-defendant is involved, and if the client is anxious to help that co-defendant, a competent lawyer would be derelict in his duty if he did not assist in that regard. At the same time, the lawyer is bound to advise his client fully as to his rights, as to the alternatives available to him, and of the fact that neither the lawyer nor the prosecutor nor anyone else can bargain for the court. There is nothing wrong, however, with a lawyer's giving his client the benefit of his judgment as to what the court is likely to do, always making it clear that he is giving advice, not making a promise.

"The important thing is not that there shall be no 'deal' or 'bargain', but that the plea shall be a genuine one, by a defendant who is guilty; one who understands his situation, his rights, and the consequences of the plea, and is neither deceived nor coerced."

to really make effective contributions either to their clients or to the courts and other agencies in the guilty plea system.[9] Furthermore, the typical lawyer is commonly unaware of the range of his possible contributions once he confronts a client who neither needs nor wants a trial. A large majority of defendants are also ignorant of the facts of the process. In waiving their right to trial they usually also waive their right to counsel almost as a matter of course. As long as counsel is considered important only at trial by defendants and by lawyers themselves the contribution of the practicing bar to the nontrial system will be likely to remain minimal. Realization of the contributions lawyers can make and the skills necessary to function effectively in the guilty plea process should provide a major and important challenge to law schools[10] and to local bar associations.[11]

Each of these issues — the formalism of the guilty plea process, the central overseer role of the trial judiciary, the propriety of plea bargaining, discretion in adjudication, and the role of defense counsel in the guilty plea process — will in all probability continue

[9] See Slovenko, Attitudes on Legal Representation of Accused Persons, 2 Am. Crim. L.Q. 101 (1964), and Storey, The Legal Profession and Criminal Justice, 36 J. Am. Jud. Soc. 166 (1953).

[10] The University of Wisconsin Law School currently has two experimental programs in professional responsibility designed to familiarize law students with operational problems and procedures at traditionally unfamiliar parts of the criminal justice system. One project, concentrating on the postconviction stages of the process, involves placing selected and specially trained law students in correctional settings for three months of work during the summer between their second and third years in law school. This project, supported by a grant from the National Council on Legal Clinics, has been possible only through the full cooperation of the Wisconsin Division of Corrections. The other project, supported by the Ford Foundation and focusing on the early, police stages of the criminal justice process, involves similar summer placements of selected students in police agencies. The field experience of the students in both projects is preceded and followed by courses and seminars offered in the law school curriculum. For a preliminary report on the Correctional Intern Project see Kimball, Correctional Internships — A Wisconsin Experiment in Education for Correctional Responsibility, 18 J. Legal Ed. No. 1 (1965). See also Remington, The Law, the Law School and Criminal Justice Administration, 43 Texas L. Rev. 275 (1965).

[11] Professor Kadish, making the point that lawyers of less than the highest caliber have been most active in criminal law work to the detriment of both their clients and the profession, and in all probability would, under present circumstances, predominate if allowed to participate in such postconviction processes as parole determinations, comments: "It is particularly in the administration of criminal justice in this country that the bar as a group has failed to discharge its responsibilities. The highest minded and the most competent are not, as a group, the lawyers most attracted to criminal work. The jail-house lawyer is a reality and not a bogeyman of parole administrators. But the presence of many bad lawyers is not a dispositive argument, any more in parole proceedings than in criminal trials, for excluding all lawyers. . . . The challenge is to the bar as well as to the agencies involved. . . ." Kadish, The Advocate and the Expert — Counsel in the Peno-Correctional Process, 45 Minn. L. Rev. 803, 840 (1961).

as major concerns of criminal justice administration. It is perhaps unnecessary to say that further, more intensive research is needed. Yet it seems apparent that the nontrial conviction process, which is superficially quite simple and direct, is actually very complex, involving a relationship of practices and consequences of practices which deserve full and continuing attention. Although the guilty plea process is undergoing change, there is little doubt that it is here to stay, that the great majority of criminal convictions will continue to be by pleas of guilty. Unresolved issues concerning the propriety of plea bargaining, the proper role of the trial judiciary, and the functions of defense counsel must be viewed from the perspective of the guilty plea process and confronted and analyzed within this system.

Index